H·E·A·V·Y
TRAFFIC

&

High Culture

New American Library
as Literary Gatekeeper
in the Paperback Revolution

THOMAS L. BONN

Southern Illinois University Press
Carbondale and Edwardsville

Printed in the United States of America
Edited by Carol A. Burns
Designed by Joanne E. Kinney
Production supervised by Natalia Nadraga
92 91 90 89   4 3 2 1

Library of Congress Cataloging-in-Publication Data

Bonn, Thomas L.
    Heavy traffic and high culture : New American Library as literary
gatekeeper in the paperback revolution / by Thomas L. Bonn
      p. cm.
    Bibliography: p.
    Includes index.
    ISBN 0-8093-1478-9
    1. New American Library.   2. Literature publishing—United States–
–History—20th century.   3. Paperbacks—Publishing—United States–
–History—20th century.   4. Popular literature—Publishing—United
States—History—20th century.   5. Authors and publishers—United
States—History—20th century.   6. Books and reading—United States–
–History—20th Century.   I. Title.
Z473.N39B66 1989
070.5'0973—dc19   88-18517
                                                                        CIP

The paper used in this publication meets the minimum requirements of
American National Standard for Information Sciences—Permanence of
Paper for Printed Library Materials, ANSI Z39.48–1984. ♾

For Fred and Amy, from "This Happy Rural Seat"

Contents

Illustrations

Acknowledgments

During its many years of preparation this book has had the assistance of a wide variety of people unfailingly gracious with their support. At the top of this list must be the staffs of the two archival sources from which it was drawn: Frank Walker and his staff at the Fales Library collection, New York University; Gene Gressley and the library staff of the Archives of Contemporary History, University of Wyoming. For these warm and enthusiastic people I will, as I have throughout the text, call on Victor Weybright and endorse his 1960 observation to Erskine Caldwell, "I am becoming more and more enchanted by the genuine literary and scholarly concerns of dedicated librarians of the United States, and I only wish that they were better supported, financially, and better paid."

Portions of my research have received support from agencies of the State University of New York. The SUNY Research Foundation supported my visits to the New York University Archives. Without its financial assistance this project would have never begun. Through the NYS/UUP program I was able to travel to the archives in Laramie, Wyoming.

Truman M. Talley's personal interest and professional skills directly influenced the shape and perceptions presented to the reader. His advice and concern span a time period even longer than the research itself. He provided reassurance, confirmation, and correction during the initial drafting of the text. Throughout his professional career he has received the public and private appreciation of some of the finest writers in the world. I would like to believe that mine matches theirs in depth of gratitude.

Special thanks should also go to New American Library, particularly to certain persons currently or formerly associated with the company. First and foremost is Ken Agnew whose appreciation of softcover history and tradition is largely unmatched in his or any other New York publishing house. Thanks to that grand young man, Harold Laskey, and to Bill O'Connell.

Thanks to Parker Ladd of the Association of American Publishers, to Jean Peters of Bowker, and to bookseller Charles Garvin of Ithaca. Two gracious ladies have been especially supportive: Mrs. Margaret M. Enoch and Mrs. Virginia Caldwell.

Throughout these six years my colleagues at the State University of New York have provided interest and encouragement. Thanks especially to Dawn Van Hall, Leonard Cohen, and Selby Gration. Special thanks to Van Burd whose continued scholarly inquiry and accomplishment serve as an inspiration and model to all Cortland faculty.

On pages 73–74 Peg Cameron best expresses my appreciation to Carol Burns and Company at SIU Press.

Finally and foremost my deepest appreciation to Elaine Galaska who has been wedded to my research and writing for twenty years. And to Murph who has been wedded to me for twenty-five years. Through these years I have sorely tested their patience, skill, and understanding with "final drafts" that were never final. As portions of this volume underscore, those who edit, proof, and correct serve us better than we serve ourselves.

Grateful acknowledgment is made to the following individuals and companies for permission to quote from correspondence: William Arrowsmith, Isaac Asimov, James Avati; Marian G. Bissell for the correspondence of Richard Bissell, Alice M. Piper for the correspondence of James M. Cain, Virginia M. Caldwell for the correspondence of Erskine Caldwell; Random House, Inc. for the correspondence of Bennett Cerf, Ralph Daigh, Joseph C. Lesser, Harry E. Maule; Whitney Darrow, Jr. for the correspondence of Whitney Darrow, Sr., Margaret Enoch for the correspondence of Kurt Enoch, Edgar M. Branch for the correspondence of James T. Farrell, Bruno Fischer, Lois Gruber for the correspondence of Frank Gruber, Leonard R. Harris, Marc Jaffe, Keith Jennison; Margaret Melcher and Frederic Melcher II for the correspondence of Frederic Melcher, Henry Miller, Walter Roth for the correspondence of Willard Motley, Charles Scribner, Jr., Leon Shimkin, Curtis Brown, Ltd. for the correspondence of Lord Snow; Roger W. Straus, William Styron, Arthur H. Thornhill, Jr. for the correspondence of Arthur H. Thornhill, Sr., Don Von Elsner, Irving Wallace, Helen M. Weybright for the correspondence of Victor Weybright.

H·E·A·V·Y
TRAFFIC

1

Introduction

Paperback book publishing in the United States came of age in the fifteen years following World War II. A handful of companies emerged from the welter of hardcover and softcover reprint operations that existed during this period. They became the leading imprints within mass market book publishing and have to this day directed the course of the popular book industry in America. These companies were the brain children of visionaries, men and women who also brought to their respective imprints solid experience in marketing, production, and editorial practices. At various times and to various degrees each of these companies affiliated with other publishing operations, including hardcover publishers. All experimented with a variety of trade paperback and hardcover arrangements. Each developed highly competitive monthly publication lists of books in various categories or series. New American Library, publisher of Signet and Mentor paperbacks, is one of these companies. Its postwar advancement in strength and in influence within the American publishing industry is representative of the rise of mass market publishing as a whole.

NAL began late in 1945 in all but name when Victor Weybright joined Kurt Enoch at Penguin Books, the New York branch of Britain's most successful softcover publishing company. In January 1948, NAL was legally founded by Weybright and Enoch and separated from the British imprint. NAL's initial publications list absorbed and was built on the reprints of the American Penguin branch. In the formative years of contemporary mass market book publishing, NAL stood out from the other softcover imprints because of the quality and diversity of both its fiction and nonfiction series. Claiming to have become the largest softcover publisher in the world, the company sponsored in the fifties and early sixties what, to many minds, was the best list in the American book industry. Matching record-setting bestselling writers Erskine Caldwell, Mickey Spillane, and Ian Fleming were authors such as William Faulkner, Truman Capote, James T. Farrell, Jack Kerouac, J. D. Salinger, James Jones, Christopher Isherwood, William Styron, Norman Mailer, Gore Vidal, and Flannery O'Connor. NAL reprinted most of the notable black novelists of the period including Ralph Ellison, James Baldwin, Richard Wright, Ann Petry, and Willard Motley. The pages of the company's *New World Writing* literary review, issued throughout the fifties, showcased the talents of the brightest young writers of the time. The Signet Classics series, and in particular its freshly edited Shakespeare volumes, set new standards for quality reprint publishing. Finally, NAL quite rightly could claim that its highly regarded Mentor imprint was the precursor of the dozens of trade paperback series that exploded on the American publishing scene in the latter part of the fifties. The company slogan, "Good Reading for the Millions," that appeared on each publication was no barren claim.

This book is based on and built around the paperback company's editorial correspondence of 1945 to 1961. I look at the company's rise especially in terms of its relations with authors, agents, and other book publishers, concentrating on softcover publishing concerns and practices that directly affected both the content of the books that it sponsored and the presentation of that content to "the millions." Throughout the book I refer to the "gatekeeper" theory of communication control. In recent years there have been several important surveys of the editorial selection process in book publishing. Sociologists Michael Lane (1980), Lewis A. Coser, Charles Kaduskin, and Walter W. Powell (1982), and Powell (1985) have all prepared extended studies that describe this process at work within several branches of today's publishing industry. Powell credits Kurt Lewin for having coined the term "gatekeeper," which has been used to describe the selection process. Lewin noted that "information travels through particular communication channels and that specific areas within these channels function as gates, governed either by impartial rules or by individuals empowered to make the decision of whether information should be let 'in' or remain 'out'" (qtd. in Powell 212).

The gatekeeper theory itself as applied to contemporary book publishing is painfully self-evident; its applicability needs no further defense. However, the publishing environments and the selection and editorial processes that determine the content and the presentation of a writer's work are less obvious and widely misinterpreted. These environments and processes have been covered by the studies noted above for scholarly, college text, and trade book publishing. These studies and others are based on close examination of unidentified publishing companies. Necessarily

2

they also examine the tension within each organization created by the conflicting goals of literary contribution and profit making. Sociologists have labeled this tension as culture against commerce. In his frequent attempts to bring the goals into harmony, Victor Weybright viewed them as the "luster and lucre" of publishing, "heavy traffic, high culture."

By contrast this book focuses on an identified publishing operation, NAL, citing by name editors, agents, and authors as well as cooperative and competing publishers. As a mass market paperback publisher, the company is a branch of the book industry largely ignored in gatekeeper studies. The written materials—letters and memoranda—help explain the motivations and circumstances that influenced editorial decision making and shaped the character of the publishing company and its publications. I argue that despite the fact that the large majority of mass market publications were reprints, gatekeeper considerations were operative and were often as complex as in other branches of publishing. The culture-commerce tension was equally pronounced as well.

The bulk of the correspondence was dictated by or addressed to Victor Weybright as the editor in chief. Indeed, along with the company itself, he is this book's central figure. Weybright and his partner, Kurt Enoch, equally shared the overall operation of the company, but Weybright was responsible for the company's editorial directions during its formative years. He generally had a final say on which reprint and original book projects NAL sponsored. He was the company's principal gatekeeper. A New Deal liberal and devoted anglophile, Victor Weybright was a multifaceted personality who, through his letters and memos, exhibits both the values and prejudices of American and English societies. At the height of his career, the wide range of his knowledge, interests, and taste was probably unmatched in the United States publishing industry.

In 1965 Victor Weybright arranged to have seventeen years of company editorial files deposited in the special collections of Fales Library at New York University. Totaling fifty-five file drawers, they were sealed for fifteen years. Arranged either by author and title or by publishing company or agent, the files contain the basic record of how Weybright and his editorial department operated up to and shortly following the Times-Mirror Company purchase of NAL. Financial, marketing, and production records, including print runs and royalty statements generally are not part of these files; interoffice memoranda to and from editorial staff, and letters to and from authors, agents, publishers, and readers are. By and large the greatest number of files at New York University concern titles that were proposed by individual authors, agents, or other publishers to the company but were rejected. The personal papers of both Victor Weybright and Kurt Enoch are part of the manuscript collections of the Archives of

Contemporary Civilization at the University of Wyoming and the New York Public Library, respectively. Since these materials by and large post-date the historical coverage of this book, I have not often cited them.

In his autobiography, *The Making of a Publisher*, written in the bitterness of separation from the company, Victor Weybright's rancor was directed chiefly at his partner, Kurt Enoch, who had been assigned to broader duties within the Times-Mirror organization following the NAL acquisition. The archival correspondence, however, bears out Enoch's own summary of their premerger relationship appearing in his incomplete and posthumously issued *Memoirs of Kurt Enoch*.

> Victor and I worked in close liaison. Since a successful publishing operation depends on a close coordination of a great diversity of functions and the pooling of many talents, Victor had to be involved in important considerations of book design, covers, promoting, etc., and I had to be in on editorial planning, decisions on royalties, assignments, commitments, contracts, etc., which required a good deal of reading on my part. In general, all major decisions affecting the company as a whole were shared by both of us. These practices reflected the actuality of the partnership interest by both of us to the company and they worked well. (Enoch 174)

As implied in this quote, Enoch's daily responsibilities were with book production and sales. His analytical personality was a perfect complement to the flamboyant Weybright. Enoch's partnership in operating the company is not extensively documented in the New York University editorial files. Where appropriate, I have included examples of Enoch's coproprietorship. Kurt Enoch's professional career is one of the most remarkable in all of twentieth-century book publishing. It deserves greater recognition than the limited scope this volume permits.

Book industry colleagues and friends of Victor Weybright were troubled by the resentment and acrimony that appears in the last third of *The Making of a Publisher*. Many have judged the memoir not worthy of the man. This book, while not pretending to be a biography of Victor Weybright, hopes to provide some objective insight into both his editorial genius and very complex personality. If nothing else it will show him to be, like Shakespeare's Cleopatra, "of infinite variety."

Chapters 2 and 3 outline the history of the company. Following its separation from Penguin Books, NAL dramatically grew gaining commercial strength through the record-setting sales of Caldwell and Spillane and backlist income from the steadily selling Mentor imprint. Profits in these areas allowed the publication of more speculative kinds of writing, including a very large number of new novelists who appeared in the heady postwar environment. NAL also set early industry bid records for reprint rights to the bestsellers of Norman Mailer and James Jones. Weybright's friendship with Bennett Cerf of Random House and the company's unsuccessful wooing of Scribner's for Ernest Hemingway are also highlighted. In the late fifties, competition from the trade paperback imprints of established publishers steered the company toward an ever increasing number of proprietary contract arrangements, particularly with West Coast writers. The company's independence and profits spurred its acquisition by the Times-Mirror Company. This in turn allowed NAL to enter all phases of general book publishing including hardcover and trade paperback. Succeeding chapters take up various themes and relationships introduced in these first chapters and develop and document them in greater detail.

Chapters 4, 5, and 6 explore softcover editorial selection concerns and procedures of the time and review some of the considerations that entered into the acceptance or rejection of a publication for softcover, mass market reprint. These chapters accent Weybright's personal gatekeeper role and point out how others both inside and outside the company supported this role. Chapters 7 and 8 move slightly away from the routine editorial processes to review two aspects of NAL's publishing history: the censorship troubles it encountered in the early fifties and their effect on book selection as well as company efforts to uncover fresh writing talent and line up lucrative media tie-in projects. Chapter 9 examines two areas of a mass market publishing operation that technically lie outside of the editorial department: distribution and design. This chapter includes author and reader reactions to specific cover designs describing in detail the troubled circumstances under which covers for J. D. Salinger's *Catcher in the Rye* and *Nine Stories* were created.

The final chapter is a return to a review of basic author-editor relations. It centers on three writers: Erskine Caldwell, Mickey Spillane, and Irving Wallace. Each author helped to shape how the company, indeed how the softcover publishing industry, was viewed and viewed itself at the opening of the sixties. A brief epilogue closes the book summarizing events that occurred within the company after the correspondence ends.

Because this book frequently jumps back and forth in chronology to develop particular themes, the word *company* is used to denote the Weybright-Enoch partnership in an attempt to avoid distraction or confusion. It should be noted that my use of *NAL* denotes a company vision, stance, or policy, that is, the mutual position of both Weybright and Enoch. Whenever it was more accurate to specifically cite one partner or the other, this was done.

2

Shaw at the Automat

On the evening of 25 July 1946, many of postwar America's best-known literary and dramatic figures gathered at the Waldorf-Astoria Hotel in Manhattan to celebrate George Bernard Shaw's ninetieth birthday. The black-tie event, under the auspices of the *Saturday Review of Literature*, included most of the New York book publishing establishment, including Dodd, Mead & Company, Shaw's American hardcover publisher. Dodd, Mead had also prepared a small commemorative volume for the occasion. Company president, Howard C. Lewis, sat near the podium and addressed the assembled luminaries.

Victor Weybright was at a table in the audience with colleagues and friends of Penguin Books, Inc., the New York branch of Penguin Books. Penguin, where Weybright was editor in chief, had three Shaw plays under paperback reprint contract (see fig. 5, p. 108). Before the event, he had sought permission to distribute at the dinner a Penguin paper edition of *Major Barbara*. Approval had been denied, and Dodd, Mead threatened to pull out of the affair if the twenty-five cent editions were given away.

A few days after the affair, Weybright mailed copies of the softcover *Major Barbara* to the guests. He also sent the following summary of the Waldorf-Astoria event to the head of Penguin Books, Allen Lane in London, who was keeping a close eye on the activities of the New York office.

> Shaw's birthday was a big event in America, and Penguin was identified with the event in practically all of the literary comment in the press and at the big birthday dinner at the Waldorf in New York. By chance, I had a brief chat with John Mason Brown, master of ceremonies at the Shaw dinner, and contrived some

felicitous remarks about both Penguin Ltd. and Penguin Books, Inc. Shaw editions. I also told John about Dodd, Mead's attitude toward our inexpensive editions, and John included in his inimitable opening remarks the fact that Dodd, Mead regarded this as automat publishing. Your old and heavy-handed friend, Howard Lewis, in his turn on the podium gave a cheap commercial spiel about Dodd, Mead, opening his remarks with: "Speaking for Shaw's conventional publishers, not the Horn & Hardart variety . . ." [Horn & Hardart are the proprietors of the Automat, a nickle-in-the-slot restaurant chain]. You will recall that earlier I wrote to you that if we gave our Penguin editions to each guest at the dinner Dodd, Mead was going to withdraw from the affair and suggest the dinner be held at the Automat instead of at the Waldorf-Astoria. (29 July 1946)

In 1946 few people on the New York literary scene were likely to have felt much sympathy for Weybright's umbrage. For over a hundred years, four generations of the Dodd family had directed the firm's fortunes, making it one of the longest established publishing imprints in the United States. In contrast, the English-based Penguin Books was barely ten years old. Its New York staff numbered fewer than a half-dozen people, some of whom wore two and three hats. The Automat might indeed be the proper place for a softcover celebration. In England, after all, Penguins were sold from a variety of places including vending machines whose slots resembled the food dispensers of a Horn & Hardart.

In 1946 only a handful of paperback publishers existed. All were reprinters issuing previously published hardcover works, and therefore, all depended on the good graces of established hardcover book publishers to obtain suitable reprints. Softcover reprinters also depended on the good will of the leading hardcover reprinter of that time, Grosset & Dunlap, to whom proprietary hardcover publishers still looked in order to sell first republication rights. Hardcover publishers, fearful of alienating what for many years had been their chief source of secondary income, often sought permission from Grosset before selling "pocket book" reprint rights. When Grosset did select a book for its own series, softcover publishers were usually required to wait at least two years after the release of the hardcover reprint before issuing a paper reprint edition.

In 1946 the legitimacy of softcover reprinting was still suspect. Publishing industry skeptics in the United States pointed to a long list of short-lived paperback experiments that had failed during the previous half-century. Those that were still publishing were seen as having World War II to thank. (The general belief was that during wartime, provided you could find enough paper to print it, you could sell almost anything published.) Pocket Books, the most established of the current crop of United States softcover reprinters, was only seven years old and appeared to be succeeding only because of its strong connections with Simon & Schuster and benign ownership by newspaper publisher Marshall Field III. Rival paperback houses of Avon, Dell, and Popular Library had all been founded during the war. Each was tied directly to separate, mass circulation, pulp magazine publishers. Each sponsored fictional reprints that were lengthier versions of popular mysteries and romances then appearing on drugstore magazine racks. In retrospect, had Victor Weybright not been preparing softcover editions of three Shaw works, it is unlikely that his status as a softcover publisher would have merited him a place in the audience of the Waldorf celebration.

Allen Lane, with brothers John and Richard, founded the softcover Penguin Books series in the middle of the thirties' depression. At the time its prospects for success were seen by the London book publishing establishment as bleak. But Allen Lane's talent for predicting what the English reading public would buy plus his ability to surround himself with very able and dedicated staff created a fresh recipe for publishing books in Great Britain. Within a few years his company was secure enough to support a sales distribution branch in the United States. Import restrictions and paper shortages occasioned by World War II forced the American branch, established in New York City, to become indigenous publishers as well as distributors of British-made productions. Under the guidance of Ian Ballantine and Kurt Enoch, Penguin Books, Inc. (as opposed to Penguin Books, Ltd. of England) issued throughout the war years a relatively undistinguished list of British and American reprints. More or less independent of British control, the two chose to publish mainly murder mysteries and light fiction designed to compete directly with existing American softcover reprinters. In 1945 Ian Ballantine left Penguin in a disagreement with Lane over future directions for the American branch. In a very short time a book industry consortium including several established publishers underwrote the founding of Bantam Books under Ballantine's leadership. Grosset & Dunlap's head became Bantam's board chairman.

After Ballantine's departure, the operation of Penguin Books was left in the hands of Kurt Enoch. Enoch's experience with paperback publishing dated back to 1931. He had helped to found and manage Albatross Books, which quickly became the dominant reprinter of English-language books on the Continent. Forced out of Germany and eventually off the European continent by Hitler, Enoch arrived with his family in New York in 1940 virtually penniless. Shortly afterward, Allen Lane secured Enoch's book production and financial expertise for Penguin Books, Inc.

To assist Enoch in reorganizing the New York office after Ballantine's departure, Lane sent his administrative aide and "principal literary midwife," Eunice Frost (Morpurgo 127). Lane also sought assistance from Victor Weybright with whom he had forged a close wartime friendship during the latter's State Department service at the American Embassy in London. Weybright's past editorial experience and connections with the American intellectual and literary community made him an ideal candidate to permanently direct editorial matters in New York. After Weybright left the London Embassy in late November of 1945, he came to New York and took up duties as editorial director and later became editor in chief. Enoch and Weybright also worked out a partnership arrangement with Lane whereby each carried equal minority shares in the American branch. Each also assumed corporate titles: Enoch became president and treasurer; Weybright became chairman and secretary.

A dramatic change in the appearance and quality of publications issued by the New York office occurred in 1946. A larger-sized book format (4¼ by 7⅛ inches) had been introduced along with full-color, more professionally drawn covers with distinctive headbands and footbands. The company's intention to appeal to an audience different from other American softcover reprinters is revealed in a Weybright status report to Allen Lane composed just after the year had ended. "On the basis of 1946 successes, in 1947 we will continue to aim for the consistent rather than the casual reader. Our books will be of permanent value rather than 'one-shot' " (24 January 1947).[1]

The Penguin series imprint presented authors like E. M. Forester, D. H. Lawrence, John Dos Passos, Ignazio Silone, Sherwood Anderson, Carson McCullers and, as already noted, featured three plays by Shaw. The New York branch also began publishing a Pelican series that featured classics like Walter Lippmann's *Public Opinion*, Ruth Benedict's *Patterns of Culture*, and V. Gordon Childe's *What Happened in History*. The most dramatic occurrence of all, however, was the publication in March 1946 of Erskine Caldwell's *God's Little Acre*. It became one of the early paperback "blockbusters," and cemented the Enoch-Weybright partnership.

By late 1947, however, differences between Lane and his two American managers led to negotiations in London and to the takeover by Enoch and Weybright of the New York Penguin-Pelican list under a new and independent corporation called The New American Library of World Liter-

---

1. Financially, however, the company was operating in the red. Records in the Weybright files at the University of Wyoming indicate that at the close of the fiscal year on 30 June 1946, Penguin, Inc. had a deficit of ten thousand dollars. Enoch and Weybright each personally loaned the corporation five thousand dollars.

ature.[2] With the change in corporate name, official on 14 January 1948, came changes in the names of the two publishing series imprints. The Penguin series became "Signet Books" and the Pelican series was renamed "Mentor Books." Signet titles were generally works of fiction that competed directly with the majority of mass market publications being published. Sold at twenty-five cents, they were given the widest possible distribution. Printed in smaller quantities, Mentors, priced at thirty-five cents, were sold more selectively. Chiefly made up of nonfiction and some literary classics, they were most effectively displayed in college and general trade bookstores as opposed to the more numerous drugstore and smoke shop racks.

One of the earliest statements of a company publishing philosophy was drafted only a few weeks after the completed negotiations with Allen Lane for independence. It is part of a Weybright solicitation letter to Joseph C. Lesser, treasurer of Alfred A. Knopf. An attempt to convince hardcover publishers of the quality of NAL's publishing program, the letter was a model for hundreds Weybright drafted during his twenty-year tenure. It contains several themes that the company's editor in chief sounded in his missionarylike messages to hardcover publishers: the similarity between his company's publishing philosophy and the hardcover publishing philosophy, the literary quality of the current and future list, and the large and profitable mass market that would be tapped effectively through innovative company design and distribution practices. Finally, Weybright argues that mass market cultural aspirations and commercial goals can comfortably coexist in the same book publishing program. In this letter Weybright was negotiating for exclusive paperback reprint rights to James M. Cain.

> We wanted you to know, and to hear first hand, of our interest in *Past All Dishonor*, and in the paperbound reprint rights to Cain's major current and future books. As Mr. Enoch explained, our publishing policies resemble your own. We are not one-shot publishers, but we do believe we know how to get the most out of a literary property in the mass market. We prefer to develop constant reorders, and reprintings, rather than artifically forced distribution (and the consequent returns). We have already worked very hard to make Cain a dominant author on our list and, as we explained, have even worked and reworked the cover on our Cain

2. Weybright and Enoch each owned 42½ percent of the company. The remaining shares were equally divided between company lawyer, Rudolf Littauer, and the O'Shaughnessy Trust, which represented the interests of the company's Chicago-based book manufacturer, W. F. Hall Co. In 1965 the company corporate name was shortened by dropping "The" and "of World Literature."

books so as to give them a characteristic Cain flare. We have just decided to give a substantial reprint order on *Mildred Pierce* and *Serenade* with new artwork for the covers. This effort, of course, is designed to give continual impact to Cain's sales in our market, in anticipation of developing the property further when other Cain titles become available to us. . . . It would fit right into a very strong list which we are developing without sacrificing the standards which identify us with the book business, even though our distribution is mainly magazine-wise. (8 December 1947)

The company's ambivalent if not servile status within the book industry in the early years of its history is captured in an almost plaintive letter that Weybright wrote to Robert L. Crowell. Crowell was head of the 115-year-old T. Y. Crowell Company, a company no longer in existence today. Apparently the trade book publisher wanted little to do with NAL.[3] A note followed the phone conversation that Weybright had with Crowell. "I am sorry, however, that you were unable to make a luncheon appointment, or even an office appointment, in the near future, as I should like to have discussed personally with you the unique sales which we can achieve through our technique of editorial selection and dynamic merchandising" (18 November 1949). Weybright was anxious to convince Crowell that NAL was the best publisher for *Cheaper by the Dozen*, then scheduled to be made into a film. Weybright concluded this same letter with an irresolute written offer that could not have reflected well on the emerging publisher. "Therefore, since we are convinced that a book of that quality and character [*Cheaper by the Dozen*] will have the best chance on our list, under our trademark, and under our promotion and distributing set up, we offer an advance of say $5,000, but would like this amount to be considered as subject to review if, in your opinion, it seems entirely inadequate, or your thoughts are tempted by the possibility of a higher advance from another quarter. Indeed, we are tempted to suggest that you name the figure yourself" (18 November 1949). The reprint eventually went to Bantam.

NAL's wooing of the Viking Press in quest of John Steinbeck, whom Weybright recognized as having great paperback sales potential, exhibits much of the same low-key approach. Their semicaptive position in relation to hardcover publishing is clearly underscored in this very early memo (on

---

3. NAL publishing records show, however, that in the formative years of 1947–52 most of the major trade book publishing houses did business with the company. These included Appleton-Century-Crofts; Dial; Doubleday; Dutton; Duell, Sloan & Pearce; Farrar, Straus; Harper; Houghton Mifflin; Knopf; Little, Brown; Macmillan; New Directions; Prentice-Hall; Random House; Rinehart; Scribner's; Simon & Schuster; Vanguard; Viking; and Yale University Press.

Penguin letterhead) from Weybright to Enoch. The editor in chief discusses the fear—then shared by all original, hardcover publishers—that two Viking executives had of a reprinter's paper edition undercutting sales of their hardcover edition or any hardcover reprint editions also negotiated.

> Marshall Best apparently recommended a rather hard bargain on *Tortilla Flat*, which I discussed with Harold Guinzburg today, and confirmed our acceptance for immediate scheduling in April.
>
> Since Steinbeck's usual royalty guarantee has been $5,000, Harold thought it wise for us to come to that amount—although he agrees with me that the guarantee is meaningless if Penguin really can sell as many books as anyone else in the field.
>
> The real catch—which actually doesn't disturb me too much—is . . . that, if we impair the sales of the trade edition, and of hard cover reprint editions, to an extent beyond that of our own earnings for the publisher and the author, Viking can at the end of a year terminate the contract on six months' notice.
>
> I think we should be quite willing to take a chance on such a proposition, and, indeed, I told Harold that we welcomed the experiment. . . . In no case, if Viking exercises this option, will the book be resold to any other twenty-five cent publisher.[4] (18 February 1946)

The company was awarded rights to the novel. With visions of other Steinbecks firmly fixed, Weybright wrote Marshall A. Best a year and a half later a letter (also on Penguin letterhead) that in essence defines for that postwar stage of mass market publishing the ideal working relationship between an original, hardcover publisher and a paperback reprinter of serious books. This letter is interesting in another respect as it confirms that as early as 1947 the company was active in placing nonfiction manuscripts with hardcover publishers for initial publication.

> I was struck by the story in today's *Herald Tribune* which quoted you as saying that the cost-price squeeze threatens to kill off publication of many worthwhile books. This has a bearing on Penguin's relations with trade publishing. We are, in the course of both our Pelican and Penguin programs, providing trade publishers

---

4. This is one of the earliest examples of correspondence between the two partners found in the archival files. Weybright addressed it to "Mr. Enoch." Harold Guinzburg, head of Viking, was a wartime colleague of Weybright in the Office of War Information. Marshall A. Best was Viking's general manager.

with some modest subsidiary revenue on books in the field of Belles Lettres, science and history.

In a half dozen recent instances, we have even cooperated with trade publishers on the development of significant non-fiction, assuming our share of the costs from the outset, so that the trade publisher and the author can count on more than ordinary popularity for such titles in advance. For example we have placed an important book on American Indians by John Collier with Norton; a scholarly historical volume by Henry Steele Commager with Random House; a religious symposium edited by Bishop Scarlett; and an outstanding new book on American ballet by [George] Amberg of the Museum of Modern Art with Duell, Sloan & Pearce. In each case we have worked with the author and the author's publisher. . . .

In working closely with the trade publishers, and in helping to avert the tendency towards specialization in quick best sellers, we'd like to feel that Penguin can count on the cooperation of trade publishers ensuring with Penguin some of the genuinely popular titles which admittedly are necessary in the reprint business as well as in the trade publishing business. Even then we like to think that quite apart from and in addition to the subsidiary income derived from reprint royalties, we also stimulate interest in an author's work by genuine book readers. (10 July 1947)

In the company's early years the reading tastes of United States paperback buyers were still being explored on a more or less hit-and-miss basis. The wartime sales of Penguin were not a good measure of postwar reading tastes. Paper restrictions imposed by the federal government reduced the number and quantity of titles printed. New reading material was scarce; practically everything published could be sold to wholesale distributors and presumably to the public at large. At the close of World War II, competition for readership heightened. New softcover publishers, like Bantam, entered the field. Those already in the field expanded reprint programs, producing more titles and larger printings. But as early as the spring of 1946, return rates ballooned as wholesalers began to send back cartons of paperbacks that had rested unsold in their warehouses throughout most of the war.[5]

5. Return rates that were 2 percent or lower during the war rose to averages that probably equaled 15 to 20 percent of annual gross sales. Today mass market return rates average between 35 and 55 percent of initial sales depending on the publisher and the distribution channel. This has created enormous marketing problems for an industry that accepts the stripped front cover of a paperback as credit verification.

The problem that Weybright and Enoch faced as they reorganized the company immediately after the war was endemic to the industry: identification of its mass market readership. Embarassing selection mistakes were made. Reprint rights for the bulk of the novels of Edna Ferber, who had a string of bestsellers to her credit, were negotiated by the company in early 1946. At first, it appeared that American-based Penguin had made a major coup in obtaining exclusive paperback reprint rights to Ferber's major novels. However, it became apparent by the spring of 1948 that after paying out substantial advances and publishing six Ferber titles, the company was losing substantial amounts of money on the arrangement. NAL, newly separated from Allen Lane's Penguin imprint, undercapitalized, and burdened by a large debt with its book manufacturer, sought relief from the Ferber contract that the company estimated would cost it fifty thousand dollars in losses. In a lengthy aide-mémoire prepared during termination negotiations with Ferber's agent and with her hardcover publisher, Doubleday, Weybright summarized two years of selection experience as editor in chief. "We began to see that the titles which were most substantial on our list were those of genuine literary quality or dynamic contemporary appeal, and that, for the most part, magazine writers of the Ferber type . . . had limited appeal" (19 April 1948). No additional Ferber titles were published by the company, but problems in determining readership preference were not associated only with "magazine writers of the Ferber type." Even writers with established literary reputations were not meeting company sales expectations.[6]

Also in the spring of 1948, Sam Rapport of Appleton-Century-Crofts was asking why NAL had not scheduled for publication three books sold to the reprinter some time earlier: Edith Wharton's *Age of Innocence* and *Hudson River Bracketed* plus Stephen Crane's *Red Badge of Courage*. At this time the multiple Ferber contract was still being reviewed. NAL had become cautious. In his reply to Rapport, Weybright first dealt with the Crane title, which Pocket Books had earlier reprinted in 1942. "When we contracted for this title we did not realize the attitude of the trade—the magazine wholesalers—toward the assumption of a title previously carried by a competitor. Pocket Book returns of *The Red Badge of Courage* have been used to service their school program so that it would be embarrassing for us to publish the work in the near future" (21 June 1948). In the same letter to Rapport, Weybright outlined why the two Wharton novels were not scheduled. "Ordinarily, instead of contracting for two titles, we would—now—endeavor to contract for one title only by an author with

6. In mid-1947 Weybright also asked Doubleday for release from multiple book contracts on O. Henry and Joseph Conrad titles negotiated a year and a half earlier.

an option on subsequent titles. In a number of instances where, in the imprudent days of 1945 and 1946, we made multiple contracts, we have consolidated them and adjusted them downward with other publishers— on the assumption that it makes for a more profitable long-term program, freeing funds for more practical new contracts on other works. With this in mind I am surveying the Appleton-Century-Crofts list" (21 June 1948). Weybright proposed a settlement of two thousand dollars; it was rejected by Rapport, who pointed out that his company in the past had also been stuck with unprofitable contractual clauses but "carried them out as a matter of policy." Enoch then took over negotiations, explaining that NAL "would not have asked you to make adjustments if circumstances beyond our control would not have made the publication of the three books completely uneconomical, a condition which we could not foresee when we signed the contracts." He settled with Rapport for slightly less than five thousand dollars. None of the books were published by NAL under the original agreement.

Early in the summer of 1948 the company was very anxious to acquire Steinbeck's *The Wayward Bus* from Viking. However, high returns plus large printing bills led the partners to try to link the royalty advance Viking would demand with royalty overpayment they had made to Viking on two Graham Greene thrillers, *The Confidential Agent* and *The Ministry of Fear*. They proposed advancing little if any money to Viking for the new Steinbeck in consideration of the money they were losing on the two Greene titles reprinted in 1943 and 1944 respectively in a small-sized American Penguin format. Replying to the reprinter's proposal, Marshall A. Best lectured, "With an author of Greene's stature, who is reaching an ever-widening audience, it would seem astonishing if you could not find an audience for him now or later, even though you failed to reach it before." Recommending new distribution of the Greene titles, Best pointed out that redistribution had been successful for Steinbeck whose "older titles have benefited in the cheap edition market from the success of the newer titles." He also rubbed more salt by concluding, "If you want me to take it up with Ian Ballantine on the chance that he would be interested in acquiring these titles, I will do so" (6 August 1948). Mildly chastised, Kurt Enoch replied:

> As I explained to you in our last visit, we are extremely eager to
> make our relationship a more satisfactory and profitable one for
> both of us. We would like very much to add books from the
> Viking list to the number of outstanding successes which we have
> had with quality titles from other publishers. Unfortunately, our
> cooperation in the past has suffered from a number of adversities.

We made certain mistakes in selecting books or in assessing guarantees which lead to our asking for adjustments not less embarrassing to us than to you. We certainly appreciate your cooperation in this case. However, as a whole, I believe we have been more the sufferer than you, and, although I realize that it has to be so because we and not you made the mistakes, we feel that it should be taken into consideration that, as the chart turned over to you at our last meeting shows, our losses on your books have been quite substantial, whereas we have been at least partially successful in creating income for you and your authors. In our opinion, the sales potential of these two books in the mass market is more or less exhausted for a long time to come. We have printed roughly 250,000 copies of each of them and we have received returns so far of 85,000 of one and 106,000 of the other, during a time when we sold through the same outlets millions of copies of other titles. Although an outstanding success of Greene's new book in the mass market might result in some additional sales, it remains extremely questionable whether the wholesalers would accept again a large distribution of our two titles, a possibility which in any case could not be considered in the very near future. (25 August 1948)

Best, however, continued to resist any adjustment that Enoch proposed, including a return of part of the Greene royalty advance. Two days later he replied, "We don't feel ready to pay this money back to you now, though we don't refuse to reopen the question later." On 30 August Weybright took over negotiations by first pleading, "Let's not permit bygones to interfere with mutually advantageous business in the future." Continuing, however, he heavy-handedly pointed out that NAL's current standard reprint contract with hardcover publishers contained a clause requiring the original publisher to agree to return the overpayment of royalty figures when the reprinter has forwarded too much royalty money caused by unexpected returns. Weybright states that "so far, no trade publisher has demurred" and ended his letter with another pitch for *The Wayward Bus*. Weybright ignored their original reprint contract for the two Greene titles that probably did not contain a royalty return clause. Further, Weybright ignored the fact that many hardcover publishers were striking this sort of provision from contracts submitted to them by reprinters, a fact that Viking's Best certainly would have known. NAL never acquired another Greene or Steinbeck title from Viking during Weybright's tenure with the company. Both became Bantam authors, and therefore for a time, Ian Ballantine reprinted them. Viking did, however, allow NAL to continue to reissue *Tortilla Flat* in softcover.

In these early tentative and tenuous years the reprinter gave little allegiance to an author or to preserving an author's words. Out of necessity, appeals for contractual relief were based on economies required for company survival. In turn, hardcover publishers were understanding but not inclined to accede to the reprinter's request for relief, citing as primary their authors' own financial necessities (with whom as proprietors they divided reprint subsidiary income equally). Survival of the reprinter and the income it generated was at best of secondary interest to the hardcover publisher. However, by the turn of the decade there was indication that the tide was shifting. With an eye on Willard Motley's *Knock on Any Door*, NAL again approached Sam Rapport of Appleton-Century-Crofts for reprint negotiations. Apparently unembarrassed by his company's past nonperformance on Crane and Wharton for Appleton-Century-Crofts and with much assuredness based on outstanding newsstand successes with authors like Erskine Caldwell and Mickey Spillane, Weybright not only underscored NAL's newly acquired marketing strength but also its apparent commitment to enlarging an author's audience and reputation.

I am certain that the decision on Motley's work will not be based purely on the amount of the advance, which by no means warrants that the highest bidder is the best reprinter for a book. In addition to total royalty income, there is the intangible value of the trademark under which the reprint appears. Here, immodestly, we can boast. We have gained acceptance for substantial literature in the mass market to a degree not approached by anyone else in our field. Indeed, it is now perceptible that the flavor and personality of the three major paperbound houses, distributed through the Independent Wholesalers [Pocket Books, Bantam, and NAL], are recognizably different—and in the trade and among ultimate readers, we have developed acceptance and enormous sales for authors, like Motley, in the top flight of contemporary literature.

I scarcely need amplify in this letter the conversation I had with you quite a while back, on our sales organization and our method of merchandising through magazine outlets, bookstores, chains, export, etc.; of our publishing policy of deliberately restricting the number of new releases each month and thereby achieving the greatest number of sales per title in our field; and of the established acceptance of our distinctive Signet and Mentor books by the trade, consumers, and reviewers. But I do want to repeat myself on one point: the development of author-consciousness, and the planned handling of all of an author's work, as we have done with Caldwell, Faulkner, Cain, Farrell, etc. (9 February 1950)

17

Weybright succeeded in his bid. *Knock on Any Door* became the first publication in NAL's highly touted Signet Double Volume series and Willard Motley shared with Appleton NAL's advance of twenty-five thousand dollars. Within the next ten years, two other Motley novels were reprinted in Signet editions. With a stable financial base to rest on, the editor in chief was now able to offer royalty payments substantially larger on average than those negotiated only a few years earlier.

Paperback reprinters were generally discouraged from dealing directly with an author they were reprinting. A gentleman's agreement among book publishers permitted a reprinter to consult with an author only through his proprietary, hardcover publisher or, with knowledge of the hardcover publisher, through the author's agent. In March 1948, shortly after its 31 January separation from Penguin, Weybright hastily wrote to the editor of *Tide* magazine correcting a recent report that NAL had recently signed a contract with James M. Cain to act as exclusive publisher of his books.

> This is an error which I should like to correct. We have a contract with Alfred A. Knopf, Inc. for the paperbound reprint rights of Mr. Cain's major current novels which are published by Knopf. As you know, a reprint publisher never approaches an author directly if the rights to a book are held by a trade publisher, and your statement, as quoted above, is therefore embarrassing to all concerned.
>
> We can readily understand how the information given to you by a member of our staff on forthcoming Cain books to be reprinted under our imprint may have been abbreviated to omit the vital reference to Mr. Cain's original publisher. I would appreciate it if this correction were published so as to correct any impression that we have violated the protocol for publishing by short-circuiting a publisher and approaching the publisher's author directly. (31 March 1948)

And this protocol for a time grew even more rigid when in early 1950 Fawcett Publications began issuing original paperback publications under a Gold Medal Books imprint. By issuing original books, Fawcett was realistically viewed by hardcover publishers as undermining the established order within publishing, that is, an author's work should first appear in a hardcover edition before becoming a paperback. These same hardcover publishers, along with most of NAL's softcover rivals, were even less enamored by this new development when they discovered some of their authors were negotiating contracts for Gold Medal originals. For a time NAL was suspect of complicity with Fawcett.

To reach the eight hundred or more independent wholesalers who in turn sold, shelved, and serviced paperback books in the newsstands and drugstores around the country, mass market publishers employed a national distributor who was already selling national magazines and newspapers to the wholesalers. From 1945 to 1955, Fawcett Publications magazine publishers and distributors also served as national distributor of Signet and Mentor paperbacks. In a note to Random House's Bennett Cerf in 1947, Weybright explained simply that "Fawcetts, like the atomic scientist, are expert at promoting a chain reaction when we deliver the uranium." A clause in its distribution agreement prohibited Fawcett from publishing "any general line of books, retailing at 25 or 35 cents," competitive to books issued by NAL. However, Fawcett decided to publish a line of softcover original books not deemed competitive with NAL's reprints. And when in November 1949, through a letter of agreement, NAL amended the distribution arrangement to specifically allow Fawcett to publish material that had first appeared in its magazines or original manuscripts that did not compete with the nonfiction categories of the Mentor line, the Fawcett Gold Medal was born. The agreement still restricted Fawcett from publishing "reprints or adaptations of publications of other publishers."[7]

Shortly after the 1949 amended agreement was reached, NAL began to receive reactions like those of Richard G. May of Rinehart & Company, "I am greatly disturbed by the news that Fawcett is going into original reprint." He asked Weybright to account for the new Gold Medal line. Weybright's reply tries to separate NAL from the magazine publisher and align it more closely with hardcover publishing aspirations.

> We have no connection whatever with Fawcett's publishing program.
> We ourselves would not want Signet or Mentor books to be identified with Fawcett's Gold Medal books for the self-same reasons which you mentioned—i.e., their policy of publishing 25¢ editions of original fiction is antagonistic to established practices in the book publishing industry with which we enjoy the happiest of relations; and their editorial criteria are certainly at variance with ours.
> Let me state, categorically, on behalf of New American Library, that there is no direct or indirect, financial, editorial or any other

7. It further restricted Fawcett from using cover design formats similar to those used on Signets and Mentors "consisting of a series of vari-colored bands which run horizontally across the front, spine and back of the upper and lower part of such covers." Three documents that deal with Fawcett national distribution for New American Library and Penguin Books, Inc. appear in "The Victor Weybright Collection," Archives of Contemporary History, University of Wyoming.

connection between our books and Fawcett's books. They are competitive, in the paper bound book field, with everyone else in the business.

We have, from the very outset of our publishing program, prided ourselves—as you at Rinehart must do—on our independence. We are not linked to a book publishing combine, as Bantam is, or to any other single publishing house, as Pocket Books is. We are not linked with a printing concern, as Dell is, or with a hodge-podge of publishing activities in the manner of Avon or Popular [Library]. We have prided ourselves on being single-minded specialists in our job—the re-printing of the best literature in every field. We have not originated fiction, except for a few anthologies, and we have not originated non-fiction when reprint possibilities have existed. In practically all of the instances in which we have originated non-fiction, we have worked cooperatively with an appropriate trade publisher—with Houghton Mifflin on bird re-cognition, with Holt on wild flower recognition, with Norton on American Indians, with Random on a [Henry Steele] Commager book, etc.

I have put all of this on the record so that you will appreciate how deeply I feel about the questions raised in your letter. We value especially the high regard of the better trade publishers for us and for our books. We are recognized as the most "bookish" paper bound publishers, even by trade publishers who are represented on the board of one of our competitors. (30 May 1950)

Fawcett use of Signet and Mentor display racks caused irritation and embarrassment to NAL as well as confusion within the industry. The 1949 letter of agreement did allow Fawcett, which had not yet decided the extent to which it would enter the paperback field, to use NAL display racks. It appears that this clause was quickly retracted as Fawcett rapidly developed a full-fledged marketing program by the close of 1950 and Signets were being mixed with or upstaged by Fawcett Gold Medal titles on NAL racks. In addition, both original hardcover publishers and their authors objected to having their reprinted publications displayed next to the more sensa-tional and seemingly more ephemeral Gold Medal originals.

The hardcover publishers, especially those that regularly issued cate-gory fiction, were beginning to lose many of these authors. Some writers discovered that their income from Gold Medal original publication could exceed the combined royalties of a traditional hardcover and paperback reprint arrangement. Jim Bishop, then Gold Medal editor, was promising experienced and prolific writers publication of everything they could turn out. After lunching with one hardcover editor, NAL editor Walter Freeman reported back. "By taking some books turned down by hardcover publishers Gold Medal has built up considerable good-will and may be expected to continue to do so, tending to draw more mystery and western writers. Publishers don't do a thing for mysteries and westerns as far as advertising and promotion are concerned and this fact makes it easy for Gold Medal to persuade writers to come to them directly—once the prestige factor can be disposed of" (5 June 1951). Observing that the reviewing media ignored softcover originals, Dutton hardcover editor Sherman Baker recognized in the spring of 1950 the quandary serious writers faced, and he conceded in a note to Weybright: "There is no other choice for a writer who will do three books a year. But he cannot have both critical acclaim as a serious writer and security."

Along with the other established hardcover and paperback reprint publishers, NAL was losing some authors it had earlier reprinted. This included Wade Miller (Bob Wade and Bill Miller) whom Weybright enjoyed referring to as "the boys." The editor in chief candidly summarized the situation for company lawyer and minority partner Rudolf Littauer. "I learned that our mystery writing team, Wade Miller whose trade books are published by Farrar, Straus, are writing original material for Fawcett. I told their literary agent that, if Wade Miller books are published else-where than Signet, we shall seriously have to consider dropping Wade Miller from our list. Incidentally, that is a pretty feeble threat—when the authors and agents receive full royalties from Fawcett and only half of the royalties from our reprints—the full royalties are likely to exceed the combination of ours and Farrar, Straus royalties" (14 December 1949).

Wade Miller managed to do what few other authors on the NAL list accomplished: to have their new softcover editions issued by both NAL and Gold Medal. Fawcett continued to get their originals, while NAL published Wade Miller reprints obtained through Farrar, Straus. The chief reason that Wade Miller remained on the Signet list is contained in NAL editor Marc Jaffe's observation at the time that "the boys have never set the world on fire saleswise, but so far as I know, we have not had a single flop with one of their books—which is a record to consider when approaching the whole problem."

By mid-1951 NAL was in a quandary. The Wade Miller Gold Medal efforts, though deemed both by NAL and Farrar, Straus as "trashy" and not worthy of their separate imprints, were being published and sold in quantities that far exceeded Signets.[8] Weybright had a simple explanation,

---

8. At this time Gold Medal's first printings of Wade Miller titles averaged 450,000. NAL's first printings of Wade Miller were less than half of this figure.

which he shared with Roger Straus, Jr., that "the Gold Medal Wade Millers are, to be frank, very spicy" (11 June 1951). The writers' cantankerous agent, Donald MacCampbell, who was highly supportive of the original Gold Medal line when it was founded, caustically described NAL's sales as "disgraceful." Weybright was quick to respond, "We put Wade Miller on the escalator—now you want to see them step off on someone else's floor" (11 November 1950).

But throughout the early fifties, Fawcett continued to stand at the escalator handing out invitations to other NAL authors, including two for whom its national distributorship achieved "bestsellerdom," Erskine Caldwell and Mickey Spillane. Spillane was particularly vulnerable. Acknowledged as his own best press agent, he seems to have taken great pleasure in promoting his books among the Fawcett salesmen at marketing conferences and among wholesalers on field trips. Spillane's name began appearing on Gold Medal covers on promotional blurbs for books that for one reason or another neither NAL nor Dutton, Spillane's hardcover publisher, were anxious to issue. (See chapter 10.)

Fawcett's initial success with its Gold Medal list in the early fifties and other original paperback imprints that soon followed like Dell's First Editions series did not seem to tempt NAL to seriously consider a proprietary publishing program of its own. The files show NAL declining many direct overtures from writers. A typical response was Arabel Porter's reply to a William Saroyan query. "If the idea of a book you propose appeals to your regular publisher, however, we should be happy to consider it a possibility jointly with your publisher, but we do not believe that it would be to your advantage to contemplate 'first book publication in an inexpensive form,' without a regular trade edition and the publicity, advertising and reviewing that accompany publication through regular channels. In any case, we do appreciate your interest and enthusiasm" (19 September 1950).

At this time, however, NAL editors were establishing personal working relationships with many of the writers whom they were reprinting. The exchanges were generally to the mutual advantage of both reprinter and author. NAL editor Truman Talley and author Alfred Bester enjoyed a strong friendship that was secured in 1951 after Talley read Bester's *Demolished Man*, which was destined to become a science fiction classic. He described the book to Victor Weybright as "perhaps the most brilliant science fiction novel I have read" and convinced NAL to select it for reprint. Three years later Talley wrote to Theodore Purdy, then editor at G. P. Putnam, concerning Bester who was unhappy with his current hardcover publisher, Shasta. "Only a few people know that he is in the process of breaking off with his former trade publisher for delay in payment of royalties. Bester has had other inquiries about his next book. I have told

1.0 — ~~Bottom~~

2 ~~$25~~ Bottom History + V.W
~~5~~ Both Pages
~~56~~

1 ~~#~~ Roma
176 — 117 Bond
~~#9 — 115~~

√176 — ~~177~~ — NAC — death

~~224~~ — ~~ICE~~ VW.

194 — 195 Cover
~~TH~~ ~~Roma~~
~~TOC~~ ~~Pin~~

SOUTHERN ILLINOIS UNIVERSITY PRESS
Post Office Box 3697
Carbondale, Illinois 62902-3697

 We submit herewith for review

TITLE   <u>Heavy Traffic and High Culture:</u>
<u>New American Library as Literary</u>
<u>Gatekeeper in the Paperback</u>

AUTHOR   <u>Revolution</u>

    Thomas L. Bonn

PUBLICATION DATE
        July 31, 1989

PRICE $19.95

We shall appreciate receiving a copy of any notice that may appear.

him that I favor you and the Putnam imprint for a variety of reasons and he is pleased with the idea" (23 March 1954).

Street-smart authors were themselves not hesitant to fertilize their initial encounters with mass market reprinters. Isaac Asimov, whose prodigious output over the last thirty-five years could not have occurred without cooperative publisher relationships, reflects this in his warm "bread-and-butter" letter to Truman Talley, composed shortly after NAL had contracted to reprint *The Currents of Space*, Asimov's first softcover publication. "In particular, I want to thank you for the cocktails that Gertrude and I enjoyed with you. It was a big thrill for the girl. It has been the dream of her life to move in lit'ry and artistic circles and one of the ways in which I won her hand was to assure her that once married to me her life would be one gay round of publisher's cocktail parties" (16 May 1953). A few weeks later Asimov sent Talley a carbon of his letter to Walter I. Bradbury, his hardcover editor at Doubleday. At the time NAL was failing to convince Doubleday's subsidiary rights department to retain an option clause placed in the reprint contract for *The Currents of Space*. This stipulation would have required Doubleday to give NAL the first opportunity to bid on Asimov's next book. Asimov, however, was obviously pleased with his dealings with NAL; he saw it in his best interest to assist the reprinter in acquiring *The Caves of Steel*, his next scheduled book with Doubleday. In essence, Asimov was asking that hardcover editor, Bradbury, become an advocate on behalf of himself and NAL with the Doubleday subsidiary rights people.

> By the way, I haven't yet had a chance to say how happy I am over the fact that Signet Books is going to put out a quarter edition of *The Currents of Space*. I am very grateful to Doubleday for making the sale and to Signet Books for taking it.
>
> Of course, I realize, contractually, that Doubleday has full power of disposing of quarter book sales as they please, but I think very highly of Signet Books and I hope that in the case of future books, particularly *Caves of Steel*, you'd decide to give Signet first crack. In fact, I strongly urge it. And it would please me to have you do so. (13 July 1953)

Two years later *The Caves of Steel* also appeared as a Signet.

Because of the growing number of direct exchanges between author and paperback reprinter and in light of the original softcover publishing programs of Fawcett, Dell, and others, it is understandable that hardcover publishers would begin to question the future editorial directions Weybright and Enoch might take. This concern is acknowledged by Weybright in a 1951 letter to Whitney Darrow, Sr. of Scribner's; it clearly states the prevailing softcover reprint publishing philosophy.

I very much appreciated the opportunity yesterday of discussing with you some of the basic aspects of the relationships between a reprinter and a trade publisher. These relationships, and the personalities who reflect them, are fundamental to our specialized field of publishing.

We have, on a foundation of solid relationships with the major trade publishers, built a unique organization in the reprint field, one of the largest in net sales at home and abroad, and certainly one of the most creative in exploiting the market for a wide variety of literature to the great advantage of trade publishers and their authors. As specialists in our job—with no financial or managerial link with any printing or distributing outfit, or with any combination of periodical or book publishers—we are particularly proud through our close association with the more distinguished trade publishers to reflect the traditions of publishing at their best.

We have never regarded our reprints of important literature as mere byproduct of trade editions, but as a sort of planned protection in the handling of literary property—frequently a means of interesting a wider audience in an author's future work, and in most cases, a source of accrued revenue over the years when the trade sales have declined to a point where the revenue from a reprint is, in the opinion of a trade publisher, more desirable than a marginal trade sales effort. In certain instances, too, indeed in most instances, we have found that New American Library editions have revived interest in, rather than competed with, trade editions of fiction of the sort which has an enduring classical or semi-classical claim on a long-term audience. These tangible and intangible factors cannot always be resolved on the auction block, but, in our opinion, can profitably be discussed in terms of the overall development of a particular literary property.

We don't want to encroach on the trade field, and do not short-circuit trade publishers with direct or original deals; but rather, we regard it as our function to extend your projection of an author's work, and your and your authors' fortunes in the literary market place at our level of price and efficient mass distribution. (27 June 1951)

3

Shakespeare at Hampton Court

In June of 1950 NAL moved from offices on lower Fifth Avenue to the heart of Madison Avenue and a building also housing Alfred A. Knopf, Inc. Despite a thirteenth-floor location, the move was considered favorable by Victor Weybright as they were within easy walking distance of other major hardcover publishers such as Random House, Scribner's, and Simon & Schuster. A 5 May 1952 *Newsweek* article labeling the paperback company as the "biggest in the business" shows a photograph of the genial-looking editor in chief with his copartner, Kurt Enoch.[1] The article concluded with a lyrical characterization of Weybright and the people who surrounded him:

> . . . a sociable individual whose daily round often includes three or four literary cocktail parties, and who collects at his apartment best-selling novelists, visiting English editors, Greek translators, advance-guard poets, science-fiction experts, reviewers, publishers, and agents. He has recently remarried, his second wife the widow of the producer and head of Fox Movietone News; and his literary gatherings, with his handsome stepdaughter and stepson mingling with the poets, suggest a pleasant combination of art and enterprise.
>
> But no bellow of despair from a baffled poet is likely to disturb this salon. The people concerned with publishing the literary reprints are people with a mission, profoundly convinced of the

---

1. Financial records in the Weybright file at the University of Wyoming show that the assets of the company increased from $142,902.92 as of 30 June 1946 (while it was still Penguin, Inc.) to $2,688,504.12 by 1952.

worth of their work, ultimately hopeful of getting the works of the poets to millions of readers—or at least hopeful that the possibility will inspire them to write better. They believe that making good books available for everyone is the most important work in the world. (5 May 1952)

The first half of the fifties saw the company polishing this *Newsweek* image as it combined art and enterprise by identifying and signing up for reprint most of the leading young American writers of fiction including Norman Mailer, James Jones, Truman Capote, Gore Vidal, William Styron, Flannery O'Connor, and J. D. Salinger. Weybright was especially sensitive to the new black writers. The names of Ralph Ellison, James Baldwin, and Richard Wright appeared on Signet covers at this time. NAL also made a specialty of reprinting postwar Italian realists. In 1952, under the watchful care of editor Arabel Porter, NAL sponsored the first mass market literary magazine, *New World Writing*. While never making much money, *New World Writing* received widespread accolades from the American literary establishment during the eight years it was produced by NAL. It also served as an excellent entrée for the company to early consideration of the longer works by the talented novelists, dramatists, and poets who appeared in the serial publication.

Equally praiseworthy and undoubtedly more profitable were the scholarly works, mainly nonfiction, which made up the Mentor series. As noted earlier, these received more limited distribution than the Signets. They found their way to serious readers by appearing on the shelves of retail bookstores, particularly those on and around college campuses. Many of the books in the Mentor series had their origins in the NAL editorial offices. Usually the paperback publisher tried to find a trade publisher willing to produce a hardcover edition to be issued before or simultaneously with a softcover Mentor appearance.

In blazing contrast with the scholarly Mentor series and the literary *New World Writing* magazine were the seven blood-boiled detective novels of Mickey Spillane published by NAL. Beginning in 1948 with *I, the Jury*, the widely publicized and criticized thrillers found the crew-cut author succeeding Erskine Caldwell in his publisher's claim of being "The World's Best Selling Author." The figures were impressive, with each book selling into the many millions. In the five years between the publication of Spillane's first and last book, NAL's gross sales more than doubled.

As with "midlist" book publishing today, certain categories of literature presented predictable financial difficulties in the early fifties. Some of these are outlined by Victor Weybright to Harvard professor and NAL adviser Howard Mumford Jones after Jones had urged NAL to reprint some lesser-known works of American literature. Weybright's cautious reply to Jones' suggestions reveal how culture and commerce were regularly pitted head to head.

> You pose a tough problem for a publisher of inexpensive editions who must depend on an audience of at least 75,000 for a short book and considerably over 100,000 for a long book, which is more costly to produce. I have been mindful of our neglect of significant and important American literature of the 19th and the first few decades of the 20th century. The brutal reality of the situation is that, except for the old established works which are constantly kept in print, a sufficient audience does not seem to exist for the quantity of printings that must be undertaken to justify the price of 25 cents or 35 cents. We are constantly studying the possibilities of a slightly higher price for the commercially border-line sort of titles which you suggest should be made available. I agree with you—they should. Whether we are equipped to cope with the problem is the big question.
>
> Mark you, Howard, although I don't quarrel with your comments in general, I do claim credit for rescuing a number of out-of-print books and giving them a wide currency in our Signet and Mentor editions. Most of them, however, have been non-fiction. (22 September 1950)

Seen as a much larger problem, however, was the manufacture and publication of works with greater than average paperback page length. Signets, like their rival softcover imprints designed for unlimited mass distribution, remained priced at twenty-five cents, the amount that Pocket Books initiated in 1939. The cost of manufacturing and marketing soft-covers had steadily risen, however, particularly the price of paper, the largest single item of expense in the production of paperbacks. By the late forties, paper costs alone made the prospects of reprinting a book over two hundred pages, without abridgment, very slim. A few publishers were experimenting with "Giant" editions priced ten cents more than the quarter norm. To counter perceived consumer resistance to higher cover prices, publishers also began to abridge or condense publications, particularly works of fiction. Sometimes the work was shortened by 50 percent or more.

Kurt Enoch proposed publishing a series of "Double Volumes" priced at fifty cents. These were designed to convince buyers that they were getting the equivalent of two books worth of reading for a half dollar. The first of these Double Volumes, Willard Motley's *Knock on Any Door*, was published in 1950; it was followed by a string of thicker Signets.[2] Early in the following year, Weybright mailed a lengthy letter of invitation to several hardcover publishers with whom he was anxious to do business, and he confidently informed them of that.

We know you'll be interested to learn that our fifty cent Signet Double Volumes are a huge success. The first four titles—*Knock on Any Door* by Willard Motley, *Forever Amber* by Kathleen Winsor, *The Young Lions* by Irwin Shaw, and *The Naked and the Dead* by Norman Mailer—are selling so well that, even though their first printings and initial distribution were substantial, we've already had to go back to press several times. Wholesalers and retailers throughout the country have enthusiastically accepted this new kind of paper-back book. They are pleased to be able to handle an even wider variety of good books now made possible by our solving of the length plus cost problem, with larger profit on each book, and with elimination of price confusion by the use of the double spine as identification on each Double Volume.

I want you to know these facts because we believe the success of our Double Volume project may also offer certain advantages to you. It has not been possible, until now, for your more important longer books to be considered as ordinary full-length reprint candidates. Now worthwhile books that are unusually long have the same opportunity to achieve wide popular newsstand circulation and acclaim as do books of normal length. This can bring you and your authors both a wider audience and additional subsidiary rights income (the royalty is two cents for the first 150,000 net copies sold and three cents thereafter). We intend to continue to select, for our Double Volume project, titles of unusual quality or special appeal—and do not intend to dilute the attention these Double Volumes are attracting in the trade and with the special reading public. Obviously, fifty cent Signet Double Volumes have higher visibility than regular twenty-five cent books or thirty-five cent Giants.

You may want to go over your back list for possible long books of outstanding interest, and you may want to think about your future books, in terms of a new reprint market. We shall be glad to discuss with you reprint possibilities in our striking new

2. In 1953 with the publication at seventy-five cents of Ayn Rand's *The Fountainhead*, Triple Volumes were inaugurated.

Double Volume format, whenever you feel you have books that
will be suitable. (9 February 1951)

In negotiating for Mailer's *The Naked and the Dead*, one of the Double
Volumes cited in the letter, Weybright set a publishing precedent that
changed the relationship of the mass market reprinters to their hardcover
suppliers. Mailer's bestselling tale of World War II demanded and received
an advance against royalty that far exceeded anything paperback publishers
had paid up to that point for reprints, thirty-five thousand dollars. Without
realizing it, the editor had christened with dollars the first literary blockbuster. This acquisition captured headlines in newspapers and trade jour-
nals at the start of the decade. It began to redraw the image of paperbacks
in the minds of the public, but more immediately for original hardcover
book publishers who usually divided these reprint royalties evenly with
their authors. (Two years after the Mailer deal, Weybright paid another
record advance, $101,000, to Scribner's for James Jones' *From Here to
Eternity*. The lengthy novel was reprinted in its entirety in 1953; a Signet
Triple volume, it was priced at seventy-five cents. This advance stood for
several years as the record high paperback advance. In later years Weybright
would be less apt to take credit for these precedents as he lamented with
some frequency the "astronomical" bids hardcover publishers were demanding for softcover reprint rights.)

Weybright's 1950 solicitation letter for *The Naked and the Dead* to
Richard May of Rinehart contained the basic elements of the message NAL
was trying to deliver to hardcover publishers; that is, he stressed the literary
nature of the Signet imprint and predicted monetary reward to both author
and original publisher, the "luster and lucre" as he would frequently capsu-
late it for friends and colleagues.

I'm not trying to tell you how to make decisions at Rinehart—
I'm only trying to make it clear that we have something to offer,
financially and quantitatively, which transcends the amount of an
advance guarantee. Qualitatively, for example, Mr. Mailer would be
in excellent company on our highly selective list. This, in turn,
means that his book in a Signet edition would not get lost in a
welter of eight or ten average or mediocre titles each month, but
would be part of a compact, fast-selling and distinguished line of
paper bound editions. His literary standing, in the popular market,
would be upheld, which in turn would undoubtedly mean increased
sales of his trade editions. By virtue of having the most *bookish*
reprint list, we have the most *bookish* and most rapidly growing audience.

I won't clutter this letter up with a lot of detailed statistics on how we have developed a vast new audience—with revenue for authors and publishers—by concentrating on the most selective literary properties and promoting them in Signet editions. . . . (9 February 1950)

The Naked and the Dead remained on the NAL publications list for thirty years. In 1981, over NAL's vigorous protests, this profitable publication reverted back to Holt, Rinehart & Winston and was put into their Owl trade paperback imprint. In taking it back, Holt, with publishing traditions that reached well back into the nineteenth century, commented in a 9 January 1981 *Publishers Weekly* article that the book was worth more to its paperback list "in terms of prestige value" than it was to NAL.

In the early fifties with financial stability and recognition came the confidence to reject ardent reprint offers from established hardcover publishers, proprietors who were beginning to weigh original publication of new manuscripts based on their mass market reprint potential. For a major trade publisher to be turned down by a reprinter when the hardcover publisher was strongly convinced of a mass market for the work was particularly nettling. This vexation appears to be exhibited by the caustic observation of Random House editor Harry Maule following a 1951 Weybright rejection.

And yet you'll be the first to agree that one of the responsibilities of the trade publisher, and indeed a good reprint publisher as well, is to develop the new talent which one day will take the place of such authors as you have mentioned.

Not that I am kicking about the policy of New American Library, because you have been outstanding among the reprint publishers in the recognition of new talent and in the daring and imagination of your publishing. I am perfectly content that 99 times out of 100 you will recognize in your own substantial way real talent when we find it. (11 December 1951)

Informing the literary world of NAL's marketplace strength and its editorial directions became the mission of everyone in the publishing company. Truman Talley reported to Weybright one instance following a lunch with Leonard R. Harris, newly employed at Prentice-Hall.[3]

3. Harris later joined Bantam Books and still later formed his own publishing company, maintaining close ties with NAL. He is now an executive in corporate relations and corporate development for the New York Times Company.

Len is the new subsidiary rights man at Prentice-Hall. Normally, he would not be of uncommon interest to us—since we have dealt freely with Ken Giniger and Myron Boardman. However with Ken now back in the army, the new editor-in-chief, Howard Goodkind, is not as yet well worked into our groove as was Ken.

Len is a magazine direct-sell and promotion-trained man who admits he knows nothing about paperbound books. Len is oriented toward us but he says he has been left a legacy of promises to various paperbound firms for the future and on basis of his reprint ignorance he is somewhat confused as to who gets what, when. Thus we should spend some time with him over the next few months. He believes, though, we will have little trouble getting what we want. (11 December 1951)

Weybright had an opportunity to follow up on Talley's advice to continue Harris' education when two months later he bid on Louis Armstrong's *Satchmo,* an autobiography of Armstrong's early years then in the editing stage (reprinted by NAL in 1955).

Not only is our volume of sales—at home and abroad—far greater than any of our competitors, but it is achieved on a selective program of many fewer titles per year. Our momentum on best-sellers of unique quality, in every category, cannot be matched.

We have one other unique asset of special relevance to Prentice-Hall in the ultimate disposition of reprint rights on Louis Armstrong. That is our outstanding position in the field of literature by Negroes and about the Negro in America. Five years ago, with the publication of James Weldon Johnson's *Autobiography of an Ex-Colored Man,* we launched a special effort to distribute our books, and especially those of racial interest, in the Negro communities of American cities. . . . We publish such books as *The Street,* books by Richard Wright, Willard Motley, Chester Himes, and such books as *Strange Fruit,* and encourage major wholesalers to add book specialists to their staff for Harlem, South Chicago and the colored sections of scores of cities, North and South. This represents an enormous plus to the normal market for a book such as Louis Armstrong's autobiography. (15 February 1952)

If there was any doubt about the effect of the NAL correspondence school, it must have been dispelled by this Harris acknowledgment drafted a year later. Directed at Kurt Enoch it follows an NAL rejection of a Prentice-Hall reprint suggestion.

31

I just wanted to underline my appreciation of the telephone call we just concluded. Although your message was obviously disappointing, I am glad you took pains to make it clear to me why the new novel does not seem a good high-price gamble for NAL. My regret is that the money and promotion in large quantities are now going to go down the drain—or will rebound to the benefit of another house. I guess the next cause for regret is the come-down from the elation I felt when three or four of your people agreed with my first hunch that this new book was the best in the series.

Please don't feel hurt, Kurt, that this will in any way alter our profound respect and affection for NAL. We are too experienced in this matter of turning thumbs down on projects ourselves to consider it anything more than a simple understandable business decision. (13 March 1953)

Authors in the early fifties with one eye on the original paperback publishing programs and the other on the advances being offered by paperbound reprinters were feeling exuberant, as NAL author James Aswell revealed in his *Houston Post* newspaper column, an excerpt of which was mailed to Weybright. "My grapevine tells me that with one exception every publishing house in New York would have operated in the red last year had they not been able to share the author's subsidiary rights—pocketbook, movie and bookclub. Which means clearly that they have, for practical purposes, all become 'vanity' houses, with authors financing their own books. This ridiculous and dishonest situation cannot and ought not to last. So I say, let her rip!" (1 June 1952). In his short piece Aswell recognizes what had become even clearer to hardcover publishers: the potential a manuscript had in attracting softcover republication was directly influencing hardcover selection.

Early winter of 1952 World Publishing Company's editor in chief asked Weybright to consider a new manuscript of Elliot Paul that he could not make up his mind about sponsoring. The World editor confessed: "Frankly, I would not want to undertake the publication of this particular book without A. a reprint contract in advance, and B. an option on the other books to come." By spring 1955 Roger Straus, Jr., for one, was willing to confirm the new trade publishing practices. In a letter to Weybright he conceded that "the reports, as you well know, across the industry clearly show that in the trade publishing field the differences between profit and loss for trade operations is the subsidiary income flow."

As paperback publishing rapidly expanded in the first half of the fifties, one major marketing hindrance threatened to bring about the collapse of the entire industry: high book returns. During the years 1953–57, most softcover imprints either drastically reduced their output or, in a few cases, ceased publication altogether. In 1954 NAL recorded a dramatic increase in domestic returns from the previous fiscal year. Slightly over 44 percent of its books "sold" (ordered and received) in the United States were returned for credit. Returns from the local independent distributors through the Fawcett distributing arm were almost 48 percent.[4] However, NAL, which was about to change national distributors, seems to have recovered quickly, as Weybright notes in this paragraph to Erskine Caldwell. "This frightfully bad year now seems to be on the mend, as far as the magazines and paperbound books, especially Signets and Mentors, are concerned. Even Doubleday couldn't stand the gaff after a loss on Perma [Permabooks] totalling millions, and NAL has achieved an even more dominant competitive position in the field" (28 October 1954).

By mid-decade Weybright, who concisely and confidently labeled his company "the world's largest and most selective publisher of inexpensive editions," could take great satisfaction in the progress that the company had made in the ten years since he joined it. Supporting this gratification was the 12 July 1955 report from Truman Talley of his lunch with Harcourt, Brace subsidiary rights director, Ed Hodge. Weybright was told that Harcourt was not even considering Grosset & Dunlap's offer to do a hardcover reprint of Orwell's *1984*, a Signet since 1950.[5] The parent company of NAL's competitor, Bantam Books, Grosset no longer carried the clout of ten years earlier, that is, determining whether a book was released for softcover. Grosset soon withdrew from the hardcover reprint business altogether.

Equally satisfying was a second report from NAL's direct trade sales manager, Maizie Halpern. It dealt with another early and chronic softcover publishing problem—the belief within the book industry that paper editions significantly harmed hardcover sales of the same title.

Walter Oakley of Oxford University Press told me on the telephone yesterday that their sales for 1954 of the book (*The Sea Around Us*) did not decline by one copy. Naturally, they and the author are pleased with this information, and since this is a fine example to quote to other conservative publishers, the story should be put to full use by all at NAL. If practical A. J. P. [Arabel J. Porter] can tell

4. This figure is taken from financial records in the Victor Weybright Collection in the Archives of Contemporary History, University of Wyoming.

5. This book remained on the NAL list through the "commemorative year" of 1984 when over two million copies were issued. In 1985 NAL reported that it reprinted over twelve million copies of the Orwell classic during its lifetime with the company.

Walter that *The Sea Around Us* was, as far as the trade department is concerned, our best selling book—Signet or Mentor!—last year. Excluding the 14,000 the Teenage Book Club purchased in 1954, trade [sales made directly to bookstores by NAL, i.e., not through wholesalers] sold 54,000 copies of the book. (26 January 1955)

Throughout the latter half of the fifties, NAL continued to be selective in the numbers of titles it published. This reflected Weybright and Enoch's policy of publishing fewer but better titles than their major competitors. Weybright, with an eye on the large advances that Fawcett had recently been paying, summarized this key to NAL success in a letter to Arthur H. Thornhill, Sr., president of Little, Brown during bidding for Richard Bissell's novel, *Say, Darling,* a title that eventually went to Bantam.

I realize that some of the reprinters are interested definitely in trying to secure a few highly visible loss-leaders to regain their situation in the distribution picture. That is probably good promotion for the publishing house, but it certainly makes the pattern of publishing cockeyed and confusing. I have a hunch, indeed, I know, that we can sell more of Bissell. Last year we published 96 new titles, compared with 152 for Pocket Books, and 118 for Bantam, and 130 for Fawcett. I would like to show you the statistics on unit or dollar volume sales in outstanding whole-saler organizations. You would be convinced that we can sell more copies per title, and more per pocket in a rack, because of our carefully diversified and selective choice of titles. So, when we hesitate to take an immediate plunge on $50,000 for *Say, Darling,* we are doing, I suspect, about what you would do if you were in my or Kurt's chair. (1 March 1957)

The NAL archival files show the evolution of comfortable working relationships with a number of major established hardcover houses. None is more interesting than the intercourse between Weybright and Bennett Cerf, the colorful and imperious head of Random House. With Madison Avenue publishing offices only one block south of NAL, Cerf was already a highly successful publisher and celebrity at the time Weybright and Enoch founded NAL. Their association through the years steadily increased and became more personal, although it appears that a translucent cover of wariness and skepticism glazed most of their dealings.

William Faulkner perhaps benefited most from their intercourse. With the exception of *Mosquitoes*, Faulkner's only mass market appearances in the forties and fifties were under Weybright sponsorship. Random House's commitment to NAL by making it the exclusive mass market reprinter of Faulkner is reviewed in a 1951 Weybright letter to Cerf. At the time Weybright's company had contracted for and published seven Faulkner works and was negotiating for still another, *The Unvanquished*.

> I am pleased that you were as gratified as we were by the little summary I gave you of the reception of the various Faulkner titles which we have reprinted. The advanced and accrued volume, substantial as it has been, only partially reflects the effect of our bold introduction and promotion of Faulkner as a universal writer for a universal audience. I like to feel—and hope you agree—that we have had more than a modest effect upon the direct Random House and Modern Library sales of Faulkner's books to a number of people who, having enjoyed a taste of an author they once considered esoteric, have come back for more in your editions as well as in our reprint series. Ultimately, we hope to trail your entire Faulkner list with Signet editions of all his major work in such a way that we shall nourish rather than compete with your imaginative hard-bound program in both Random House and Modern Library editions. This means that we hope to alternate some of the more difficult books with some of those which are more immediately fathomable and followable by the ordinary reader. I therefore welcome your assurances that Faulkner will not be placed in competitive reprint directions. (21 May 1951)

Cerf's generosity had its limits, however. A study of Faulkner's sizable output shows that with possibly three exceptions those Faulkner works that NAL did reprint were less significant than the fiction Cerf preserved exclusively for the hardcover reprint series on which Random House was built, Modern Library, and for its trade paperback series, Vintage Books.

Early in his book publishing career, Weybright had good reason to be wary of Bennett Cerf. Random House was part of the book industry consortium that controlled Grosset & Dunlap and with the Curtis Circulation Company financed Ian Ballantine's founding of Bantam Books in 1945.[6] The following Weybright letter penned not long after the start of his tenure as Penguin editor in chief was addressed to Eunice Frost, Allen Lane's administrative assistant in London.

> There is one very good reason why I haven't been in any hurry

6. Besides Random House, the publishing consortium included the Book-of-the-Month Club, Harper & Brothers, Scribner's, and Little, Brown.

with Random House: I don't trust Bennett Cerf. He has been Ballantine's principal brain truster, has appeared at many meetings as a spokesman for Bantam Books, and is a magpie in every sense of the word as far as picking up other people's bright ideas or books and putting them in his own nest.

His best selling book, *Try and Stop Me*, was largely purloined from other people's quips and writings. In recent months, as Penguin has tended to outstrip both Pocket and Bantam in sales in a number of important cities, including Chicago, it has been inevitable that Bantam would snoop around to see what titles we were interested in so that they might imitate that segment of our editorial formula (they have no concept, of course, of the overall integrity of Penguin quality). For us to have approached Random House for any title would simply have meant that it would have gone to Bantam a little more quickly.

Some time ago Bennett Cerf mentioned to Harriet Pilpel [Penguin lawyer] that Penguin must think that Random House stinks since they haven't been in touch. I telephoned Bennett Cerf and made a luncheon date for November 4th. We will see if they let us have a bit of Faulkner. But I am quite certain that what Cerf really wants is to pick our brains and pry into our plans. I have good reason for believing this, I can assure you. (21 October 1946)

That suspicions were mutual is clear from this Cerf negotiation letter to Weybright centering on Truman Capote's *Other Voices, Other Rooms*. It was sent only four months after NAL's independence from Penguin. "Thanks for your note of May 14th, but your offer of an $800 guarantee on Capote strikes me as altogether out of line—particularly if it is to include an option on his next novel and also his book of short stories. I think a guarantee should cover the first printing of 200,000 copies. In fact, I think you quarter-book boys—and that includes my friend Ian [Ballantine]—are getting away with holy murder. Further details will be furnished upon request" (17 May 1948). The advance was raised to one thousand dollars and the objectionable reprint option clause was omitted as Weybright acknowledged a few days later. "You will note that I have not included an option, since there is a firm understanding that if we do well with Capote we're in the front of the queue for the next" (20 May 1948).

As observed in earlier quotes, Weybright often went to some length to demonstrate to the original publisher why NAL was the best choice for the reprint when bidding on a literary property. By the start of the new decade, there was no need for extended polemics with Cerf. Below Weybright uses flattery rather than fact to try to gain from Random House both John O'Hara's *A Rage to Live* and Irwin Shaw's *The Young Lions*. The publisher's prediction in the final sentence was borne out with the rise of movie novelization, "nonbook," and "brand name" publishing in the seventies.

> I am writing you a brief background letter with both the O'Hara and Shaw bids, reinforcing our feeling that not only do these books naturally fit our list, but that we can do better for you and the authors on them because of our selective handling of a limited number of important titles.
>
> Although it sounds pompous I would like to use this occasion to tell you how much of a lift it gives to our enjoyment of publishing to have a chat with you. Actually, you've blazed a trail, which we have followed, with faith in the general public intelligence more consistently than some of your own protégés would probably like to acknowledge. This community of interest between those of us who, without any snobbery, recognize the fundamental integrity of a book is going to be increasingly important in the next few years, when opportunists will be packaging every sort of paper product into the appearance of a book in the newsstands. (11 January 1950)

With Random's 1949 publication of *A Rage to Live*, John O'Hara, whose works were at the time considered somewhat risqué, moved into "bestsellerdom." In 1945 Penguin had taken over publication of his *Appointment in Samarra*. Pocket Books had dropped the reprint when it become contemporary paperback publishing's first censorship controversy immediately after publication in 1939. Another O'Hara on the Penguin list had been allowed to go out of print and Avon Books actually had more O'Haras to its credit. Therefore, any moral commitment Random may have felt toward a particular paperbound publisher was at best diffused. Weybright grudgingly acknowledges as much to Cerf after he had successfully contracted for *The Young Lions*, Irwin Shaw's 1947 bestselling, first novel. O'Hara's *A Rage to Live* went to Bantam.

> I take great pleasure in sending to Random House, herewith, our contract for *The Young Lions*. It's a marvelous book; we are proud to have Irwin Shaw on our list, and I'm sure we will do well by it, for ourselves, for you, and for the author. We really don't consider it a consolation prize for losing *A Rage to Live*.
>
> But, Kurt and I are both terribly sorry that the Bantam squeeze-play knocked out our well-laid plans for O'Hara. We are

giving O'Hara, and *A Rage to Live*, fresh acceptance in our market through the popular re-issue of *Appointment in Samarra*, which will rebound to the advantage of a competitor—a competitor, at that, whose president [Ian Ballantine] makes the most odious remarks throughout the trade about the realistic language in some of our best books. Yet I suppose in Ian's case imitation can be accepted as the sincerest form of flattery. I genuinely understand and sympathize with your situation in determining the reprinter of O'Hara, and I am grateful to you for giving us a chance at *A Rage to Live*. I hope that, having lost it through no fault of our own, we shall have an opportunity to reprint your next big Random House literary property, and thus carry to new dimensions the extremely pleasant and profitable relationship we have had on our projects to date and contemplated under our recent agreements. (27 January 1950)

Cerf's involvement with the book industry consortium that controlled Grosset & Dunlap and shared control of Bantam put him squarely in the middle of the acquisition and sales wars that mass market paperback houses were waging against hardcover reprinters. In September 1950 Grosset announced that to meet softcover competition it would publish a new paperback reprint series, Reviewers' Selection, priced at seventy-five cents. In its announcement, Grosset denigrated their "lowest-priced" rivals by strongly inferring that mass market paperbacks were not appropriate for retail book outlets. Mass market publishers who were raising cover prices of newer, larger editions to fifty cents and contemplating seventy-five cents were naturally concerned. Weybright was able to help impede Grossett's plans when, a month after the Reviewers' Selection announcement, he made a reprint offer to Bennett Cerf on *World Enough and Time* by Robert Penn Warren. This letter is also interesting for the distinction that Weybright makes in the final paragraph between the reading preferences of "regular" book readers and those that presumably make up the bulk of mass market paperback audiences.

I'm very grateful to you for the chance to study this book more thoroughly as a literary property ideally suited for a new incarnation in our Signet Double Volume editions at 50 cents. Confirming my telephone conversation, we make a firm advance guarantee offer of $7500 for publication a year after your trade edition release date, with royalties at the rate of 2 cents on the first 150,000 copies and 3 cents thereafter. If Grosset and Dunlap should undertake a hard cover edition at $1.49, therefore delaying our edition to two years after your trade release date, we would have to reduce our guarantee to $4,000.

But, if Grosset and Dunlap should do the book in a paper bound Reviewers' edition at 75 cents, we would, with great reluctance, have to stand aside altogether. The price and the format are too close to our own, and the distribution would overlap too greatly in the drug and variety syndicate store field. I would be very sorry to see this occur for two reasons: first, in our desire to license reprints of outstanding modern authors, we would not want to omit a Warren, especially now that we have proven acceptance of the Double Volumes and no longer need edit and abridge for economic reasons. Second, and even more important, we like to engage in teamplay with Random House, because you are one of the creative publishers who does not regard an inexpensive edition as a by-product but as a positive projection of an author's work and audience and revenue.

If the early sections of *World Enough and Time* were easier for the uninitiated book reader to get into, we would up our guar-antee—but I think you and Robert Penn Warren both would agree that the commencement of the novel is a little difficult for readers who are not regular book readers, but who are lured into a good piece of literature by widespread availability of an attractive edition at a price they can afford. (27 October 1950)

Two years later Weybright issued the book at fifty cents in the Signet Double series. The new Warren title did not go to Grossett. Its softcover Reviewers' Selection series lasted only a short time and soon afterwards the company also exited the hardcover reprint business.

The Random House file in the NAL archives bulges with correspondence between the two publishers, supporting Weybright's observation made to Cerf at the close of 1950 that "it is gratifying to know how many of our better books, past, current, and future, come into popular incarnation from your Random House list." Truman Talley, however, believed that it was veteran Random House editor Harry Maule, rather than Bennett Cerf, who functioned as their real ally. After a lunch with Maule in late 1953, Talley reported on their discussion of reprint rights to Christopher Isherwood's *The World in the Evening*.

He [Harry Maule] said that there was no question in his mind but that Isherwood belonged on our list. He thought that one other paper house would make an effort to get the book—Dell— apparently on the basis of a former personal relationship between

Frank Taylor and Isherwood. Harry said if we wanted to make an offer now it might be of some help getting the book. I hadn't realized before to what extent Bennett Cerf oversees all subsidiary rights decisions. The submitting around that Random House does . . . is the policy of Cerf to extract every last nickle for a reprint advance. (15 December 1953)

Despite these assurances and further lobbying on the book's behalf by Maule, Weybright remained unconvinced of the merits of this Isherwood title and softcover rights went to Popular Library. (For more on this incident see chapter 5.)

For a long time Weybright seemed equally unconvinced about the first novel of a writer with far less literary stature than Isherwood, Mac Hyman. This was in spite of (or perhaps because of) the Random House dust jacket that carried Cerf's self-serving testament that it was the funniest book he had ever read. A hardcover bestseller for Random House in 1954, *No Time for Sergeants,* with the help of successful television and Broadway adaptations, achieved this status again in 1955. Yet it was twice rejected as a Signet reprint by the editor in chief. Then a holiday greeting arrived from Bennett Cerf, as Weybright later reported to Harry Maule. "Bennett called me on New Year's Eve to wish me a happy New Year and to suggest that if we wanted a happy 1956, too, we ought to have sense enough to reprint *No Time for Sergeants.* In the warm glow of January 3rd, I telephoned Bennett and we struck a bargain. With your blessing, done and done" (3 January 1956). The NAL softcover, which subsequently sold over two million copies, helped inspire Weybright's Christmas greeting to Cerf twelve months later.[7] "Throughout our organization there is a great feeling of goodwill toward Random House at the end of the year in which we have done an amazing amount of business on reprinting some of your outstanding literary properties" (17 December 1956).

And two months after this greeting, Weybright attempted to return the favor, following one of his trips to London and a visit with actor-playwright, Peter Ustinov. Weybright, who also suggested the actor as a perfect guest on the television panel show "What's My Line," where Cerf was a fixture, urged the hardcover publisher to examine Ustinov's new play, *Romanoff and Juliet.*

I don't know who Peter Ustinov's representative is, and I certainly

7. Weybright's greeting could afford to be all the more effusive because when NAL released *No Time for Sergeants* in March of 1956, the Random hardcover edition was selling at the rate of one thousand copies a day. At the time Random House considered this NAL softcover edition a "premature release."

have no right to pass the script around. . . . However, I should think that, if Random House is interested, the best approach would be the direct one to him at home: 215 Kings Road, London. It is Ellen Terry's old house, and he maintains a small secretariat of personal and professional helpers, in a constant and delightful frenzy of activity. He is certainly one of the most gifted actors and dramatists in England, and he has occasionally done spectacular character roles in Hollywood. Here again, a major film development would make a reprint interesting. Otherwise, the play probably better belongs in a drama library series such as yours. (13 February 1959)

Cerf published the play the following year.

Like any successful publisher, Cerf regularly scanned the lists not only of his hardcover competition but also of those to whom he sold titles for reprint. As publishing moved into the sixties, Cerf wrote to express concern about an apparent decline in the quality of NAL's new releases. Weybright's reply to Cerf was dictated during the time he and Kurt Enoch were negotiating the details of their merger with Times-Mirror, and it refers to Cerf's yet to be announced acquisition of Alfred A. Knopf, Inc.

> I wonder if you have occasion to see our trade order form—since you have a notion that our list "used to be better than it now is." We are definitely not developing a lot of second class movie trash on the West Coast, but trying to work with the finest authors there are who are uncommitted and who want to write some first class books.
>
> It was a great pleasure to see you yesterday and to know that our distinguished neighbors upstairs at 501 [Alfred A. Knopf, Inc.] have enjoyed the continuity of their good works through their line up with Random House. (1 April 1960)

NAL's relationship with another member of the hardcover publishing establishment, Charles Scribner's Sons, was more checkered. As early as 1944, Kurt Enoch was unsuccessfully wooing Scribner's for permission to reprint Ernest Hemingway in a Penguin, Inc. edition. The quest for Hemingway would continue off and on for more than a decade. The young company's early inexperience with hardcover courtship, however, was dramatically revealed in early 1945. Penguin had scheduled a Ring Lardner anthology for publication later that year. In a letter to Kurt Enoch, Scribner's executive Whitney Darrow, Sr. complained about being hounded for permission to use a Scribner's-published, Lardner short story. Darrow, one of the most respected and avuncular members of the New York publishing establishment, patiently lectures the upstart reprinter.

You may use *Alibi Ike* in your reprint of *The Love Nest* and other stories by Ring Lardner. The message regarding this came to me on Friday. I was the only one in the office Friday and could not make any inquiry until this morning after ten o'clock when the managing editor came in.

When anything like this comes to me I handle it in the quickest possible time. To be interrupted by repeated phone calls only delays my work and gets me nowhere. I know you will understand, but I'm going to give you an illustration of what this means. The first moment I could get an answer for you on your question was at 10:15 this morning. After that I had three emergency jobs and then called in my secretary to take my morning dictation including to have her call you with this message and to write you a note. To show you how busy we are, I will tell you that I am signing all payroll checks in the office while I am dictating. In the midst of this we were called three times on the telephone by you and each time had to stop my work.

I want to cooperate with you and when anything comes up I will give you every attention possible but won't you please, after I've said I will do something, give me an opportunity to do it at my earliest convenience and not by telephoning which is just one of the reasons I couldn't get your answer. I think you will recall how many times I was interrupted on the phone when I had my last talk with you. (15 January 1945)

Enoch's apology for his doggedness gives an interesting peek into the scheduling requirements of mass market publishing that are similar to those of magazine publishing and that continue to this day.

First of all please accept my sincere apologies for disturbing you by my frequent telephone calls. I know perfectly well how much a nuisance telephone calls are and on my last visit I noticed how busy you are. I can assure you that I myself hated to call you so often. It was, however, an emergency situation due to the fact that we wanted to schedule the Lardner book for publication in February. There was no other chance to meet this date unless I gave the printer immediate instructions about this book. We are releasing our new books on pre-fixed monthly dates as monthly magazine publishers do and everything in the distributing machinery is geared to these dates. Therefore it was important to get your decision in time. I hope that on the basis of this explanation you will understand my insistence in this matter. Thank you very much for your cooperation, which we deeply appreciate. (17 January 1945)

No other hardcover publisher at this time matched Scribner's in its list of American authors of genuine literary merit. Hemingway, Fitzgerald, Wolfe, Lerner, Rawlings, the golden nuggets of Maxwell Perkins' fabled editorship, constituted an Eldorado for a struggling postwar paperback reprinter. However, Scribner's had helped found Bantam Books. When Scribner's occasionally leased backlist nuggets for reprint, Bantam generally was the beneficiary. In a letter to Darrow, one in the sequence of NAL's unsuccessful quest for Hemingway, Weybright acknowledges Bantam's special status at a time when NAL itself was gaining strength and financial stability. Weybright also refers to two Thomas Wolfe works, an anthology of short stories published under the Penguin imprint, and a section of *Look Homeward, Angel* entitled *The Adventures of Young Gant*.

Is there any possibility we shall have a chance at the works of Hemingway other than *A Farewell to Arms* and *The Sun Also Rises*, which have been issued by Bantam Books? For some six years going back to our Penguin days our company has endeavored to secure from Scribner's the reprint rights to Hemingway's fiction. Now that we have developed the fastest selling line of paperbound books per title in the country, and, in doing so, secured rights to the works of practically all the greatest modern authors, we are especially disappointed not to have had a chance at the works of Hemingway. I realize that your house is intimately involved in the Bantam set up and therefore in a position to favor Bantam— although I do appreciate the fact that, in the case of Thomas Wolfe, you chose our imprint for popular reprinting, as Random House has done in the case of William Faulkner and other authors of literary importance.
. . . We have sold Caldwell, Faulkner, Farrell, Cain, and other writers by the millions—some 18 million Caldwell books in three years—and I genuinely believe we could have put Hemingway in our top bestseller class if we had had any chance at all with *A Farewell to Arms* and *The Sun Also Rises*. (2 August 1949)

A few months later, following still another Scribner's rebuff on Hemingway, a form solicitation letter arrived at the NAL offices on behalf of the

Girl Scouts of America. It was addressed to "Penguin Books" and signed by Charles Scribner, Jr., then president of the hardcover publisher. The reprinter's terse response read: "Your letter of January 28th . . . is hereby acknowledged by us. Our corporate name was changed early in 1948 when we severed our connection with the English company." No contribution was enclosed.

Occasionally Scribner's actively sought reprint royalty advances for second-rate or uncommercial works of their prestigious authors. One example is Fitzgerald's *Last Tycoon*; NAL turned it down in the spring of 1953. About this same time Weybright replied with pious lament to a Scribner's invitation to bid on rights to reprint a less popular Hemingway novel and an anthology of the author's short stories. "I greatly regret that we do not feel it would be an adequate Hemingway program for us to reprint *To Have and Have Not* and/or *The Green Hills of Africa* considering the placement of more typical and universally admired books in other competitive reprint hands" (24 April 1953).[8] In 1958 another Hemingway creation, however, gained fresh attraction. Weybright had learned through freewheeling Hollywood producer Jerry Wald that a film was being designed around Hemingway's Nick Adams stories. Weybright wrote directly to Charles Scribner, Jr. (Darrow had retired; his subsidiary rights responsibilities eventually fell to George McCorkle, whom Weybright would hire in 1959 as NAL's financial vice-president.)Weybright offered twenty thousand dollars in advance plus a 10 percent royalty rate, unusually high for a mass market reprint. On the same day he made this proposition to the young Scribner, Weybright alerted Wald and summarized his twelve years of dealing with the sensitive publishing house on ticklish Hemingway proposals.

> You probably don't know that Charles Scribner is very touchy about publishing overtures to Scribner authors except through Scribner's. Hence, I had to put my proposal to him in writing yesterday afternoon. He said that he had written to Hemingway and, although he usually is guided by Hemingway's wishes, he was not certain that Scribner's would reverse its policy and permit a Hemingway reprint. I cannot predict the outcome of my overture.
>
> I consider Charles Scribner a friend, a very fine person. But we take different views of publishing. He favors a monopoly under the Scribner imprint of all important Scribner authors. All licenses on Hemingway, Thomas Wolfe, Scott Fitzgerald and many others. Because of his high attitude toward New American Library we continue our reprint of Alan Paton's book, one [C. P.] Snow book,

8. The Bogart-Bacall film of *To Have and Have Not* was then almost ten years old.

all of James Jones' books, and certain others. Therefore, it is not advisable for me to pressure Charles any further as he is easily irritated by intrusion upon the areas which he considers exclusively the province of his publishing house. (18 October 1958)

Scribner replied the following week with the negative response Weybright seemed already prepared for.

In the day following receipt of your letter of October 18th I was in touch with Mr. Hemingway about the possibility of licensing the stories in a reprint to sell at 50 cents. I'm afraid that neither of us are in favor of such a reprint, since it runs so obviously counter to our policy of preserving a highly satisfactory sale of these works in their original or Scribner Library editions. In any case no arrangements for a motion picture have been made so I guess the whole matter is pretty much a matter of producer putting the cart before the horse. Please understand this often happens in Hollywood! (24 October 1958)

Scribner's had for some time issued a series of quarto-sized paperbacks for college classroom adoption, Student Editions. This series reflected Scribner's long-standing reluctance to publish anything that might inhibit the hardcover backlist sales of its prominent authors. In the late fifties, however, it began to publish paperbacks for the trade bookstore market in the same quarto-sized format as the Student Editions. These bookstore editions carried a "Scribner Library" imprint and a price tag significantly higher than that of mass market paperbacks.

Years earlier the absence of a Scribner Library trade paperback series plus dogged persistence paid off for Weybright after his discovery of Scribner's South African novelist, Alan Paton. Following a lunch approved by Scribner's that Weybright had with Paton in New York, the editor in chief wrote to the author in care of Whitney Darrow, Sr. "I am sending you with a packet of books published by our company most of which will never be available in South Africa because of the racial themes which are apparently banned in your country. Through arrangements with British publishers we export a modest number of books to South Africa, but because of the self-censorship of our distributor there, the titles consist mainly of innocuous history and American westerns" (2 November 1949).[9] Paton's reply two months later acknowledges receipt of the books and

9. Based on the level of the literature exported, American paperback publishers, with some justification, had been accused of using some English-speaking countries as dumping grounds for their overstock. However, this explanation offers some argument for rebuttal.

observes: "I believe you expressed the hope that my novel [*Cry, the Beloved Country*] would one day be published in your series. This, as I am sure you well know, is a matter for Scribner's who at the moment do not seem inclined to permit it." Four years later after receiving a review copy of *Too Late the Phalarope*, Weybright made a more direct assault, this time to Scribner's executive Norman H. Snow.

> I am very grateful to you for the pre-publication copy of Alan Paton's *Too Late the Phalarope*. I read it over the weekend, and I'm still under its haunting spell. Though you sent me the book as a personal gesture, and I do not construe it as a submission for ultimate reprint, I should like to go on the record again as hopeful for the privilege of eventually reprinting Alan Paton's novels. Their poignant message—as well as their great literary quality—should have great currency in today's literary world as millions of magazine readers are aware of Paton's involvement in the political aspects of South Africa's tragic racial conflicts. I hope that if and when the time comes to think of an Alan Paton reprint you will think first of New American Library. He is too distinguished an author for the auction-block. I don't like to make a derogatory mention of a competitor, but I certainly was dismayed by the Dell presentation of Hemingway and, even more recently, Dell's reprint presentation of Faulkner's *Mosquitoes*. I am not boasting when I say that as the reprinter of more genuinely distinguished contemporary fiction than any other competitor in our field, we can give Alan Paton the natural extension of his proven audience of your trade edition. (27 July 1953)

This letter is notable not only for the casual swipe it takes at Dell's "packaging" of recent Faulkner and Hemingway reprints but also for Weybright's description of the complementary gatekeeper role that a reprinter can play to a hardcover publisher.

Weybright apparently made his point. NAL issued the *Too Late the Phalarope* reprint in 1956. By 1960, however, the trade paperback Scribner Library series was well established. When NAL offered Scribner's, in view of "the sequence of events that occurred in Little Rock," a substantial advance on Paton's *Cry, the Beloved Country*, the offer was rejected with the fear that the cheaper edition would seriously harm the sale of its Scribner Library edition. One can conclude that Scribner's vision of the complementary role of mass market paperbacks to its own editions again differed from Victor Weybright's.

The Scribner Library series unsettled for a time the close friendship

Weybright had with another major Scribner writer, C. P. Snow. In 1960 Weybright was preparing a revised and expanded edition of Snow's controversial *Two Cultures and the Scientific Revolution* for the mass market. In the following excerpt Snow refers to this edition and to *The Search*, an early and less important novel that Weybright also had permission to reprint. It seems clear that Snow also wondered for a time why Weybright was not reprinting titles in his widely acclaimed Strangers and Brothers fictional series, parts of which were reprinted under the Scribner Library imprint. "I am delighted you are doing this, my dear Victor, and also *The Search*. I had hoped that we might do more together, but that was before I heard of the Scribner Library. I wasn't told anything about this until it had actually happened, and was mildly surprised that you had not acquired one or more of the series. Now I see the explanation" (23 June 1960).

Scribner's was more indulgent with its "front list." The editor in chief successfully obtained, albeit for a record-setting price, James Jones' critically well-received *From Here to Eternity*. It was a hardcover bestseller in 1951, and NAL was allowed to reprint it two years later. (See chapter 6.) Other bestselling Scribner's titles that gained a Signet imprint were Thomas Chamales' *Never So Few* and Morton Thompson's *Not as a Stranger*. Only a comparative study of royalty figures could give accurate analyses of whether Scribner's paternalistic control of its established literary authors achieved greater remuneration for its writers than would have been obtained by more liberal distribution of softcover reprint rights to the mass market. It seems certain that by restricting or eliminating mass market sales, Scribner's limited access to its authors' works to large segments of both American and world populations.

The mid-fifties saw the dramatic rise of trade paperbacks, books that bridged hardcover and mass paperback markets. Doubleday's Anchor Books, begun in April of 1953, led the rise of this book category, higher priced paperbacks sold exclusively through the book trade to the same retail bookstore outlets in which Mentor books were successful. These bookstores were generally in or around college campuses. Doubleday and the other hardcover publishers like Scribner's who entered trade paperback publishing employed the term "quality paperbacks" to distinguish their softcover series from lower priced and more widely distributed mass market paperbacks. The term annoyed most people in mass market publishing, and in particular the folks at NAL who pointed out the more established roots, history, market, and editorial quality of the Mentor line.[10]

10. In a letter to Weybright, 8 July 1960, Edward Watkins of the University of Michigan Press defined "quality" when used by trade book publishers as "a piece of double-think, i.e., it means 'quantity.' This is the kind of paperback you sell fewer of, and charge more for."

By the mid-fifties most of the major hardcover publishers and many university presses created new softcover imprints to take advantage of the market that Doubleday's Anchor Books had successfully highlighted. In a memo to his partner, Kurt Enoch, Victor Weybright formally expressed his concern, citing the challenges that the new trade paperback imprints presented to Mentor nonfiction and Signet fiction.

> Note also (in *Publishers Weekly*) Van Nostrand's Anvil books (originals) at $1.95, Noonday's Meredian Books. Some of these will have some effect on Mentor in bookshops and college bookshops. Pat Knopf reports that Viking and two or three other houses are embarking on a Vintage-type series of their own. The effect will be felt first on Mentors—but also, combined with the condensed book clubs development, on the availability of both strong immediate fiction and backlist fiction for reprint.
>
> I don't worry about Mentor which can do an original with all the prestige of an Oxford University Press type of imprint; but I would like to discuss with you some of my observation on the position of Signet fiction. (22 November 1954)

Further cause for concern by mass market publishers was shortly evidenced by the discovery that hardcover publishers like Scribner's were again becoming reluctant to sign over softcover reprint rights to mass market houses, preferring instead to issue these titles in their own higher priced softcover series. Even more serious were the decisions of the original hardcover publishers to cease renewing existing reprint contracts on steadily selling mass market titles. This permitted paper edition reprint rights to revert back to the original publisher and allow for softcover, trade editions to appear. In almost all efforts to retain paperback rights, the mass market publishers claimed credit for finding a new, larger, and generally more profitable audience for the author. When their arguments were successful, a new agreement was drafted. It usually included a fresh and sizable royalty advance plus an increase in the royalty rate. Obviously reversion to hardcover publishers most severely threatened the profits of those mass market publishers who had developed strong backlists, books that were not likely to become immediate bestsellers but that would sell steadily and profitably over a period of years. Many of the literary Signet titles and all of the Mentors fell squarely into this category.

Apparently hardcover publishers did try somewhat to redress the double injuries of trade paperbacks and reversions by conceding that certain categories of fiction were appropriate for original appearance as mass market paperbacks. These categories were the genre fiction—romances, westerns, and mysteries—that grew out of the magazine publishing backgrounds of many of the smaller reprinters of the time and had already been championed in the Gold Medal and Dell First Editions series. One recorded instance of this concession is contained in a report to Weybright and Enoch made by NAL executive Theodore Waller.

> He [Harold Guinzburg of Viking Press] indicated that in his own judgment there is a field in which the hard bound publisher performs no real function and where the present pattern is, therefore, anachronistic. He said that although there might be some industry objections, he didn't see how any hard bound publisher could seriously, and for long, object to the loss of the hard bound edition of westerns and mysteries which, after all, is undertaken wholly for the reprint income and to which there is no editorial advertising or other special publishing contribution in the hard bound operation.[11] (29 September 1953)

And Roger Straus, Jr.'s 1955 comments to Weybright endorse this table scraps support for mass market original publishing. "I also think to answer your last point about original publishing that I feel un-dog-in-the-manger-ish about this. If you can pick up pieces and bits from British, foreign and fringe American writers for your original publication, more power to you, and I do not consider this at all competitive, for we are publishing authors primarily, and certainly in the foreseeable future, that could only be done by the trade houses, unless a paper house does, as we discussed some time ago, actually go into the hard back field with an imprint, etc." (7 April 1955).

As the fifties advanced, NAL went increasingly into proprietary publishing. Retaining paperbound as well as foreign sales rights, the company reversed standard practices. Retaining softcover rights in its author contracts, NAL sought out trade publishers to issue these titles first in hardcover. It was believed then and, to a considerable extent, is still believed today that hardcover publication for certain types of books is necessary for library sales and for obtaining the reviews and other promotional attention necessary for a new title to gain public interest. Weybright lifts some of the veils off the company's proprietary publishing program, particularly in relation to the Mentor series, in a 1957 letter to *Publishers Weekly* editor Frederic Melcher. Among other things he reveals his conception of the

---

11. The company's first original fiction title was a movie tie-in, *Kiss of Death* by Eleazar Lipsky. It was published in 1947 as a Penguin and, inside the front and back covers, contained stills from the highly regarded film.

various audiences for softcover nonfiction and the degree to which the company had become a proprietary publisher.

> Your letter of June 19th raises a question which we have lived with from the very beginning of our Mentor program (under the old Pelican imprint: January, 1946). Overall, Mentors probably are on a one-to-five ratio in volume with Signets; however, the Signet and Signet Key lists contain a great deal of general non-fiction and reference, such books as *The Meaning of the Dead Sea Scrolls*, (over 2 million), and other subject titles with the level of presentation simplified beneath the level of Mentors. We have reason to believe that most of the readers of Mentors, and more than half of the readers of Signet Key and Signet non-fiction, constitute a new audience, not an audience that has switched from fiction to subject non-fiction. . . . We don't brag about our Mentor sales as much as we'd like, simply because it inspires competition, and was in no small sense responsible for the development and expansion of expensive paperbound series by a number of trade publishers. This, in turn, has cramped reprint sources of editorial material and resulted in a constantly higher percentage of original Mentors, very much in the pattern of Allen Lane's Pelicans (except that most of our Mentors are placed with trade publishers or university presses for prior publication. Currently, for example, we are about to bring out Mentors which have been placed with Princeton, Indiana, Knopf, Houghton Mifflin, St. Martin's Press, University of California, Macmillan, Oxford, and a number of others.)
>
> It certainly adds great zest to publishing to be engaged in these creative pursuits, even though we sometimes function—to use a forgotten New Deal phrase—as passionate anonyms. (20 June 1957)

NAL's most extensive and critically regarded proprietary arrangement was the Mentor Philosophers series, which the company conceived and edited. Begun in the mid-fifties, under the general editorship of Anne Fremantle, its six volumes were copublished in hardcover by Houghton Mifflin. Very favorably reviewed and widely adopted for college classroom use, the series was only one of several multi-volume book projects that NAL guided from start to finish in the fifties and early sixties. The softcover publisher developed these projects the same way that any trade hardcover publisher would by dealing with all the editorial and production concerns an original manuscript demands and then arranging, usually before or sometimes after issuing a softcover Mentor or Signet, independent hardcover publication. Some publishing companies, however, like Harper's, had a policy of not taking on anything under contract from another publishing company. Most did not have such a policy.

In 1956 Putnam president, Walter J. Minton, approached NAL about establishing closer publishing ties. He suggested, among other things, the possibility of a dual imprint. The new head of one of the oldest and most distinguished book publishing companies in the United States, Minton saw that close cooperation could help finance some extensive nonfiction projects he was anxious to undertake. Weybright's response reflects the more aggressive attitude within NAL about proprietary publishing and the legitimate desire of the company for recognition of their editorially creative efforts.

> I don't like to sound hesitant about making a commitment, but actually we are in somewhat of a quandary ourselves about the best method of handling some of the very substantial non-fiction works, developed for Mentor, that should, somehow, be available in a more durable hardcover form. When we discussed the books with the authors, we talked largely in terms of Mentor only—though in most instances we did secure world rights in volume form at every price—and now the question arises: what to do about the hard cover possibilities? As you will realize, there is also a question of pride involved. For years we have been planting important books with university presses and trade publishers who take the bows, the laurel and the bay, leaving us in the mind of critics and public alike as uncreative rubber-stamp reprinters. Some of our people are beginning to feel very strongly that New American Library ought to get a little bit more recognition for its developmental publishing. (4 February 1956)

The pressure to go deeper and more openly into proprietary publishing, particularly into general fiction, increased as the fifties concluded. This, coupled with NAL's complementary interest in becoming connected with West Coast movie and television projects, put Weybright in touch with a large number of California writers. An NAL feeler to Viking author Oakley Hall inspired Weybright's old nemesis Marshall A. Best to declare that this represented an attack that "some of the paperback boys are trying to make on the whole structure of publishing. . . . The idea of making the cloth bound publisher the 'secondary' publisher and letting him buy his rights from what used to be called a reprinter, is totally unpalatable to us." Weybright soothed some of the concerns between the two companies at a lunch later in the year with Viking president, Harold Guinzburg. Despite getting sidetracked on the Charles Van Doren television scandal, Wey-bright's letter, a follow-up to their luncheon, reflects softcover publishing's perceived status within the book industry as well as its new aggressive posture at the close of the fifties.

> I should like to discuss with you further, some day, the cooperative role of the inexpensive paperbound publisher—i.e., New American Library—in the development of major literary and scholarly properties. The withholding of properties from inexpensive reprint (for the market mainly beyond the book shops) means that the entire paperbound field is gradually being forced to develop books from traditional sources, at home and abroad, on an increasing scale. New American Library, for one, does not poach authors. Indeed, we cannot concede that hardcover publishers have a moral code or editorial standards that are higher than our own. The impression of superiority still prevails too widely among some hardcover publishers, who frequently constitute The Establishment, to be comfortable for us.
>
> I personally find many elements of publishing as it existed prior to the inexpensive paperbound book industry as hypocritical and sometimes as corrupt as television has been revealed to be. Last year, for example, at the ABPC luncheon, prior to the National Book Awards, I was shocked to discover Charles Van Doren on the program and seated next to me. Long before that I had gone on record as convinced of his fraudulent career, made possible as a member of the biggest log-rolling family clan in American letters.
>
> There are no secret meetings of paperbound publishers to discuss hardcover attitudes, but I know of several gatherings of hardcover publishers to discuss ways and means of disciplining inexpensive paperbound publishers. I regret to say that one such discussion was graced by the active participation of the prospective president of the American Book Publishers Council. . . .
>
> Tiffany's may not like Woolworth's on 5th Avenue. And some publishers may not like the inexpensive paperbound element in their cherished profession—but I think we have to learn to live together, and I am doing my utmost to promote harmony and a common purpose. And I think you are too. . . . (24 November 1959)

By the early sixties, proprietary ownership and a paperback house's subsequent sale of hardcover rights to a trade publisher, which became known as "buying backwards," appears to have become commonplace.

Perhaps as many as thirty NAL proprietary titles were placed with hardcover publishers in 1960. This was confirmed by Truman Talley's observations to a Houghton Mifflin editor who was weighing two NAL literary properties. The waggish tone of the letter would not have been conceived of ten years earlier. "We have quite a number of arrangements now with most of the major hardcover houses on books we've sparked, and I'm quite sure that both of these will lend themselves very nicely to your list. Our 'proprietary contracts' pass along all of the normal hard-cover prerequisites and, the way they've been regularized over the last two years, are quite painless" (3 May 1961).[12]

Along with scouting for new writers for proprietary projects on the West Coast, NAL also intensified its contacts with Hollywood film producers and studios. The decision of a producer to create a movie based on a softcover publication usually meant a significant increase in the projected sales of the title. Therefore the sale price for reprint rights to books was increased manyfold if a film option was already signed. It was to the great advantage of the softcover publisher to get there first, that is, to sign the author to a proprietary contract that guaranteed softcover publication and permitted NAL to negotiate hardcover options.

To aid NAL's search for both writers and potential paperback-movie tie-in projects, Literary Projects was formed in Los Angeles under the direction of Ted Loeff, a former Hollywood press agent. In reality an NAL subsidiary, Literary Projects attempted to gain the cooperation of film studios or producers to turn story ideas into successful screenplays and books and to locate West Coast writers to novelize these assignments. NAL, as proprietary book publisher, would line up a hardcover publisher, publish the softcover edition, and collaborate on mutually beneficial promotion and reissue arrangements with the studio upon a film's release. Weybright's compact with Loeff paid early dividends when the latter introduced Weybright to Irving Wallace. Wallace's book publisher at the time was the man upstairs in NAL's office building, Alfred A. Knopf, who had published two collections of Wallace biographical profiles.[13] In the spring of 1959, Weybright was asked by Wallace to advance the author twenty-five thousand dollars for two book-length projects. The money freed Wallace from screen writing and allowed him to write a novel, *The Chapman Report*, and a full-scale biography, *The Twenty-Seventh Wife*. Weybright then approached his neighbor to interest him in the hardcover editions. Knopf

12. Today approximately 50 percent of all mass market books published are originals. Of the first editions (hardcover, trade paperback, and mass market paperback) published in the American book trade, it is estimated that about 15 percent are sponsored by imprints traditionally associated with mass market publishing.

13. *The Fabulous Originals* (1955) and *Square Pegs* (1957).

declined. Despite Knopf's refusal, reactions from many in the book industry establishment to this precedent-breaking arrangement were encouraging. Weybright quickly received feelers inquiring about hardcover rights to the Wallace projects. Both books eventually went to Simon & Schuster (*The Chapman Report* later became a major Hollywood film). NAL editor Walter Freeman reported on his lunch with literary agent Jean Detre shortly after the announcement of the Simon & Schuster acquisition was made.

> Jean tells me that *The Chapman Report* is discussed all over town (as we know) and that there has been considerable comment on the fact that we had the book before any hardcover publisher. Most of this has not been particularly derogatory but there have been the usual words about "attacks on the basic structure of publishing." Her reaction was quite favorable and she was very much interested in the possibility of getting advances on a couple of her own authors. . . . Her main interest in the Wallace book is to find out just what publishers shy away at taking on a novel from a reprint house and which ones are not adverse to the idea. (20 May 1959)

At the same time from Hollywood Ted Loeff feverishly reported to Weybright that Wallace "is our most important public relations ambassador—causing hundreds of writers to descend upon this office—demanding 'an Irving Wallace deal!' "

Two years later in a speech to the Canadian Booksellers Association, Weybright summarized this trend that he set that was then being followed by the other major softcover houses. "I don't believe it was a calculated plan for inexpensive paperbound publishers to undertake important general fiction . . . but it happened. Paradoxically, some of the fiction which we developed was so irresistibly good, or so unmistakably marketable, that hardcover publishers came clamoring for what I chose to call 'reprint' rights. At New American Library we are very discreet about these arrangements, so that our hardcover and university press friends in the United Kingdom as well as the United States do not lose face through wide-spread knowledge of the fact that we are the primary holders of the important publishing rights for the full period of copyright" (2 May 1961).

By the late fifties, West Coast contracts and projects occupied enormous amounts of company attention. In retrospect, however, Weybright's efforts to develop a West Coast salon to counter hardcover publishing reprint reversions and trade paperback imprints resulted in relatively few acceptable book projects. Focusing on Ralph Ellison's *Invisible Man*, Truman Talley expressed serious concern about future NAL editorial directions. The seeming need to drop longer works of established fiction from the company backlist in response to rising paper costs prompted this memo to the two partners.

> I understand we are thinking of dropping this title from the list. If we cannot come out financially with such books at a 75¢ price and with reprintings every year or two, I think we must start to think in terms of 95¢ or $1.00. . . . Otherwise we will be dropping soon other long titles that are not fully reissuable: *Lie Down in Darkness, Native Son, World Enough and Time, Love Is a Bridge.*
>
> Whenever we have dropped a book of some note or quality, we have come to regret it later, when raised prices on classic programs have made such a title again feasible. *Manhattan Transfer* is one such instance, our only Dos Passos.
>
> For good reasons we have dropped, or not taken up options on, books by a number of respected novelists over the last two years. We are discontinuing *New World Writing*. In the meantime, our recent lists have included many more second-rate bestsellers than ever before, with fewer big novels of quality coming to us from the trade houses. I believe we need to retain our Ellisons, Styrons, etc. We have more need than ever before. (20 May 1959)

The editorial tendency toward acquisition of more commercial and ephemeral fiction, however, was balanced somewhat by a renewed commitment to publishing books appropriate for the school and college markets. The paperback generation of the fifties saw their teachers and professors dropping expensive hardcover textbooks in favor of paperbacks, which offered more variety and freedom for instruction. New Mentor projects were undertaken as well as new scientific, religious, and art series. The institutional marketing staff was expanded. The most dramatic undertaking aimed at the school and college markets was the initiation of the Signet Classics series in the late fifties. Comprising a mix of public domain and successful backlist titles, it became the most acclaimed American paperback "classic" series of modern paperback publishing.

Shortly after the series began, Erskine Caldwell's *Georgia Boy* was scheduled for a Signet Classics edition. Weybright informed the author, whose literary reputation had suffered partially by its connection with mass distributed books, that the new edition "should do something to preserve and heighten the qualitative interest in your writing." Weybright then went on to summarize his vision of what his company had achieved of significance in the cultural sphere in this country. In very succinct fashion he states the context in which he and Kurt Enoch operated during the first fifteen years of their softcover publishing partnership. "I am all for the mass market—and live by it—but one has to be aware of critical attitudes that may be influenced by success in the mass market. That, really, is why we started *New World Writing* back in 1952—to demonstrate that NAL was not just a juggernaut catering to the great unwashed. Since then, of course, it has been possible through Mentors and many Signets, to prove that there is nothing particularly rude or vulgar about popular taste, given a chance for it to be exercised" (27 June 1960).

The 1960 acquisition of NAL by the Times-Mirror Company of Los Angeles began a new era in the corporate life of the company as well as in the professional lives of its two founders.[14] The greater financial resources of Times-Mirror immediately permitted investment in extended publishing projects and deeper exploration into proprietary publishing. Further it allowed NAL to bid even greater sums for reprint rights to hardcover bestsellers. Of particular note is the spectacular success of Ian Fleming's James Bond thrillers, which were obtained in the late fifties on a Victor Weybright hunch. With Times-Mirror backing, the company also set up a London-based subsidiary by acquiring two small English reprint companies and merging them into a new entity to be called the New English Library. The company's determination at this time to continue to grow and compete both in the foreign and domestic markets through expanded marketing arrangements but especially through a determined commitment to proprietary publishing is underscored in Weybright's observation to British publisher Charles Lewis of Allen and Unwin written only a short time after the Times-Mirror acquisition.

> This puts a great deal of extra work upon us, but we must meet the threat that the reprint material will not be as readily available as more and more [hardcover] publishers tend to issue higher priced paperbound titles from their own list. Scribners, for example, has terminated on Modern Library, as well as on us, Hemingway, Thomas Wolfe, Scott Fitzgerald; and Viking has terminated Joyce, Steinbeck, Sherwood Anderson, etc. You can't imagine that the dynamic paperbound industry of the U.S. will permit itself to be flattened by terminations and astronomical bids against royalties. (26 July 1960)

By the mid-sixties, aided by another Times-Mirror acquisition, the

14. The Times-Mirror Company acquired the company through an exchange of shares. Holders of NAL stock received $13 million in Times-Mirror Company stock as reported by Victor Weybright in his memoirs (*Making of a Publisher* 200).

company became a fully integrated, general book publisher of mass market paperbacks, trade paperbacks and, for a time, original hardcover titles.[15] No longer did the company see its earlier role in the book industry as a responsible "service organization" to trade publishers. It had become a fully rounded publisher in its own right, competing equally and effectively with the major and often long established general book publishing houses.

The Hampton Court Palace, where, at James I's order, *Macbeth* was first performed, had not been the site of a banquet for over two centuries. However, in April 1964, in recognition of Shakespeare's four-hundredth birthday, "A Midsummer Night" celebration was arranged by the Royal Shakespeare Company and NAL's London branch, New English Library. At this time the English branch was introducing in Britain the Signet Classic Shakespeare, edited by three American scholars. Early volumes in the multi-volume project were very favorably reviewed in the United States, and they were competing successfully with the long established Penguin Shakespeare editions.

Attending the Hampton Court affair (full evening dress, white tie, and medals) were over four hundred luminaries from the British social, stage, and literary worlds, including the Duke of Wellington, Sir Ralph Richardson, Dame Edith Evans, and two of the world's richest men: Nubar Gulbenkien and J. Paul Getty. Cohosting and speaking from the dais was the chairman of the board and editor in chief of NAL, Victor Weybright. He later recalled, "I was almost in tears of elation at the pagentry of the vaulted ceilings covering such a splendid and magnificent company, as I delivered my well-reported remarks." Weybright concluded that his part in the affair was "possibly the greatest honor ever accorded an American publisher in England." Regardless of the degree of the honor, it is clear that the publisher and his company had moved a long way away from the Automat of Manhattan.

15. The hardcover line, NAL Books, was soon merged with that of another Times-Mirror acquisition, the World Publishing Company. This hardcover imprint was dropped within a few years only to be reinstituted in the spring of 1980.

4

"The Publishing Side of Our Private Lives"

Victor Weybright was cofounder, chairman of the board, and editor in chief of NAL. Distinctions between his service as publisher as opposed to his service as editor are arbitrary and, for the most part, unimportant. In most book publishing operations where the responsibilities reside in the same individual, these distinctions are difficult to make as they relate to the evaluation of any one prospective publishing project. Clearly the ultimate decision on whether to sponsor a particular literary work is a publishing decision. The initial evaluations are made by editors who, in most commercial publishing operations, must judge both the inherent worth of the writing (an editorial concern) and the likelihood of the project bringing in a profit (a marketing concern). These evaluations represent the basic gatekeeper theory at work. The tension on the gate's spring is created by the cultural contribution that the work is likely to make tempered by its projected balance sheet.

Victor Weybright shared the basic responsibility for New American Library's overall publishing program with his partner and cofounder, Kurt Enoch. Enoch, however, as company president, directed his daily supervisory responsibilities to the company's production and marketing functions. As editor in chief, Weybright was primarily responsible for the company's general editorial trends; the way he unified these trends constituted the company's publishing program. Weybright was also responsible for the specific books that the company contracted to publish—their selection and their progress through the editorial department in preparation for softcover publication. When large advances were involved, the approval of Enoch, who was also treasurer of the company, was required.

The career of Victor Weybright as revealed through the editorial correspondence encourages reflection on those elements of his life and personality that contributed to his spectacular success as editor and publisher. Perhaps the one personal attribute that dominated all the rest was his far-ranging curiosity. In the correspondence, this attribute is revealed by the great variety of professional and personal interests that the editor in chief developed and maintained through the years of his leadership at NAL. Besides an almost required interest in literature—the process of its creation and the current trends it was taking—Weybright had a deep and abiding concern for contemporary political and social issues. Stemming from his apprenticeship in the mid-twenties as secretary to Jane Addams at Hull House, these concerns were heightened by his editorship of the *Delineator* and *Survey Graphic* in the late twenties and thirties and, of course, by his State Department service in London during World War II. During the course of his service, Weybright often had a firsthand look at the governmental systems of both Great Britain and the United States.

Politically, Weybright was a New Deal liberal, an enthusiastic supporter of Adlai Stevenson during the Eisenhower years, when NAL grew prosperous. Weybright's scope of personal interests seems boundless, ranging from scientific farm methods and fox hunting to gypsy lore and gourmet food. At the time of his retirement from NAL, he belonged to more than thirty clubs and associations and subscribed to more than seventy-five periodicals. Concern for and travel to Third World countries seems to have occupied an increasing amount of his time as NAL prospered in the fifties and sixties. These global regards, which continued after his retirement from publishing, kept him in touch with a wide range of society and fostered acquaintance with influential intellectual, elected, and titled personages. Both at home and abroad he was a tireless entertainer and, in turn, received invitations to numerous and varied social and professional functions. His genuine liking for people was best exhibited by a benign paternalism toward his junior editors and writers. The NAL files show numerous examples of moral and financial support for his authors. He was a kind—but seldom humble—mentor and patron.[1]

Weybright's worldwide associations, particularly in England, directly

---

1. Weybright's excessive ego seems to have generally been understood and endured by the editor in chief's friends and associates much in the same manner one tolerates the egocentrism of a very bright but impetuous child. Its most unfortunate and permanent display appears in his autobiography, *The Making of a Publisher*, completed soon after his unhappy departure from NAL. In a 16 February 1989 letter to the author, Truman Talley observed: "I suppose there was a certain amount of Mozart about Victor, an energetic genius in his manner and fashion who was also, when hard-pressed, a cauldron of spite and vindictiveness. He was never that difficult to deal with if you gave him a modicum of appreciation and praise for his extraordinary vitality and accomplishments. There were very few Victor/Kurt hassles through the '50s."

benefited his authors. These personal associations were developed to the mutual benefit of both the publisher and his authors. They were seen as service to "the publishing side of our private lives," as Weybright once summarized for Erskine Caldwell (27 December 1951). For instance, he willingly provided business and social introductions. Typical of a Weybright heralding was this request to an English friend on behalf of Kathleen Winsor. "I'd like awfully for her to know you, and if Parliament is sitting, to have a glimpse at that great institution. She has never been to England, despite the historical research which produced her bestselling *Amber*. I am very keen for her to know England and the British, and show her some of my affection for you-all" (12 May 1952).

A more colorful example is an introduction that Weybright arranged between two British scholars. His letter was directed at his friend and adviser Isaiah Berlin, who at the time was also preparing a manuscript for Mentor publication.

Joshua Whatmough is, I think, worth knowing. He has some of the qualities of a [C. S.] Sherrington, a little tincture of [Alfred North] Whitehead, and, with his deep knowledge of language, philology, linguistics and semantics, should have at least academic interest for any philosopher. He's a compact Lancashireman, with an atmosphere about him as meticulous as his brightly polished professional spectacles. He is writing a book on *Language*—that just may be a milestone volume. I hope so, as I am publishing it, and my tea-time date with him in Winchester is a reconnaissance on the progress of the manuscript. I don't want to frighten you, but I am a very persistent editor when deadlines approach. (10 November 1953)

An introduction of a different sort was provided to the entire NAL staff. Toward the end of his tenure at NAL, Weybright, in the role of editorial senior statesman, drafted a short exposition on Jane Addams. In this recollection, headed "Random Notes from The Editor," he tied himself and Addams to other personalities linked with NAL as authors and advisers. Sharing reflections like this may have helped inspire his autobiography, *The Making of a Publisher*, published in 1967.

In September we are issuing *Twenty Years at Hull-House* as a Signet Classic during the centenary year of Jane Addams' birth. Earlier in the year, Henry Steele Commager, author of our foreword, wrote a remarkable essay on Jane Addams for *Saturday Review*. Now in connection with a new biography of Miss Addams and the reissue by Macmillan of one of her important books, *Peace and Bread in Time of War,* *Saturday Review* is giving special space next to the review for the attached brief "Recollection" which they asked me to write. I was Miss Addams' secretary for two years—nearly forty years ago—while studying at the University of Chicago.

Our younger NAL people should read *Twenty Years at Hull-House* for their own edification, but those having anything whatever to do with Chicago simply must read it. As the first Signet Classic in the field of modern autobiography—Teddy Roosevelt's *The Rough Riders* is next—it is one of the most significant books in American literature. Its author is linked to many of NAL's finest and most basic publishing projects and personalities. A few examples:

Edith Hamilton (whose two sisters, Norah, a notable artist and etcher, and Dr. Alice, first woman on Harvard faculty and pioneer in occupational medicine, were constant resident-visitors at Hull-House) wrote her first book—*The Greek Way*—at the age of 60. She brought the proofs to Hull-House to read, proud as a schoolgirl. *Mythology* and others followed, and Miss Hamilton is still writing in her upper nineties.

Howard Mumford Jones, of Harvard, whose advice has been responsible for a dozen of our Mentors, was a resident of Hull-House and one of my faculty advisers.

E. C. Lindeman, our late editorial consultant, frequently sojourned at Hull-House when, with Jane Addams and Felix Frankfurter, he was a contributing editor of the old *New Republic* in the days of Herbert Croly. I met him there in 1924.

During my two years at Hull-House every major historian, educator, philosopher, poet and critic who visited Chicago (then quite a literary center) tried to make an appointment with J. A. I always managed to squeeze them in. From those days—typically, for example, breakfast with William Allen White of the *Emporia Gazette* in Kansas, lunch with Lord Robert Cecil of the League of Nations, tea with John Dewey, dinner with Sidney Hillman (once a Hull-House neighborhood boy) and supper with Gerard Swope, president of General Electric—my early training as an editor.

I wrote and published something on behalf of Hull-House nearly every week; attended the University; practically managed and budgeted the operations of Hull-House for Miss Addams; and served as secretary and fund raiser. I was not yet 21 when I persuaded Miss Addams to give me a chance in the exclusive circle of her work, so I could study at the University of Chicago which seemed so much more exciting than the Wharton School of Finance & Commerce of the University of Pennsylvania where I had previously been a self-supporting student.

Whatever privilege may have got me into Hull-House was not based upon wealth or the recommendations of others. I had read much of *Twenty Years at Hull-House* ten or fifteen years earlier in the *Ladies Home Journal*, where it was serialized by Bok, the great editor who made the Curtis Publishing Company what it was for two generations. When Bok was secretary to old Charles Scribner in the 1890s and Frank Doubleday was running the stockroom in the basement, Scribner told them both they didn't have what it took to become publishers! How different from the inspiration of Jane Addams upon everyone who ever was within reach of her influence!

Next bulletin from VW: "Sinclair Lewis." (24 July 1961)

Weybright was fond of comparing NAL authors with the great writers of the past. Common in trade book publishing, these exercises in literary association, which range throughout the archival files, heighten entrepreneurial perspectives, melding cultural and commercial visions. Weybright frequently compared Erskine Caldwell's story-telling powers with those of Mark Twain. Louis Auchincloss was seen "in the great tradition of Henry James, with an ability at the very outset which in my opinion far surpasses Edith Wharton's talent in dealing with similar upperclass material." Novelist Paul Bowles is a "major minor talent . . . certainly in the peerage of Isherwood, Tennessee Williams, etc." And he viewed Georges Simenon as possessing an "almost Dostoyevskian revelation of human motivation and compassion for human frailty."

In the early sixties, Weybright frequently associated Sinclair Lewis and Irving Wallace. In recognition of the thirtieth anniversary of Lewis winning a Nobel literature prize—the first American to do so—and to complement the publication of Mark Shorer's widely publicized biography of the author, Weybright reprinted Lewis' three best-known works as Signet Classics. At the same time Irving Wallace was completing drafts of *The Prize*, a bestselling successor to his *Chapman Report*, which describes in detail the Nobel awards ceremonies. (Both novels were NAL proprietary publications.) With luster and lucre clearly in mind, Weybright congratulates Wallace on the movie sale of *The Chapman Report*.

Your call Friday night was exciting, as if I had received the news that you had won the Nobel Prize ($40,000 isn't it?). The MGM deal, quite apart from its financial importance, reinforces our mutual conviction that Irving Wallace is one of the world's giants in the field of the modern novel—giving meaning to life through revelation of characters and dramatic crises.

I am proud to have been identified with your move from journalism and Hollywood entertainment to the stature of a creative novelist of universal importance. Those who sneer at *Chapman* will soon recant. I can see the coming recognition that you deserve as a novelist, fearless with theme, authentic and true to the characters of great importance in our world.

Although better than Sinclair Lewis, I expect you will occupy his position in international letters as a social observer with an eye and an ear for the most difficult thing there is to portray: the obvious, the venacular, the meaningful, etc. (29 May 1961)

Part of Weybright's effectiveness as an editor may be traced to his own three full-length books. This not only gave him an inside look at the process of writing, but also provided him another bond with writers. In 1955, exactly twenty years after the publication of his first book, *Spangled Banner: The Story of Francis Scott Key*, Weybright coauthored with his long-time friend, Henry Blackman Sell, a second biography, *Buffalo Bill and the Wild West*. Publication gave the editor in chief a taste of the joys of authorship and allowed him to bask for a while in the literary Valhalla where he assigned so many of his authors.

After Oxford University Press accepted *Buffalo Bill and the Wild West* for hardcover publication, Weybright boasted to Isaiah Berlin that "they rate it in the same company as Parkman, Turner, Dobie and DeVoto." NAL issued a softcover version in 1958. Three years later, when the William Cody biography had failed to achieve lofty expectations, Weybright applied his own disappointment as consolation for another NAL author, Robert West Howard, whose new work he declined to reprint, "There has been a genuine slump in western books, obviously as a result of the heavy western schedules on TV—and I could almost write myself the same kind of letter you have written me, if I wanted to split my personality and face the music on the poor showing in paperbound of *Buffalo Bill and the Wild West*."

Throughout his career at NAL Victor Weybright exhibited supreme confidence in his ability to judge the readership potential of a new book or manuscript. Complementing his editorial judgment were his speed-reading skills, which allowed him to personally review the prodigious number of literary properties his company attracted. In one letter he laid claim to reading fifty books and manuscripts per week. In *The Making of a Publisher*, Weybright lowered this rate slightly to average out to two thousand annually.[2] This speed often permitted early and rapid bids, which gave NAL an edge in acquiring attractive reprints. It earned for Weybright the appellation from Hardwick Moseley of Houghton Mifflin as "the quickest editor in all this business" (5 April 1951). And when he successfully completed the record-setting bargaining for James Jones' first novel, he boasted to Whitney Darrow, Sr. of Scribner's, "I, personally, am pleased by the outcome of a negotiation which commenced when I borrowed the galleys of *From Here to Eternity* and read them at a single sitting—probably the only reader who has managed such a feat."

His reading prowess was matched by the tireless energy he devoted to other aspects of his job. Apologizing to senior editor Arabel Porter for not yet resolving a permissions problem, Weybright described a typical business day in London.

> I haven't had a single minute to look into the Mao Tse-Tung snarl but I hope to get into it before the end of the week.
>
> I have appointments at the rate of 9 or 10 a day outside of the hotel, and it doesn't leave much time for special projects—which really should be undertaken by JBC [J. Bradley Cumings, NAL editor]. For example it is now 6 a.m. and I have a breakfast date at 7:30 and another at 8:30, then constant outside dates until 6:00 p.m. when Dennis Brogan comes to tea—then an early dinner at George Weidenfeld's and a supper party afterwards. I mention this only so you will know that I am not dodging these special requests, but trying to fit them in. (20 September 1961)

Following a manuscript or reprint acquisition, Weybright's direct concern with the project usually ceased. It became the responsibility of staff editors to see that details and deadlines involved with the preparation of text for book publication were met. Surrounding and reporting to Weybright was a stable of editors, perhaps never numbering more than a half-dozen, each usually responsible for one or more particular genres but also expected to acquire, review, or edit books or manuscripts covering a wide variety of nonfiction topics. NAL editors Donald Demarest and Walter Freeman were both writers themselves. In fact, Freeman published two novels with NAL: *All the Way Home*, dedicated to Victor Weybright, and

2. He also observed that NAL senior editor Truman Talley read about eighteen hundred titles a year (*Making of a Publisher* 288).

The Last Blitzkrieg, produced as a film by Columbia Pictures. David Brown, producer of several very successful major Hollywood films, worked at NAL in the early sixties, helping to launch the company's first, short-lived hardcover list.

One of the best-known of all NAL editors, E. L. Doctorow, came to NAL in 1959 from Columbia Pictures.[3] Demonstrating the expected working range of paperback publishing, he specialized in philosophy and science books during his five years with the company. He was also in-house editor of the highly regarded Signet Classic Shakespeare series as well as the less academic *Mad Magazine* cartoon books and the later Ian Fleming Signet reprints. Best-loved among the ranks of editors who served under Weybright was Arabel Porter. On the company payroll even before Weybright, both she and Donald Demarest were hired in 1945 to replace editors who left Penguin to go to Bantam with Ian Ballantine. Porter was particularly sensitive to contemporary writing and worked with most of the young writers whom NAL featured in the late forties and early fifties. She was also the editor of the widely praised *New World Writing* series, which appeared under the NAL imprint in the fifties.

Several very successful executives in the publishing world learned the complexities of mass market publishing under Weybright's tutelage. Among these are Edward Burlingame of Harper & Row and Marc Jaffe. After leaving NAL in the late fifties, Jaffe played a major role in the rise of Bantam Books to softcover dominance in the sixties and seventies, succeeding the legendary Oscar Dystel as president. For most of the fifteen years he was with the company, Truman "Mac" Talley, who arrived at NAL in 1949, was senior among the NAL editors under Weybright. Talley was Weybright's stepson and heir apparent as he advanced through the company to the editorial vice presidency. Comfortable in most areas of literature, Talley had a special fondness for science fiction and was chiefly responsible for the company's initial ventures into the as yet uncharted area for paperbacks. Authors he worked with included Robert Heinlein, Brian Aldiss, Isaac Asimov, and Alfred Bester.

In the formative years of the company, Weybright also received advice and support from a kitchen cabinet that both suggested and reacted to proposed editorial projects. These counselors included Judge Jerome Frank and Sir Isaiah Berlin. Berlin contributed two titles to the NAL list and was advisory editor for the very successful Mentor Philosophers series. The most influential and admired of Weybright's early advisers was Columbia University and New School of Social Work professor Eduard C. Lindeman.

---

3. Weybright also used author Saul Bellow as an outside reader and reviewer in the early days of the company.

An authority on adult education, Lindeman directly shaped the nature and content of the Mentor imprint. As the company grew, Weybright, like most general publishers, also sought guidance and opinions from a great variety of authorities—specialists and academics—on specific editorial projects. From time to time, he hired consultants to give extended evaluation on editorial ventures in which the company was making a large investment of time or capital.

Little happened in the editorial department that was not shared by all of its members, including routine problems that might find nonbinding advice dispensed by Porter or firmer direction from Talley. As NAL grew and devoted more effort toward proprietary publishing, the details surrounding the publication of individual manuscripts multiplied. Three morning editorial meetings a week, chaired by Talley, helped to keep track and follow up on myriad editorial matters.

These details, often technical in nature, centered on the best methods to present the material to a mass market. More or less routine, most of the technical problems were solved by the staff editor, often in verbal consultation with the author as well as others in the department. These decisions are generally unrecorded in the archival correspondence. In 1957, however, because of the number of Erskine Caldwell titles under NAL sponsorship and the complexities they created, Truman Talley was required to document for future reference some routine matters common to daily editorial decision making.

RE: Dedications, introductions, blurbs and critical apparatus: Caldwell titles.
1. Dedications
   For some time now all author dedications in NAL editions have been deleted.
2. Introductions
   There is one, brief introduction by Caldwell in *Tobacco Road*. This should be dropped in the book's next printing and a half-title [page] used to replace it.
3. Postscripts: NAL and Modern Library have, in *God's Little Acre*, the Magistrate's Court, City of New York decision. RML [Rudolf M. Littauer, NAL lawyer] feels its inclusion has outlived its usefulness. The present reissue will last, probably until the appearance of the movie, when a replated reissue can substitute advertising matter for the ruling.
4. Author's photograph: All new reprints and reissues employ the same Caldwell photograph. This will be continued until such time as another shot, or use of the portrait, is decided upon.

5. Brief cover IV biography: J. T. [Jay Tower, head of NAL publicity] feels that a standardized biography would become very dull. She would prefer to continue the present practice of varying details of the author's life with mentions of books and sales.
6. Proofs of front matter: Sending such matter is now standard NAL practice. (26 February 1957)

Staff editors under Weybright were also responsible for answering reader complaints and queries. Some complaints received what might be considered today an unusual degree of personal consideration. Not least among readership targets was *The Catcher in the Rye*, singled out by an American journalist vacationing in Canada. "I have come across, in a house where I chance to be lodging, a book published by you, entitled 'Catcher in the Rye.' I do not know how much more of this kind of filth you have turned out, but it seems to me that only in a country where the general moral-standard has sunk to a very low level would people of your kind be permitted to foul the moral and cultural atmosphere in such fashion and keep out of jail" (24 June 1955). Walter Freeman drafted a carefully worded, almost friendly reply.

Frankly, I'm astonished that a journalist has such an unfavorable opinion of J. D. Salinger's novel, *The Catcher in the Rye*. Of course we are all entitled to express our opinions and the editors of the New American Library are just as anxious to know the views of those who dislike a book of ours as we are to hear from those who approve of it. It was particularly surprising to see you describe the book as "filth." . . . [Freeman then goes on to quote some leading critics of the day.] The consensus seems to be that the book is important because of its brilliant style and characterization so rarely found these days. When these qualities are found they should be welcome.

Regardless of the nature of your opinions, however, I should like to repeat that we welcome your letter. I am enclosing a catalog of our books in print. From it you should receive an indication of the high quality of our list. (1 July 1955)

No author on the NAL list, however, seems to have matched Mickey Spillane's ability to generate heated reader reaction. Critics often received an analytical rebuttal from Spillane's editor at NAL, Marc Jaffe. The following is typical as it brings into focus that classic moral problem for which book people have generally assumed a Janus-like profile, that is, the effect that reading matter has on the reader.

> There has always been a tradition of the individual assumption of responsibility for revenging crimes against society and other individuals. The familiar cliché of mysteries has been the battle between police and an amateur detective. From Sherlock Holmes on down, mystery readers have identified themselves with strongly drawn fictional characters whose job it is to track down a murderer. In this sense I think Mike Hammer is simply a contemporary extension of this long-established tradition. Second, I don't think that the average reader is quite so affected by some of the moral implications—even the psychopathic implications—of *One Lonely Night*, as you seem to be. The Spillane fans, ranging from university professors and Washington journalists to college students, house-wives, servicemen and a wide variety of reading Americans, consider these books mere entertainment of an exciting sort. I really don't think that reading about violence can make an individual more violent than he would be ordinarily or in terms of total development, which would take place whether or not a particular kind of reading matter had been absorbed and enjoyed. (29 August 1951)

Much of NAL's early correspondence came from readers in the armed services and reveals how paperback titles passed from hand to hand in the military. "While reading through Irwin Shaw's *The Young Lions*, my buddy and I came to a debatable point. Said point appears on page 457 (Signet Pocket Book). I would like to know if Cawley was shot then drowned, or did he lose his balance and drown. I would appreciate it if you could give us a definite answer. The whole barracks waits your decision. Hoping to hear from you soon" (18 July 1952). Marc Jaffe replied warmly to this query from a Navy outfit.

> Sorry to have kept the whole barracks waiting for so long for this note, but I have had to take a vote of the editorial staff here on the problem of interpretation which has troubled you in regard to *The Young Lions*.
>
> It seems clear that in the scene on page 457 Cawley was shot just as he reached the top of the bank. Note the sentence, 'Then there was a burst of gunfire' and following that, Cawley whirls and falls back. It seems to us he has been shot before he falls and subsequently drowns.

I hope this answer is satisfactory. If there is further discussion in the ranks don't hesitate to write again. (28 July 1952)

A book's cover could be subject to scrutiny as critical as the text as this tongue-in-cheek query from an Army corporal who had also recently completed *The Young Lions* supports. "You have probably received many letters on the same subject. The cover of your very fine book is in error. Why is a certain Pfc. (I would like to be in his shoes) wearing stripes and also officer's brass on his lapel? The guy might be AWOL or something, and I would sure hate to get the GI in trouble. Is there an answer? (3 December 1951). In this case Jaffe's reply was more conventional in explaining that the error was "just one of those things that creep in when a large and complicated publishing program is under way."

Editors at NAL took their cue from Weybright who rightly believed and proved throughout his career that widespread social, educational, political, and business contacts were the nurseries for profitable books and book ideas. NAL editors joined clubs and civic, trade, and professional associations. They attended receptions and parties sponsored not only by their own company but those hosted by hardcover publishers. Lunches with authors, their agents, with other paperback and hardcover editors, and subsidiary rights people were frequent. When a particularly interesting reprint possibility emerged, the report might also recommend a Weybright follow-up, as when Arabel Porter urged action on Rachel L. Carson's *Sea Around Us*, a book that later became one of NAL's most successful nonfiction reprints. "I think the time has now come for you to write one of your presentation letters reviewing our past record and our position in the whole reprint paperback field, and making some fairly concrete, but adjustable, offers" (10 April 1952).

Empathy and understanding of the trials and rewards of authorship are the basic equipment of an effective editor. Although these attributes may seem to be secondary in a company that does a high percentage of reprint titles, the NAL files reveal numerous instances of editor involvement with the sorrows and celebrations of their authors' personal lives. Novelists like Doctorow and Freeman could empathize convincingly with their authors. For those editors who were not writers, there was always a willing writer to explain the process. Suspense writer Don Von Elsner describes it to Weybright assistant, Davis Crippen. "Nothing could be simpler than writing in Hawaii. You put a son in college, buy a new car, contract to paint the house, retain a landscape crew to refurbish the yard. You set the alarm for 6:30 and, after a hasty snack, you enter your study. Your wife cheerfully shoots home the bolt on the outside of the door. The landscapers have boarded up your windows so you're not distressed or depressed by all the beauty out there. You light a couple candles, and after a couple hours, what is there to do but write? Christ, you can't see to read!" (19 October 1961).

Truman Talley was provided with an equally facetious glimpse by Isaac Asimov whom he was trying to lure from his Boston home to an office conference in Manhattan. "As soon as I told Gertrude that I would probably be taking a trip to New York, they all got sick. First David got tonsilitis, then Gertrude had a sinus attack, then Robyn developed a mysterious fever. However, they are all recovering (it was a mistake in tactics on their part, they started it too soon) so barring unforseen accident, I ought to be able to take off on the 23rd" (13 March 1960).

Although not a writer himself, Truman Talley seems to have particularly excelled at advice and support. Following the 1952 Signet publication of William Styron's first novel, *Lie Down in Darkness*, NAL was anxious to acquire the future full-length works of this young, talented, and critically acclaimed writer. When Talley learned through Styron's agent, Elizabeth McKee, that he was at work on a new project he quickly wrote.[4]

> Elizabeth mentioned that you were pretty well decided on making your long story into a novel. I don't want to let a day go by without telling you how happy I am to hear it, and I am sure Arabel and Victor will feel the same way. One first rate novel by you will ultimately be worth all the short stories you might write, particularly since you are already within that small group of young authors who will not be forgotten between books. We will always be eager to do a Styron story in *New World Writing*, but the thing that makes us happier, with a writer already known, is to do a stretch, if at all possible, from a forthcoming novel. That way everyone wins.
>
> Good luck on the novel. You are smart not to spread yourself too thin through many articles and stories. Your problem for the next few years looks as if it will be resisting the blandishments of plausible young men wanting "just a short piece" here, there and everywhere. (11 February 1954)

As NAL increasingly undertook more proprietary projects, concern for writing deadlines became a frequent subject for letter exchanges between writer and editor. From Weybright on down, the editorial response to

---

4. Unnamed in the correspondence, this project was probably *Set This House on Fire*, which was published six years later and reprinted by NAL in 1961.

author delay is a mixture of the sympathetic and the firm. The importance of the writer and his standing within the company generally prescribed the proportions in the mixture supplied to each writer. In 1955 one of the more colorful responses was written by Weybright to adviser Isaiah Berlin who was then editing the fourth volume in the Mentor Philosopher series. Its arrival had been long delayed and the subject of anguished correspondence between Weybright and Houghton Mifflin. NAL had arranged for publication of a hardcover edition through the Boston publisher. Houghton, however, felt "squeezed between the upper and nether millstones" by Berlin's delay. Berlin's letters to Weybright at this time contained a variety of reasons why he was not able to get everything pulled together. Mailed to Berlin's Riviera address on April Fool's Day, Weybright responded to one of Berlin's letters in this series. "This is to acknowledge, with appreciation, your progress report. . . . We are all waiting breathlessly for the manuscript, not only because of the urgencies and exigencies of our publishing project, but also for the personal enrichment of our education" (1 April 1955).

Not surprisingly, an author's need for money to continue writing was often cited as the central reason for failure to meet publisher deadlines. Requests by writers for additional advance money that would enable them to stick with writing full-time persist throughout the correspondence files. For most of its early history, NAL seems to have been more tolerant of delays than liberal with additional money.

The control that a reprint publisher exerts over the output of an author is by the very nature of the publishing activity different from that exerted by a proprietary hardcover book publisher. At the beginning of a reprint project, the softcover publisher, assuming it is not the proprietor, usually is separated from direct contact with the author by one or more layers of screeners or evaluators. As seen in chapters 2 and 3, these initial gatekeepers are usually the original book publisher and, if the writer has one, his agent. Their knowledge of and relationship to the paperbound reprinter is part of a selective process that, when functioning, brings the author's manuscript, proof, or hardbound text to the attention of the reprinter.

Several factors appear to influence this "secondary" selection process. One is simply the publishing record of the reprinter: What kind of books has it published in the past, and how successfully has it published them? A reprinter with a small, new, or nonexistent science fiction list, for instance, is not likely to have the first option for reprinting the latest narrative of a popular-selling writer in the field.

A second selection factor is the personal contacts between editors of the publishing companies involved or between the agent and the softcover editor. Have there been successful negotiations in the past between them? Are there any particular favors that one owes the other?[5] A hardcover editor or agent will feel some degree of obligation to a reprint publisher who has successfully published the author in the past. When a new work appears by the same author, perhaps one with greater commercial potential than the first, a sense of gratitude may have developed in the recognition that the reprinter aided in getting the writer "exposed," that is, in building his or her literary reputation. And in turn, reprint publishers will call on this indebtedness when attempting to secure a later work of a writer they have previously published.

Obligation can also be a factor when time and the balance sheet demonstrate that a highly touted title that commanded a large advance has not lived up to expectations as a paperback. On a subsequent negotiation with the proprietary publisher, the softcover publisher might ask for more favorable terms, "a little reciprocity" as Victor Weybright closing a deal once requested of the Dial Press. Reprint editors will, of course, court agents and publishers who control talent or who have gained reputations for being strong in certain categories of literature that are compatible with the reprinter's own list. Further, the identification of trends and of writers to deal with these trends is basic to the survival of any book publishing operation, the recurring melody in the dance of agents and hardcover publishers with paperback houses.

Once a book or manuscript has been selected by a publisher, control shifts directly to the material itself. This control can be generally classified as either external or internal to the work itself. The external control, if not better known, is perhaps better understood. It is primarily concerned with "shaping" and "positioning" the book "product" for its appearance in the marketplace. It is not directly concerned with the book's content but rather how to package and market the contents to attract the greatest number of buyers. Though this control does not affect the content, it does affect how the content is interpreted by others. These external controls encompass design (typeface and size, page design, cover illustration, and the technical details described earlier in this chapter) and distribution (promotion, advertising, and sales). (These concerns are discussed further in chapter 9.)

Internal control of the written work is primarily the responsibility of the editorial department. Here the publisher deals with text, shaping it with a final eye to the audience that the publisher and the author envision. In the offices of a proprietary publisher, these editorial activities are line editing and copyediting. Performed on the manuscript before type is set,

5. This second selection factor is discussed quite thoroughly in chapter 3 of Coser, Kaduskin, and Powell.

their general aim is to make the work clearer, more readable, stylistically consistent, and accurate.

Line, paragraph, and section revision and reorganization are alterations usually made by the editor who acquired the book for the publisher or to whom the book project was turned over after contract negotiation. Irving Wallace's *Chapman Report*, a proprietary work of NAL, was sold to Simon & Schuster for hardcover publication. Walter Freeman, who was given the responsibility of line editing the book, suggested to Wallace a number of changes that he believed would improve the manuscript. His efforts were rewarded with this candid response.

> Working from the manuscript of *The Chapman Report* that you returned to me, as well as your letter of September 25th, I have finished that part of the rewriting that involved largely a general toning down. As you will see, I accepted the majority of your suggestions. In most cases I accepted them because I felt they improved the book. In other cases I accepted them because they seemed important to you and were not important to me. In a few instances I made the changes regretfully—and frankly, only as a bargaining lever—so that I could say, if necessary, look, I've trusted your judgment down the line—now give in to me for the little I want. And, understand the little I want to retain I do not wish to cut or modify, I feel quite strongly about from a story-telling and literary standpoint.[6] (16 November 1959)

Copyediting seeks a different depth than line editing, by checking grammatical correctness, accuracy of detail, and clarity. Very often this work is given to a free-lancer who in turn exerts a different sort of control over the author's creation. This influence is not always appreciated by the author, as free-lance copy editor Peg Cameron laments in a note to Truman Talley in which she also summarizes the supportive and harmonious relationship that should exist between editing and writing.

> And don't you sometimes wish that an author would regularly remind himself that the editor, and the copy editor too, are on *his* side and are above all interested in helping him to succeed with the reader? It would be easier for everyone too if authors understood

6. Irving Wallace was also incensed with Walter Freeman's surgery of a reproductive organ reference in *The Chapman Report*. "I'd love Gallup to run a word poll—I'd wager most Americans would define 'uterus' as a saltwater fish, a minute insect or a school attended by boys and girls," he fulminated.

that the process of editing is as gradual in its way as the process of writing. The few points I mentioned in that letter to you do not nearly cover all the problems in the manuscript, just as the rewriting you initially asked him to do does not necessarily thoroughly complete the demands to be made on him. One naturally picks out the first glaring omissions or faults that come to mind, and then the focus gets closer and closer, and gradually other details emerge. But this is obviously difficult for the writer to appreciate and heaven knows what can be done about it. (18 August 1960)

Some alterations to an original work are superficial and, to an author, may appear to be arbitrary. Following one minor editorial change, Arabel Porter received this droll reply from scholar and classics translator William Arrowsmith, then at the University of Texas. "If you think asterisks look chic, why, let them stay. I must admit, I had never thought of them that way. Perhaps they do; here in Austin one loses the sense of fashion" (5 August 1959).

Reprinted publications do not usually require the kind of internal editorial scrutiny necessary for original works. (Some kinds of reprinters, such as book clubs, contract for use of the proprietary publisher's printing plates or film to produce replicas of the original text.) As already noted, in the early years of their history, mass market publishing was almost exclusively engaged in reprinting. With approval of the original publisher and usually the author, abridgment exerted a form of internal control that, for a time, became a recognized peculiarity of the softcover industry.

From the 1939 inception of the first successful modern paperback series, Pocket Books, a quarter was the universally recognized price of mass market editions. After World War II, inflation pushed up the price of paper—the largest single cost item in the production of paperbacks—to a point that larger books became too costly to produce at twenty-five cents. Publishers feared that increasing the price to cover increasing paper costs would alienate buyers and doom these more expensive titles to failure. Cutting out portions of the original text seemed a practical alternative.

"Abridged for the modern reader" on the front cover not only alerted the reader that parts of the original were missing but also left an impression of doing the reader a favor by the elimination of unimportant detail. In truth it allowed publishers to control page count and maintain a margin of profit.

At the turn of the decade, with continued rise of paper costs, publishers broke various price "barriers" with Giants at thirty-five cents and, with NAL leading the way, Double Volumes at fifty cents and Triple Volumes at seventy-five cents.[7] Even with the flexibility offered by new price levels, however, mass market publishers through the first half of the fifties continued to abridge books when it appeared necessary. Some categories of literature had prescribed page counts which, if exceeded, would lose their attractiveness to dedicated readers of the genre, or so publishers believed. Examples are mysteries and westerns that for a long time held to their twenty-five-cent price. Publishers also believed that titles in these categories could not exceed a certain number of pages, somewhere between 144 and 192. Most writers of these genres knew the page proscriptions and wrote accordingly. However, general fiction not aimed at any closed set of habitual readers has page limitations set solely by the imagination and energy of the author. As a consequence, paperback publishers when bidding on these titles often had to weigh the effect that the length of the work would have on profit margins. If the book was long and the author relatively unknown, the likelihood of abridgment increased significantly.

In the fall of 1952 Victor Weybright wrote to Truman Talley from London about a new first novel that had been rushed across the Atlantic for consideration. The book under scrutiny was written by the then blind John Howard Griffin.

I read the unbound copy last night (Tuesday) immediately after it arrived—and I congratulate you upon detecting and discovering this unusual work of a gifted author, unconventionally published. I think that NAL should take on the book and—despite the handicap of an abridgment notice—edit it to Giant or even twenty-five cent length. It hasn't got the weight or momentum for a Double Volume. If it casts off with sufficient margin for a Giant, then I think it should be optional whether or not the book is edited— since, if it achieves fame, we may not want to touch it. Is NAL in the position to get the book for a comparatively modest advance? Say $4,000? I can't tell from your communications with whom you are negotiating—but I agree with you that a bargain should be struck before the book is launched in trade edition and, because of the circumstances of its publication and authorship, over- dramatized.

If the author is young, and at work on another book equally subjective in approach, this book is worth more than if it is a one-

---

7. At least one NAL title was issued in both an abridged and unabridged format. Ann Petry's *The Street* appeared in an abridged, "Special Edition" in 1949 at twenty-five cents. In 1954, after the quarter price barrier was broken, it was reissued, unabridged.

shot. I leave it to you and KE to thrash out since I am not close enough to actual bargaining and background. (16 September 1952)

Nearly a month later, still not having signed the book for reprint, Talley continued to wrestle with the problem of shortening the text. The original manuscript, virtually unedited, was being locally produced in Fort Worth, near Griffin's home in Dallas. The following excerpt of Talley's letter to Griffin's Texas agent highlights the reprint publisher functioning as gatekeeper, that is, recommending editorial adaptation in light of the strictures of the marketplace.

> Our best advice must remain that—unedited, whether it is reprinted by NAL or a competitor—Howard's first novel, in its present form, will not reach the widest possible paperbound audience. And as such, an unedited paperbound version would damage the subsequent reception of his later books among those who did pick it up.
>   Howard has a phenomenal future ahead of him, perhaps the most promising of any of the young writers in America today. In addition to his native talents, his blindness is both his most valuable literary resource and his greatest weakness—technically. But technique has always been the function of the editor—to be the sympathetic, though emotionally uninvolved sounding board, the friendly arbitrator between what an author thinks he said and what actually has arrived on paper. I hope we can contribute some small part toward Howard's development. I am sure we can do a great deal toward the widest possible dissemination of the final result. (4 October 1952)

For reasons that the files do not reveal, NAL was not successful in obtaining the novel. No doubt the company's desire to edit down the book had an effect on the reprint award. In 1954 an unabridged Cardinal Giant edition of *The Devil Rides Outside* was issued by Pocket Books at fifty cents. But Talley's prediction for "an unedited paperbound version" seems to have held true. The book was not reissued in softcover during the remainder of the fifties, and no other Griffin novels found their way into softcover during this period.[8]

Weybright and Talley remained in contact with Griffin, however, and the third issue of *New World Writing* contained his short story, "Sauce for the Gander." Their families became quite close, to the point that Victor

8. In 1956, Houghton Mifflin published Griffin's *Nuni* in hardcover.

Weybright's wife, Helen, sought medical aid for Griffin's war-caused blindness. Eventually this handicap was cured. Griffin went on to write his stirring autobiographical odyssey of race relations in the United States, *Black Like Me*. Its Signet edition is one of mass market publishing's all-time leading bestsellers and one of the mainstays of the NAL backlist.

Ralph Ellison's *Invisible Man* was considered for abridgment by Weybright when NAL was negotiating with Random House for reprint rights in 1951, the year after NAL introduced fifty-cent books to paperback shelves. Bearing in mind that the royalty income from the sale of a fifty-cent book was usually twice that of a twenty-five-cent title, Weybright presented to Harry Maule of Random House a best case scenario. His intent was also to provide the proprietary publisher with added incentive to promote the book's hardcover sale. (It has not been uncommon in the history of softcover reprinting for a proprietary hardcover trade book publisher to ease up on the promotion and advertising of a new title once profits were assured through the sale of softcover reprint rights.)

> I am resolved that we should cope with this remarkable book by a remarkable author in reprint—and I would like to suggest, tentatively, a formula that has shaped up in my mind. If your trade edition achieves the velocity and vibration of the marketplace to make a Double Volume Signet reprint a good risk, then we should like to have it as a Double Volume—at, say, an advanced guarantee of $6,000. But, if the trade edition achieves a more limited acceptance—despite the critical acclaim which it will merit—then I should like to propose an abridgment, of 25¢ Signet length, for an advanced guarantee of, say, $4,000. In any event, [we propose] to pay the $4,000 guarantee in toto at once—and to use our discretion a year after your publication whether to undertake it at a 25¢ length or complete and unabridged at 50¢.
>
> It would be our desire, obviously, no less than yours, to see it as a 50¢ item. But I think you will agree that, without the build up of the Random House edition into the general consciousness outside of ordinary book circles, it is very risky. (13 December 1951)

A contract was completed two weeks later under the terms Weybright suggested. Along with a signed document, Weybright sent Harry Maule some counsel, which reflects attitudes then existing within the retail book trade. Booksellers, generally, were unenthusiastic about first novels by relatively unknown authors and, therefore, did not place large first orders. When it was known before initial publication that an inexpensive softcover edition was already arranged, their orders were likely to be even smaller, anticipating that many readers would wait for the paperback edition. However, having fewer copies in the marketplace inhibits the building of a book's reputation through word-of-mouth sales. For a book like Ellison's to ultimately succeed in both hardcover and paperback, a literary reputation was essential.

Herewith the contract on *Invisible Man*, which I hope is in order. I am emphasizing in an internal memorandum that, if for any reason I should not be present when *Invisible Man* is scheduled, only in a desperate situation should an abridged edition at 25¢ be contemplated.

A word of advice: I don't know Ralph Ellison, but word has reached me from a mutual friend that he is very pleased that NAL will eventually reprint his Random House book. I think that somehow the advantage of you and us, as well as the author, would be served if his Random House editor could advise him discreetly not to mention the fact of the reprint at this stage, when word of it would annoy the book trade. We lean over backward to keep all such arrangements confidential and I know you do too—and I hope you don't mind this word of caution for the author.
(31 December 1951)

In April of the following year, confirming Weybright's earlier faith, *The Invisible Man* appeared supported by overwhelmingly positive reviews. (On 16 April 1952, the *New York Times*' Orville Prescott, the most influential book reviewer of his time, described it as "the most impressive work of fiction by an American Negro which I have ever read.") NAL issued the book the following year as an unabridged Signet. This volume also initiated a longtime friendship between Weybright and Ellison, which included visits by the editor in chief to the writer's Paris apartment.

Abridgment was a publication alternative that was especially vexsome for writers with established reputations, a vexation clearly understood by the publisher. By mid-1949 Weybright had successfully reprinted about a half-dozen James Cain novels and was trying to round up others for republication in a Signet format. One, *The Moth*, required abridgment. The shrinking was done in house by Arabel Porter. Its completion was announced by Weybright to Joseph C. Lesser at Knopf, Cain's hardcover publisher. NAL was counting on Lesser to soften Cain's predicted dissatisfaction.

At long last one of our best editors, working closely with me personally, has cut *The Moth* to a length which would make it economically a profitable 25¢ item—and I only hope that you and Mr. Cain will appreciate the exigencies of the situation sufficiently to condone the necessity for abridgment. As Somerset Maugham has pointed out, we all cut and abridge a bit as we read; and in reducing the length of *The Moth*, Mrs. Porter has read the book a number of times to spot the very sections that, no matter how unfortunately, could be dropped without really mutilating the work. (26 July 1949)

Earlier that year, Weybright had studied a Porter memo regarding *The Moth*, informing him that fifty thousand or more words would have to be cut to get the book down to the 192-page, twenty-five-cent Signet limit. His studied response to the Porter proposal was handwritten on the bottom of her message. "It should be borne in mind that Cain is an author's author, very sensitive to editorial or other interference with his own conception of writing. It will be a delicate task to edit *The Moth* and to secure his approval. Knopf assures us of their best efforts with the latter." Cain's own reaction to the abridgment, contained in a letter to William A. Koshland at Knopf, is a combination of disconcertion and resignation. "I must say that I am somewhat bewildered as to the stuff that has been taken out. All the stuff about the oil fire, which apparently sold the book, and created great interest in it in California is out, as well as most of the hobo stuff. On both phases I worked until my tongue hung out writing and researching. They are completely out. However, I shall not make any objections, for I shall be curious how the thing is received with these changes. It may be that what I thought of value and what the reader does are two different things" (28 August 1949).

In 1957 NAL was weighing whether to bid on James Jones' second novel, *Some Came Running*. At this same time Fawcett was attracting a lot of notice for its new Crest reprints series through record-setting bids for the acquisition of bestselling titles. It had broken an earlier advance record that NAL had set with Jones' *From Here to Eternity*. (See chapter 6.) Concerned with the financial risk of a large advance on *Some Came Running*, Truman Talley's lengthy memo to Victor Weybright, centers on the price at which the book should be sold.

It can be argued that *Some Came Running* reads along, that it should have something ᴏf a trade sale, and that if this book just happened to be the first novel reworked, it would be premature to let Jones go elsewhere in reprint. True enough, but we could take an awful beating on this book.

If no delay is possible with Scribner's, I suggest an advance not exceeding $40,000. We should not offer a higher royalty rate. A $1.00 or a $1.25 price might allow more of an offer—but there are just too many unfavorable intangibles: brief trade bestsellerdom, Scribner-type length of time we'd have to wait to reprint, a movie that conceivably may never be done. I now, too, begin to have doubts about Jones' future. A subsequent combat novel would make a fine commercial title, when and if; it could also mean that the groping direction of Jones' career has come to a halt.

We have a number of precedents concerning second novels that failed to benefit from the reputation and sales of the first. Motley's *We Fished All Night* comes particularly to mind, as does Mailer's *Barbary Shore* and Shaw's *The Troubled Air*. Too, a 75¢ price seems to be about as high as we can go for the mass reprint sales, even during recent prosperity. If the present stock market slide continues, Jones' meandering hero will seem even less sympathetic, and the $1.25 will be spent elsewhere than on this book and NAL will be holding the bag—perhaps even losing the "option" on future books that has been our rationale for taking this. (16 December 1957)

After NAL acquired it, a reduction of 50 to 60 percent was deemed necessary to meet the seventy-five-cent price that Talley envisioned. The reduction, done by a freelancer hired by NAL, required the approval of Jones' hardcover publisher, Scribner's. Predictably, it was not greeted with enthusiasm by the author who believed that "the overall meaning of the book has been seriously damaged," as reflected in the editing out of the "breakup" scene of the character, Bama. Jones also believed the editing "by your young lady makes me sound like a latter day James M. Cain in style!"

In his response, the editor in chief quickly passed over Jones' reactions to the abridged Signet. Perhaps stretching the truth in reporting readership reaction, Weybright got to matters that reflected more auspiciously on his company's gatekeeper activities.

I agree with you to a considerable extent on the Bama business, but something had to go to make the economics of the book feasible. I am happy to report that—purely on a materialistic side—the reprint project has been an enormous success. We shall earn royalties at the rate of 10% of the cover price, which may well total $100,000. A great many readers have written fan letters saying that they never would have paid the full price of the hard cover edition, and they are grateful to New American Library for bringing the book to them, even in shorter form, at a price suitable for the average Main Street reader. (12 May 1959)

When abridgment was deemed necessary, the preferred arrangement was to have the author do the cutting. This presumably would greatly reduce discontent after the abridgment was completed. If author abridgment was not possible, another approach was to enlist someone known to the author and sympathetic to his writing. When preparing Robert Penn Warren's first Signet reprint, *At Heaven's Gate*, for the mass market, Weybright found such person in "George Mayberry, a friend of Warren's and an appreciative critic of his work." Mayberry apparently was able to satisfactorily reduce Warren's *At Heaven's Gate* by 50 percent before it appeared. When Warren's *Night Rider* was scheduled for reprint the following year, Mayberry again was employed. The author, who appears from the records to have no qualms about these reductions, took an active hand in the second abridgment, exchanging some of Mayberry's cuts with those of his own choosing.

There is much evidence that the abridgment of a serious writer was never undertaken without weighing how cuts would affect the integrity of the work as well as its salability. With reference to the cutting of Warren's *At Heaven's Gate*, editor Marc Jaffe presented an assessment of Willard Motley's *Knock on Any Door* abridgment potential. This book ultimately led NAL to gamble on a new price category, fifty cents, and to begin publishing Double Volumes.

I read this book (practically in one long session) when it was first published. A re-reading would no doubt clarify my opinion about the cutting problem. Any book can be cut, but in this case I think the result would be a full-fledged condensation, not an abridgment. As I remember, there was not a great deal of extraneous material in *Knock on Any Door*—no long-winded descriptive or self-examinatory passages; and even the final trial section is a very important part of the whole thing.

Again, a cut is possible, but I feel it would be even more damaging than in the case of a book such as *At Heaven's Gate*, for instance. (20 June 1949)

In January 1950 Arabel Porter explained to Walter Van Tilburg Clark the reasons that it was necessary to abridge *The Track of the Cat*. "Though we would much prefer it if you would undertake to cut the book yourself we are prepared to assign the task to our most skillful editor." The author turned down the assignment concluding that "it's nearly impossible to be sufficiently objective about something you've lived with as long as I have the *Cat*—the fresh view is more to be trusted."

The task was given to Alice Teneyck on a free-lance basis. After studying the book, Teneyck gave Arabel Porter a summary of the approach she intended to take.

It would seem that great writing in the field of imagination makes each reader feel, see and interpret what he reads in his own terms. Such books are three dimensional, with the depth as deep as the reader's capacity. Because of the development of still another level, that of the subconscious as shown in dreams, it seems to me that this book might well be called four dimensional, if that wouldn't sound too pretentious and falsely erudite. . . . I strongly believe that the balance of elements the writer has developed must be maintained and not tampered with. Stark details plus dream-like intangibles are combined brilliantly to make up the mood intention of this book. I would want, at most, to trim out only the "side" or minor details. I can, however, give you no specific points where I would like to cut until I get into the work, as each book, I have found, makes its own cutting pattern. (6 February 1950)

When a copy of the letter was passed on to Clark, the author replied that he was "considerably reassured. The *Cat* will suffer very little in the hands of the surgeon who feels that way about it."

Since most textual abridgment was done outside of the publishing company by free-lance editors, general guidelines on how to carry out the cuts were necessary. These varied according to the book, its author, and the size of the cuts required. In 1949 Weybright sent the following instructions on Elliott Arnold's *Two Loves* to a free-lance editor.

In editing, you will reduce the length of the book to not more than 75,000 words, preferably 72,000, and in doing so, endeavor to give the work, through deletions and the technique of abridgment of portions of it, a more mature literary quality and, to the extent possible, a less "dated" feeling generally. You will not alter the time or the setting of the novel or completely remove the Lindbergh case, but you will diminish the emphasis on the Depression period and the Lindbergh case topicality.

It is our hope that the book, as edited, will be more highly thought of by the author himself than it now is retrospectively as he has developed into a more important and significant writer. (28 September 1948)

When issuing an abridged edition, the company wanted to avoid any implication that anything important was left out. Some of these editions were published with a "special edition" rather than with an "abridgment" notice on the front cover. Also, the back of the title page usually informed the buyer that the work had "been slightly shortened and especially adapted for its appearance in this Signet edition. There has been no re-writing." However, in 1950 NAL was called to task by the Federal Trade Commission for not accurately labeling the covers of its trimmed-down editions. A series of hearings and court cases followed the original FTC citation. These concluded in May 1954. As a result, NAL was required to prominently display the words, "abridgment," "abridged," "condensed," or "condensation" on its altered texts. The FTC also stipulated that any reprint for which the title had been changed clearly display the original as well and the revised title.

The original FTC charges and subsequent court determinations encouraged NAL to publish unmodified reprints and to proclaim prominently on the front covers of these untouched titles, "Complete and unabridged."[9] And when abridgment could not be avoided, the correspondence indicates that the company was very conscientious about complying with the letter, if not always the spirit, of new regulations.

Book titles, another product of the author's creativity, are vulnerable to reprinter remodeling. Title changes from the original hardcover edition to softcover are today much less common. The current market for hardcover and paperbacks have emerged at least to the point that the same title can give a hint of what a book is about and attract a broad range of buyers of both hardcover and softcover formats. In the forties and earlier, however, hardcover books were given titles to satisfy a comparatively conservative and selective hardcover reading public. The early mass market audience was then defined as having the majority of its readership drawn from slick and pulp magazines. To achieve success on paperback display racks, many books seemed to require more provocative and sensational labeling than their original hardcover editions. Revised softcover titles frequently held the promise of sexual activity lacking in the original. Rosamond Marshall's historical romances *Laird's Choice* and *Jane Hadden*, for example, were cloaked as *The General's Wench* and *The Temptress* when Signet editions arrived on the stands. Frederic Melcher's editorial criticism in *Publishers Weekly* of the Ludwig Lewisohn title switch from *The Case of Mr. Crump* to *The Tyranny of Sex* evoked this Weybright defense (see fig. 6, p. 109).

---

9. Schick reveals that in Weybright's early reply to FTC charges, thirty-five abridged titles of the three hundred NAL had in print in October 1950 were recorded as being abridged.

We hope we can dispell your apprehension that we are "leveling down" in an effort to appeal to the mass market. As you know, 25 cent books are sold almost exclusively by display without benefit of salesman, advertising, or special promotion. We, like other publishers in our field, have to follow magazine practice in designing covers and in preparing blurbs which appeal to the public who buy our books from magazine dealers. A change of title, although not a desirable practice, is sometimes unavoidable. Some titles of original editions are not descriptive enough for books sold entirely by display. As you are aware, many English novels are re-titled by American trade publishers in order to appeal to American readers—and it seems equally justifiable, on occasion, to change a title calculated for the intelligentsia or trade book audience and explained in the advertisements and by salesmen in bookstores to something which interprets the book for the ordinary reader who would not otherwise be attracted by it. In the art work on our covers, as well as in the title and blurbs, we endeavor not to misrepresent but rather to more fully describe the author's intentions or the book's content. (16 February 1949)

Far from being upset, author Ludwig Lewisohn, who in 1949 saw two additional books of his (neither title was changed from the original) appear as Signets, applauded Weybright's efforts when he received a copy of Weybright's letter to Melcher.

By this time softcover publishers believed that they had proved, through a variety of marketing demonstrations, that their twenty-five-cent paperback formats expanded a book's readership and in most cases did not harm the continuing sales of the hardcover editions. As Weybright outlines above, reprint publishers asserted that they were locating, through new channels of wholesale distribution, readers who did not frequent or have access to the relative handful of retail bookstores across North America responsible for most hardcover sales. The importance of a reprint bearing the "right title" to reach these new consumers is also patiently stressed by Arabel Porter to editor Sumner Putnam of Ives Washburn, United States hardcover publisher of *The Wine of Etna* by Englishman Alexander Baron.

We still feel a new title is extremely important if we are to effectively present Baron to the wide popular American market he genuinely deserves to reach. We do agree that *The Wine of Etna* is a beautiful title for your edition—and for bookstore sale. But we should like to reach out far beyond the normal book sale, to hundreds of thousands of readers, and to do this we have to have a title that is quickly understood, and has immediate appeal.

Actually, the title change should be very much to Mr. Baron's advantage, and your own. In our opinion, a warm and pleasing, a simpler title should vastly increase the potential market for the book—bringing greater financial returns to you and to Mr. Baron. . . . Really big sales of the *Wine* in our edition should widen your market for his next book.

Do think about it, and let me know. We suggested *A Time for Pleasure* to you before. Now we offer another alternative *A Time to Forget*. (18 December 1950)

Neither of these titles won support. After further negotiation, the 1951 Signet version of *The Wine of Etna* eventually was retitled *There's No Home*.

Harry Grey's first hard-boiled Signet was simply called *The Hoods*. For its successor on the NAL list, the company wanted an equally direct, no-frills cover inscription. Editor J. Bradley Cumings outlined the status of negotiations over the title, a Signet original publication, to Victor Wey-bright in an interoffice memo. Discussion had apparently stalled. Cumings suggested an alternative over which the author did not have contractual control. "Harry Grey rejects the title *The Mobster* and any variation thereof, including *Delilah and the Mobster*. Nor does he like *Delilah and the Gangster*, *The Gangster*, or any of the many other suggestions I have made to him. He will accept, however, *Portrait of a Gangster*. "In view of the present impasse, and the fact that the title must be made by mutual agreement, I think this latter should be the title. We could minimize 'Portrait of a' and blow up 'Gangster,' since Mr. Grey does not have cover approval" (16 May 1958). That same year the novel, a fictional account of the gangster Dutch Schultz appeared with the final compromise, *Portrait of a Mobster* (and the word "mobster" twice the size of the first part of the title on the front cover).

Bruno Fischer was one of the most successful of the early paperback mystery writers. He placed books with more than a half-dozen different paperback houses including many in Fawcett's Gold Medal series. A willingness to arbitrate and a sense of humor probably account for much of the writer's success in being published. His letter to Marc Jaffe on the retitling of his Dodd, Mead hardcover novel *The Angels Fell* seems to confirm these necessary virtues. "I have been informed that New American Library wishes to change the title of *The Angels Fell* to *The Flesh Is Cold*. As I told you when we discussed this some months ago, I have no objection. "But I think I ought to tell you that on October 5th Gold Medal (Fawcett) will publish a quarter original of mine called

The House of Flesh. That's going to be a lot of flesh under my name" (9 September 1950). Perhaps with a tip of the hat to Samuel Butler, the Signet edition appeared later in the year as *The Flesh Was Cold*.

5

"A Richly Furnished
Mind at Work"

In any commercial publishing operation, the final decision on whether to recommend publication almost always rests on the predicted profit of the book. A successful publishing company can be defined by where it places itself on the financial fulcrum to achieve a profitable balance sheet. Does it emphasize its frontlist, new books that receive concentrated marketing attention throughout a publishing season or its backlist, older titles on the publisher's price list with steady if modest sales over a long period of time?

When compiling an economic forecast for a proposed new title, a publisher considers many factors, especially the sales history of the author's books that are already on the publisher's list. The publisher also attempts to measure whether a book fits into its publishing program by considering the audience for which the book is intended, the success the publisher has had in the past in reaching this audience, and the new methods that can be employed to reach and expand the audience. A great portion of NAL's early success was based on identifying and publishing trend-setting novelists whose audience was likely to expand as the writers became more widely recognized. This chapter will examine a publisher's criteria for selection, frequently criteria external to the text itself, that indicate how a publisher views a proposed work in relationship to what it has already sponsored.

In February 1957 four different NAL editors were carefully weighing Jack Kerouac as a new Signet author. He was a writer with both short- and long-term sales potential. Seven months before the hardcover appearance of *On the Road,* Truman Talley reviewed the manuscript and concluded in a memo to Weybright, "I'm very much for the book. It's got the restless, rootless feel of younger people in this country to an extraordinary degree." At the same time Arabel Porter reported that feature articles on Kerouac and the "San Francisco Group Boom" were appearing in *Life*, the *Atlantic Monthly*, and *Time*. Reaffirming her faith in Kerouac, Porter predicted that "Kerouac is destined to become a big 'talk' item." Two years earlier, in April of 1955, a selection from his novel-in-progress appeared as the lead piece in *New World Writing #7*, "Jazz of the Beat Generation," under the pseudonym "Jean Louis."

Talley acquired *On the Road* from Viking at a bargain four-thousand-dollar advance. One month before the fall 1958 softcover release of *On the Road*, Kerouac's *Dharma Bums* was also offered to the company for reprint. Marc Jaffe ended his reader's report on the latter, "All in all, my feeling is that this book is very much for a special audience. If it turns out that this audience is large enough to absorb a substantial number of copies of *On the Road*, I imagine that we could do this one with modest success." Thirty days later, with one month's sale of *On the Road* recorded, Truman Talley also suggested a conservative course with *The Dharma Bums*. He recommended a bid that matched their royalty advance on the earlier Kerouac. "I believe that the tentative $4,000 offer is just right. We ought to do the book if we can get it cheap. *The Dharma Bums* is a thirty-five center. It isn't quite long enough to be able to expand to fifty cents. Nor will it, I think, ever match *On the Road* in sales; it's a more readable book in some ways, but *On the Road* has become the book of this whole phenomenon, and anything else Kerouac does in a sales sense will be a lesser item" (19 October 1958). *The Dharma Bums* appeared as Kerouac's second Signet a year later.

In the early fifties Truman Talley pushed hard for the inclusion of science fiction on the Signet list.[1] As a result NAL made commitments to issue books of this genre over an extended period of time. By December 1951, with two Robert Heinlein titles behind him, Talley was confident in predicting the success of Alfred Bester's *Demolished Man*. He went so far as to compare the author's style with two of the company's bestselling detective writers, parlance understood by all at NAL. "This is perhaps the most brilliant science fiction novel I have ever read. It's a dazzling, futuristic story that contains a large number of fascinating plot and character inventions, coupled with the fast-flowing writing style that, in many stretches, contains the same sort of word-by-word magnetism of Spillane and Simenon. . . . Bester is by far the best bet, from what can be judged at this point, to become the next important property in the science fiction field—and, in a creative sense, an even better one than Heinlein" (13 December

---

1. Truman Talley's pioneering efforts on behalf of paperback science fiction is given very little notice in the histories of this highly publicized genre. His success in bringing science fiction to a mass market has been unfortunately overshadowed by the more widely known achievements of Donald A. Wollheim and Ian Ballantine.

1951). Science fiction would take time to prove itself as a profitable fiction category, as Talley admitted in late 1951 to an editor at Simon & Schuster: "Science fiction is getting there. About a year or two remains before we'll know." Some years later Talley drew up some conclusions about the genre in a letter to Mina Turner, subsidiary rights head at Doubleday. "We do the four best authors in the field: Heinlein, Bester, Clarke, and Asimov. They also sell the best. However, and here's the rub, science-fiction has a limited, intellectual audience—something that the cavalier critics have missed completely when they refer to science-fiction as a popular, wide-selling, bread-and-butter category of writing. Science-fiction *seldom* goes beyond 200,000 in paperbound reprint, and a good many titles sell far less than that" (2 April 1957).

Throughout most of the fifties, NAL, like the majority of mass market publishers, focused its sights most sharply on another genre—mystery-detective fiction. During the Spillane hiatus, the company strove to find a detective writer and formula that would complement and surpass Spillane's popularity and capture long-range sales from an even wider audience. At one time or another, NAL approached various publishers, agents, and writers in their quest to "re-grind the image of the private eye." John D. MacDonald was one author courted. Another, Leo Rosten, was given an advance to follow these Weybright instructions: "Deliver within the calendar year 1954 a work of fiction not less than 60,000 or more than 75,000 words . . . which will in the development of its plot and narrative introduce an original sleuth-team: an Intellectual (psychologist-social scientist) and a Detective (officially connected, of good but undisciplined native intelligence—i.e. a typical average guy)" (n.d.). For reasons not found in the files, the manuscript was never delivered, and in 1956 Weybright was still looking for an author to develop a new model for detective fiction. In a letter to Kenneth L. Rawson of David McKay Company, he expanded on his description of the "Intellectual" as well as the publication terms under which he and his creator would be issued.

> Now that I have taken you into my confidence on our conceptual approach to a New Sleuth, I may as well amplify the thoughts which I shared with you yesterday. First, however, I should like to repeat that if you find the perfect, and perfectly qualified author, New American Library would be entitled to 50% of all ancillary and subsidiary income due the publisher, including but not limited to publisher's share of first serial rights, performance rights, reprint and other inexpensive paperbound rights, etc.
>
> It is not necessary to analyze Spillane to realize that a detective (amateur or professional) who has less dubious traits than the

character successfully exploited by Spillane, would have unique acceptance. We are familiar with the passé figure of Sherlock Holmes, or the over-exotic Philo Vance, or the pedestrian Perry Mason. I am thinking of something quite, quite different from any Sleuth hitherto developed in modern crime-and-detective fiction.

In these notes I shall, however, counter-poise our New Man against Spillane's dull-witted, slap-happy, over-compensated effeminate character. We need a new Image more in harmony with the political and social tasks of our time. The new character's relationship to crime and deviational conduct is vicarious. He must justify a minimum of private violence, treating it as a last resort that occasionally signifies a regrettable lapse of foresight on his own part. He must think of himself as supplementing official with private channels (in accord with our basic institutional structure) and indicate a rational basis for working effectively in harmony. He must not be psychopathic, but he must know all about psycho-pathology. He must be absolutely certain of his identification with the male role. If we assume—for the sake of agreement with Max Lerner—that the Spillane image, Spimage for short, associates morals with violence, then an orgasm of violence is the purge for a sense of weakness, guilt, shame, lust and doubt.

The New Eye must provide a new catharsis. He must be a well-developed personality who is strong enough and sufficiently disciplined to face his motives in all candor. He will be able to cope with them by the use of a versatile repertory of skills other than violence. This leaves no scope for hunch and punch, but, rather, shows a richly furnished mind at work. Our new man will not find himself baffled by modern knowledge, or by the scale of modern organization. (He will not be a "superman.") He will be in command of the best thought from the causes and consequences of deviational conduct. . . . It is no accident about the fatalistic Maigret appeal to Europeans. The primitive Old Testament Mike Hammer has appealed to millions of Americans. There is an opportunity for a universal and well-rounded Egghead to appeal to readers of all sorts, everywhere. In doing so, he can elevate the mystery beyond the sardonic shock of Hitchcock's TV thrillers, as successfully as mellow and picturesque Sherlock Holmes did at the constant astonishment of Dr. Everyman Watson. Maybe our New Man needs a countervailing stooge, always a useful device, from Don Quixote's day onward. I am not at all certain that he should be a professional man—Doctor, Lawyer, Social Scientist. He should be well rounded, like a great Renaissance man or Benjamin

Franklin, a serious dilettante in the best sense of the word. There is an old saying that "talent *can;* genius *must.*" Our man must be an amateur genius in the field of human nature, hence growing, always growing as a personality as each of his assignments unfolds the awesome panorama of human personality. The devices—plot, suspense, and the usual apparatus of the mystery—will not be greatly tampered with, as we see it. The secret is in the distinction, sophistication and skill of the writer. He cannot be a hack. (10 October 1956)

Gore Vidal was considered anything but a hack writer. In the early fifties, as the writer was emerging as one of the major voices of postwar fiction, NAL learned about some of Vidal's pseudonymous fiction. Pyramid, a small mass market house, published in 1950 *Cry Shame!,* a reprint of Vidal's *Star's Progress.* (This was a Dutton-published novel loosely based on the life of Rita Hayworth.) Both novels appeared under a pen name, Katherine Everard. Also in 1950 Weybright republished Vidal's serious novel *The City and the Pillar* under the author's true name. Shortly afterward Weybright learned that Vidal had drafted a light mystery that he also desired to publish pseudonymously. It needed extensive editorial assistance, however. Acknowledging its mass market potential, Dutton agreed to let NAL share the editing task and publish the softcover edition. After initial examination of Vidal's first draft, Weybright sent a summary of his evaluation to Nicholas Wreden at Dutton.

Herewith Gore's partial manuscript, and Marc Jaffe's notes which coincide with my editorial opinion of the effort. To attract mystery readers, and hold them, Gore will have to make his reader care a lot more about the outcome, about the course of his protagonist in the narrative—and, above all, to have the murder occur earlier to confront the reader with a real suspenseful puzzle.

On the constructive side—I genuinely feel that Gore could develop an interesting and profitable sideline out of this sort of thing, without sacrificing any of his dignity or distinction if his pen name were ultimately penetrated by the critics. (31 July 1951)

Two weeks later, after a follow-up lunch with Vidal, one senses Weybright's glee as he informs Kurt Enoch of the mystery and of the line editing done by Marc Jaffe, NAL's mystery book specialist. "Gore Vidal ghosted a thriller—*Cry Shame!*—which sold over 400,000 copies in paperbound reprint. He is about finished with a lush mystery, which Marc and Nick Wreden [Dutton] will be handling. It looks promising. This is a deep secret and should not be discussed with anyone at all except Marc and me in our shop" (13 August 1951). A month later Jaffe sent Weybright an update on his editorial revisions.

> About three weeks ago I had lunch with GV after reading the entire first draft of the mystery. The book had a couple of major defects—a poor beginning, for one thing—and a number of minor things. On the whole, however, it looked promising, although in a completely different vein from anything we've done in a long time. GV and I discussed the whole proposition and he went on to do a revision. Last Monday I went down to Dutton to discuss the revision with Nick Wreden and GV. Both Nick and I felt that the new beginning still did not have enough to get the reader really interested. Nick suggested a major structural change which will mean about 50 pages of rewriting; and although GV did not seem too happy about it, he realized that it would be better for all concerned. I felt justified in giving GV and Nick assurance that we'd take on the book if the beginning were done successfully, plus some additional work on the end. Naturally, you will have final say, but I think you won't be disappointed. The individuality of this book will be its style, and its casual attitude toward high society sex. There will be some carnality (added at my suggestion), but if you want more I think you'll have to buck Wreden—who wants to tone down the scene which I asked GV to spice up.
>
> A final aside: GV is most impressed with you as an individual and as an editor, with your encyclopedic knowledge of contemporary writing, general acumen, etc. (20 September 1951)

Published by Dutton in June of 1952 under the authorship of "Edgar Box," *Death in the Fifth Position* received mixed reviews including this perceptive summary: "More sex than gore in this unsavory concoction of murder in the ballet" (*Bulletin from the Virginia Kirkus Bookshop Service*, 1 May 1952). With a Signet edition still a year away, a second Vidal mystery manuscript appeared on Weybright's desk the following month. After a hasty read, Weybright quickly sent his congratulations to Vidal for delivery of what eventually would be called *Death before Bedtime*.

> Whodunit II by Edgar Box is a little dandy—with a good title, and a little tinkering here and there—it ought to surpass *Death in the Fifth Position*. I am prepared to proceed at once with a Dutton contract, as soon as they have it in hand, and I shall share my notes with Marc. I read it at one sitting, to get an approximate composite

effect of an actual reader, so I didn't take notes. Off hand, though, I don't think there will be many corrections. The initial sex scene will probably have to be edited down by a word or two. I wonder about the propriety of including such prominent actual senators as Taft and Byrd, etc. present in the Senate office building. Let's don't tie it too closely to 1952, and risk a certain datedness.

I'd like to congratulate you especially on the tone of the writing, and on the consistent and suspenseful development of clues and character. (29 July 1952)

On the same day Weybright sent a euphoric memo to Jaffe underscoring his enthusiasm for "Edgar Box" whom he envisioned lining up with other successful mystery and detective writers on the Signet list. "Edgar Box's second is a little honey—the most literate mystery imaginable; daring and sexy but not hard-boiled, and therefore ideal for family reading. I predict that we can build Edgar Box into a major S. S. Van Dine type of mystery writer. This has a bearing on Wade Miller. With two or three Boxes in sight, we have something with more prestige than Wade Miller—or Agatha Christie for that matter—and can take it easy on marginal mysteries as we develop our own team: Adam Knight, Mike Roscoe, Edgar Box, and Mickey Spillane" (29 July 1952).

Jaffe disagreed with Weybright. He did not find the manuscript as good as the first Box and appears to have given his boss some second thoughts about publishing it. In the early fall, as Jaffe was in the process of editing this second "Edgar Box" mystery, he warned Weybright that "Gore seems to think that this book is the best so far. He indicates that he doesn't have too much faith in my judgment. We'd better discuss the handling of this deal after you've made up your own mind." With the first yet unpublished in Signet softcover, but still wishing to issue the second, Weybright responded soberly. "I certainly feel that we can build up Edgar Box as a civilized mystery author, far superior to most, and certainly a lot more readable and suspenseful than Wade Miller, for example. Would you like me to deal with the author? In any event I think it should be you who functions as primary contact and communicates with him. I'll be happy to join in the discussions" (5 October 1952). The sales of *Death in the Fifth Position* must have been something of a disappointment, yet not enough to discourage Weybright in following through and reprinting the second Box mystery in 1954, one year after the first, and a third, *Death Likes It Hot*, in 1956. Records show that by the close of 1956, almost 197,000 copies of an initial printing of 335,000 of the first had been sold. The first printing of *Death before Bedtime* was lowered considerably to 207,000; 164,000 copies were sold. The final title, *Death Likes It Hot*, appears, initially at least, to have been the most successful financially. By the close of 1956, 196,000 of an initial printing of 220,000 were sold. And within two years NAL would do a new edition of each, still using the "Edgar Box" pseudonym, despite Weybright's attempts to have Vidal use his real name on the volumes.[2]

For the most part, this review of NAL editorial concerns here and in the previous chapter has focused on the company's assessment of the internal or intrinsic elements of an author's work, that is, how effectively the text attracts its intended audience and how it can be altered to make the book even more attractive. As the company matured, consideration of factors outside of textual quality gained additional weight. These external factors often overrode considerations of textual quality or defect. One dominating outside factor was the potential of the book as a film or television production. A typical example is found in a 1961 Truman Talley letter to Hollywood agent, Daniel M. Winkler. Here it is clear that a film commitment would be the deciding element in the reprinter's decision to publish the manuscript that did not yet have a hardcover sponsor.

> We are still interested in doing *The Liquid Assets of Frankie Polo*. Nevertheless, as well done as it is, the novel is in the light comedy vein—a loose category of novels that seldom have gone to large figures in the paperbound field. It would need, in short, a film tie-in to give it anything beyond 200,000 copies in paper.
>
> There might be a hardcover edition in the book. I think of Bennett Cerf at Random House. However, the experience of many trade publishers with gently humorous novels has been poor. With a film clearly in the works we'd have no hesitation in doing the book as an original, and would pay $4,000 for it.
>
> Can you tell me something more about its film prospects? I remember you telling me that Mr. Wells had a movie commitment before he could turn to *Frankie Polo*. Is his schedule now clear? Who might do the film? (20 November 1960)

It appears that the manuscript was never sold either as a book or a film. This external "West Coast" factor in editorial selection is a concern examined more closely in chapter 8.

A more traditional and common selection factor outside of textual quality is the author's reputation or future potential as a writer. In the early

---

2. After Vidal received an early royalty statement from NAL on *Death in the Fifth Position,* he remarked to Weybright that it was "not bad for a cocktail hour project . . . BUT STILL VERY LITTLE MONEY."

fifties when NAL was trying to corner the market on reprinting fresh, bright American writers, Weybright suggested to Enoch and Porter that NAL might have to bid on Louis Auchincloss' short story collection in order to get an inside track on the potentially more significant and profitable future works of the writer.

> This collection of stories reflects one of the most competent writing talents I have ever read in a first book. The stories really rate with Somerset Maugham's short stories. If we could have first crack at Auchincloss's novel, without undertaking these stories, I would be happy; but if anyone else is after this collection I think we would have to consider seriously the possibility of trying to license them from Houghton Mifflin for somewhat delayed publication. I predict that Auchincloss will emerge as a major novelist in the category of Marquand and Maugham. Too bad the people are so upperclass. But that's the way it is. (13 November 1950)

NAL reprinted two Auchincloss novels in 1953 and 1954; these were followed by a book of short stories in 1955. In presenting reasons for reprinting J. D. Salinger's *Nine Stories*, Truman Talley used similar rationale to buy the collection from Little, Brown in a memo to Enoch and Weybright.

> These nine stories, in Signet format, would come to 144 pages. They're superb. All of them have previously appeared in the *New Yorker;* as a collection, the book would grace any publisher's list.
>   The limitations are obvious: the problems of selling a short story collection; the fact that each story, while of interest to anyone who does much reading at all, is subtle and does not give the sense of fulfillment that some more obvious and contrived magazine stories do in their conclusions.
>   Nevertheless, we should take on this collection, using a new title for our edition. Salinger, as a writer, is as important to us as Truman Capote or Paul Bowles—whose second books were short story collections that we took on partially as a means of retaining the authors. *Nine Stories* should sell at least 150,000 copies and perhaps the whole of a 250,000 first printing. . . .
>   Little, Brown has indicated that we very definitely have first crack on this collection; however, from their recent mailing practices it is evident the other reprint houses received a copy of the book yesterday, as we did. (17 March 1953)

The collection, which remained entitled *Nine Stories,* was reprinted in 1954, a year after the Signet edition of *The Catcher in the Rye* appeared. It was probably the company's most successful short story compilation until both Salinger titles were lost to Bantam in the early sixties. (See chapter 9.)

Similar publishing rationales were employed when considering publication of a weaker second novel by a writer whose first book with the company was a critical or financial success. Before NAL reprinted Shelby Foote's *Love in a Dry Season*—Signet successor to *Follow Me Down*—Walter Freeman outlined to Weybright the key factor he considered when weighing reprint possibilities. "Obviously we want to keep Foote if it is reasonably possible to do so. It is apparent, too, that we will have to go a bit further than the book's probable sales really warrant. The question, of course, is whether Foote is worth it in the long run. I believe that he definitely is. In spite of the fact that *Love in a Dry Season* isn't quite as good as his previous book, it maintains a high standard of literary excellence—enough to justify faith in the author's future work" (26 July 1951). Victor Weybright outlined another consideration in the editorial evaluation of new authors to William Targ of World Publishing. World was weighing the unlikely titled, first novel of George Lanning, *This Happy Rural Seat.*

I read this intelligent, subtle, quiet and thoroughly civilized novel at a single sitting, and emerged from the experience concurring 100% with your opinion. It is, however, premature to think of launching Lanning in the mass market. Even a modest distribution would be bound to fail—at least, until we really succeed in making distribution of fiction as selective as our Mentor distribution, to heavy traffic, high culture and educational outlets. This does not mean that Lanning will not eventually be a successful author in reprint. Off the record, there is a slight parallel with a writer of much less distinction—Gerald Sykes. No one picked up his first novel, *The Nice American,* but upon reading the manuscript of his second—this is in strict confidence—I did take it in advance and agreed to follow with a modest, but not a mere token, edition of *The Nice American.* It may be that such a procedure will fit Lanning. He is bound to achieve critical acceptance upon publication of *This Happy Rural Seat.* If, by any chance, and without trying to influence you or him, his second novel should have somewhat more universal interest, I would be willing to take a chance, then, on following the more universal novel with a modest edition of *This Happy Rural Seat.* (29 July 1952)

Neither this first book of Lanning nor Gerald Sykes' even more dubiously titled *The Nice American* saw NAL publication.

When NAL considered bidding on Ross Carter's *Those Devils in Baggy Pants*, it weighed both internal and external factors surrounding the text and its marketability. The author was dead. Thus his further development as a writer was eliminated. And while well written, the book would date itself quickly. However, NAL was anxious to stay in the good graces of the publisher, Appleton-Century-Crofts. Bids on two other books—potentially more lucrative than the Carter book—had been recently submitted to Appleton, as Truman Talley revealed in a memo to Kurt Enoch.

In the final analysis one point should be clear. Despite all the trade stir coming up, this book is a one shot—the author is now dead. It is neither literary nor normally an over-350,000 copy item. If we get it by strategy rather than a large advance—fine; if not, we have our two options coming at Appleton-Century-Crofts, the Remarque and Motley books, that will be more important to us in the long run, both literarily and saleswise. If, in losing this, we psychologically solidify our options on those books—particularly the Remarque—we'll have lost to a good cause. Nevertheless, I want us to get this book, as much as to deprive the competition of anything we publish as the fact that it is, ephemerally, a little gem. (21 August 1951)

The company's carefully weighed bid was successful, and the book was published in 1952 and reissued five years later. Books by both Motley (*We Fished All Night*) and Remarque (*Spark of Life*) also appeared about the same time under Signet imprint in 1953.

Opposite from the writer whose small output has yet to earn the author a reputation is the writer who appears to have written too much within a short space of time. In 1955 after obtaining rights to Michael Avallone's *Violence in Velvet*, the company discovered that the writer "had a book popping up every six or eight weeks." After a look at the later works, a reader's report on Avallone concluded that he "might write a fair novel some day, but apparently he is not willing to work hard enough" (20 June 1955).

One unexpected facet of the NAL archival files is the quantity of correspondence that was generated immediately after the successful submission of a writer's first book. Proposal letters from the author's hardcover publisher are common. These publishers, proprietors of one or more of the writer's older works, assert the appropriateness of these earlier works for paperback reprint.

In 1956 NAL paid World Publishing Company a sizable advance for MacKinlay Kantor's *Andersonville*. Kantor was then a veteran writer with almost thirty books to his credit. However, his *Andersonville,* a critical success and hardcover bestseller in 1956, marked Kantor's breakthrough into the ranks of major American writers.[3] William Targ of World asked Weybright to consider Kantor's *Noise of Their Wings,* first published in 1938. After reviewing it, Weybright diplomatically declined.

> I read this interesting book twice, and it was read by two of our editors. The theme is fine, but not one which I think reflects the growth of Kantor's talent during the two decades since it was written. In reprint, we feel that it would have limited appeal today—and as a consequence, would add little, if anything, to Kantor's status in literature, and might well harm the regard in which he is held by readers of *Andersonville*. Indeed, a poor reception in the marketplace, might harm the momentum which we feel that *Andersonville* is bound to achieve in mass market, miles beyond the bookshops. (9 November 1956)

However, in 1958 and 1959 two collections of Kantor's western short stories did appear in Signet. Combined with the acquisition of *Andersonville,* these seem to have given NAL the inside track on Kantor's next major novel, *Spirit Lake,* which the company reprinted in 1962.

In its formative years the company was almost exclusively reprinting other publishers' originals. Rejection letters, therefore, were almost exclusively directed at hardcover publishing personnel, not at the authors themselves.[4] At the beginning of the fifties, the frequency of rejection letters sent directly to writers increased. One early example of an author turndown was mailed to Theodore Pratt. Written at the time when Fawcett was issuing its first original Gold Medal titles, Weybright's heavy-handed candor is as surprising as his follow-up recommendations.

> *The Nymph* worries my colleagues—both the editors and Mr. Enoch—a little too much for us to handle it. . . . would you like me

---

3. The Signet edition of *Andersonville* (1957) did not mark Kantor's first softcover appearance. A string of the author's earlier titles had been issued in paperback, mostly under the Bantam imprint.

4. Company records show that even as late as 1958, six NAL editors divided and reviewed only 269 unsolicited manuscripts. Less than one a day, this seems a very modest number for a major publishing operation.

to try it on another publisher? The Fawcett people, whose distribution system is employed by us, have launched a series of paper bound book originals, none of them reprinted from trade editions, and it is possible that they might find it a useful item on their list. They announced that they are doing first printings of 300,000, and I know that they are paying guarantees of $2,000 against royalties on some of the items they are commissioning—mainly of a romance sort.

. . . If the Fawcetts can't cope it is possible that Avon might want to handle it. They employ more sensational covers and blurbs than any one in our field, and frequently exploit books far beyond what the contents would justify. This we cannot do because of our identification with such authors as Caldwell, Farrell, Faulkner, Cain, etc. There's nothing censorable really, in the book at present. It retains the austerity, always, of your original draft. Please advise. I would very much like to see you reap some reward from this project.

This manuscript reminds me of a piece of semi-blighted real estate which I once owned and which was on the market for a number of years before I finally unloaded it, after some remodeling, at a tidy profit. It was a poor house on a poor location—and that seems to be the plight of *The Nymph*. She is not very attractive or very well situated in a fictional frame of reference—but she ought to bring something, considering the effort and patience that have gone into her career. (24 February 1950)

Pratt appears to have followed Weybright's advice as he became one of the mainstays of the Gold Medal list.

John B. West was a black American physician who owned and operated a hotel in Monrovia, Liberia. He also wrote thrillers. Weybright discovered him on one of his trips to Africa. In 1959 he published West's *Eye for an Eye*. This same year West submitted another manuscript, a serious "sociological" novel that Weybright did not like. In the ten years that passed since the Pratt rejection, it is clear that Weybright, while remaining plainspoken and unequivocal, had polished his author rejection letter style.

As to the more important novel you would like to write. When a minstrel (i.e. entertainer, and writer of books for relaxation) graduates to the serious novel (i.e. seeking the deeper meaning of character and life) the challenge is considerable, and the result is unpredictable. . . . Your approach to a sociological novel, in my opinion, was too melodramatic and corny. Perhaps a novel dealing with medicine in combination with the jungle, with a strong story line, is something that would come naturally out of your own observation and experience. Why not try several themes, outlines, or conceptual approaches on us? We'll be frank. I look upon you as one of the most talented men I know. Whether you can step up from the "Hot Beat" room to the Philharmonic, who knows? (24 June 1959)

In 1952 NAL published Christopher Isherwood's *Goodbye to Berlin* and, in 1954, *The Bhagavad Gita* that Isherwood had helped translate and edit. The author had two other book projects that he was anxious for his agent, Curtis Brown, and his hardcover publisher, Random House, to place with NAL. He believed that NAL had made commitments to both projects. Weybright, however, was not enthusiastic about either: an anthology of short stories and the novel *The World in the Evening*. But he was anxious to maintain good relations with Random House and with Isherwood, whom he recognized as an important American writer. Not denying the author's charge that NAL had backed out of the anthology, Weybright tries to convince Isherwood to accept the offer on the novel that included a seven-thousand-dollar advance tendered by his competitor, Popular Library. The gatekeeper concerns of the publisher are all too painfully evident.

Now comes *The World in the Evening*. It is a fine book, with the most terrifying suspenseful first chapter in any modern novel that I have read—and yet I'm afraid of its fate in the *mass market*, because of the detached subtlety which distinguishes most of the book. Three years ago, before the newsstand apparatus had become glutted with paper products of every description in book form, I know we could have given such a book visibility enough to get it launched successfully. Today, I have my doubts. So yesterday I went over to Random House and talked it over with Bennett Cerf, Donald Klopfer, Robert Linscott and Harry Maule. I explained how I had a special feeling for you and your work, and also how I had an overriding responsibility to keep our publishing enterprise dynamically solvent, which means currently avoiding obvious risks. I was told of the substantial advance offer offered by another reprint house—and after a great deal of discussion we all agreed that everyone would be better off if that other offer were accepted. This is a matter that, in today's market, must be judged financially. If another house, desperate for a literary name with which to upgrade its product, is willing to invest far beyond the bounds of prudence, I recommended the offer be accepted. There was no friction in our discussion. On the contrary, all agreed that you, Random House and Curtis Brown would benefit, and surely not be harmed, by another imprint—and our good friends at Random House went further to say that this move would not prejudice them against future offerings of your work to me. So, I implore you to proceed with approval of the other offer. We have enough mutual respect among all of us to realize that this does not compromise any of us. I have simply got to face realities so that, when the small book revolution and its claim on the new reading public shakes down—and shakes out the marginal producers—we shall be a dominant instrument between creative and scholarly imagination, and the millions of readers beyond the conventional book shops.

All these decisions are difficult, and sometimes painful, to make, especially in view of our aspirations which have frequently transcended commercial considerations when times were better. Isherwood is well represented in our current season, in a marvelous portrayal in John Lehmann's memoir in *New World Writing* and, for a long time to come, in *The Bhagavad-Gita*. So I don't feel divorced, only on a journey through this drastic Eisencropper budget country.

I hope you will understand and let me repeat my assurances that there is no grievance only regret. With best wishes, always, sincerely yours. (20 April 1954)

On a copy of the letter sent to Harry Maule at Random House, Weybright wrote, "I hope Man-Mountain Weybright hasn't labored and brought forth a mouse." The following year Popular Library published *The World in the Evening;* no further Isherwood was ever reprinted by NAL.

Directed at both authors and proprietary publishers, rejection correspondence, based on internal and external selection factors, confirms that the number of projects that NAL actually undertook was a small percentage of those initially presented for evaluation, perhaps one in twenty.[5] It also underscores that there are many more reasons for a reprinter to turn down a piece of writing than exist to support its publication or republication in softcover. Writing style, an internal factor, was among the more common.

5. Between 1948 and 1957 NAL published a total of 821 new titles. This averages out to about 80 per year. Because many of these titles would see one or more reissues during their life with NAL, the actual annual number of publications (new titles and reissued editions) issued annually was higher. These ranged between 120 and 170 titles; approximately 13,000 separate editions were issued by NAL in these ten years.

It may be too pedestrian, unimaginative, or, in the case of Malcolm Lowry's *Under the Volcano,* too difficult for acceptance by the mass market. In the early fifties Truman Talley relayed this last evaluation to Lowry's hardcover publisher, Lippincott: "Our sales staff began to raise hell. They said that they simply can't sell Mr. Lowry, and his long sentences and long paragraphs." William Faulkner's greater reputation and popular success overcame similar objections to those raised against Lowry's writing style. Nevertheless, with Faulkner's *Pylon* Truman Talley predicted other problems when he distinguished between the two kinds of reading audiences NAL attracted, the mass Signet audience and the more scholarly minded Mentor readers. "Faulkner's name and an attractive cover should sell this beyond the breakeven point, but the contents would disappoint the mass market reader. For this is a Mentor book marked "Signet." The very accurate delineation of purposelessness and vacuum in the lives and surrounding those "stripped" individuals—literally—seems good; saleswise, it seems to me that our Signet audience—most, perhaps, looking for escape, divergence and a measure of unity and purpose to fill their own void—will not take on *Pylon*" (4 November 1949).

However, *Pylon* did appear as a Signet two years later—and the publisher's perceptions of Faulkner readership were refined even further. Weybright's reply to a Johns Hopkins English professor who had offered to write an introduction to a Signet edition of *The Unvanquished* shows some of the continued examination and redefinition of the popular end of the Faulkner reading audience that took place within the company.

> If our edition were to be read primarily by serious students of literature, lay or academic, I would welcome your proposed introduction. However, our twenty-five cent edition will be sold in the usual way through mass distribution to magazine outlets. To many purchasers and ultimate readers, therefore, an introduction would somehow tend to give Faulkner a highbrow aspect and destroy natural interest. We have sold a good many millions of Faulkner's novels and stories in reprint, obviously many of them to people who are not ordinarily addicted to the reading of books, and, since *The Unvanquished* is simpler in style than any other Faulkner volume, I believe it would suffer rather than gain an appeal by an introduction. That is, in the paper bound edition— which, of course, is not comparable to the hard-cover trade edition or a hard-cover reprint. (14 December 1951)

Another Faulkner novel, *Mosquitoes,* never appeared in a Signet edition despite the fact that it was offered to NAL several times. NAL considered this early Faulkner to be among the weakest of the author's inventions. Marc Jaffe, responding for the reprinter, informed Arthur Pell of Liveright, proprietors of this work, that "the consensus is to let the book go—even if it means one of our competitors might eventually take it on." Jaffe concluded that "the book would be a great disappointment to the great majority of both Faulkner enthusiasts and general readers in the mass market" (16 April 1952). Despite *Mosquitoes*' acknowledged defects, one is left to wonder how disdainful NAL would have been had it been dealing with Random House and Bennett Cerf. With Random controlling all of the major Faulkner properties, it is not likely that NAL would have turned down a Random House solicitation on *Mosquitoes* for fear of losing other Faulkner titles in the future.[6]

As seen earlier in this chapter with the Christopher Isherwood proposals, when a publisher really does not wish to sponsor a book, elaborate, if not always convincing, rationales can be employed to cover a predicted trail of unprofitability and avoid annoying any hardcover publisher involved. A halfhearted or tempered bid from a reprinter generally indicates to the proprietary publisher that the paperback house really does not want the book and may not do much promotion and sales should it acquire the book. In this tempered reply to a bid solicitation from Putnam's Walter Minton, Weybright revealed some interesting editorial criteria that Clifford Irving's *On a Darkling Plain* apparently did not meet. In a nutshell it outlines basic gatekeeper standards for his mass market publishing company.

I've just taken on several first novels in somewhat the same category as Irving's—of middling—average literary quality with the familiar elements of bewildered youth: fornication, drinking, abortion, disillusion, frigidity (everything but homosexuality). To make a better than average success out of the book in paperbound it would have to be packaged with a good deal of color, hot blurbs and teasing color art. We are tending in the other direction. I don't care how bold the book is if it's in the grade "A" literary category, and can be justified artistically. I might add that I don't care how bold a book is if it promises to sell millions. It is this in-between category that currently has me puzzled. Some go over big, some don't. I wouldn't like to predict too much for *On a Darkling Plain,* hence my cautious and, I imagine, unacceptable offer of $3500. (9 March 1956)

6. Both Avon (in 1941) and Dell (in 1953) issued reprints of this title.

NAL did not get the book; it was reprinted by Avon later in the year.

This letter also succinctly summarizes the quandary publishers then and now face with a so-called midlist book, the title that while attracting an audience will not have a large initial sale and whose profitability for the long term is at best very unpredictable. This is the type of publication that is most difficult to "fit" between the two extremes of a publisher's offerings, frontlist and backlist. It sits dead center—at the balance point—of a publisher's range of offerings to its public.

Fig. 1.   Kurt Enoch and Victor Weybright, 1958. (Courtesy
Publishers Weekly.)

Fig. 2.   New American Library senior editorial staff, 1959. *Left to right:*
Victor Weybright, Marc Jaffe, Arabel Porter, J. Bradley Cumings, Walter
Freeman, Truman Talley. (Courtesy Archives, American Heritage Center,
University of Wyoming.)

Fig. 3.   A celebration of the sales of twenty-five million Erskine Caldwell
Signet titles, Commodore Hotel, New York City, 1951. *Left to right:* Kathleen
Winsor, Victor Weybright, Roscoe Fawcett, Erskine Caldwell, Kurt Enoch,
Mickey Spillane. (Courtesy Archives, American Heritage Center, University of
Wyoming.)

Fig. 4. *Pygmalion*. Penguin Books, Inc., 1942, second printing. Early American Penguin edition before series was redesigned in 1946.

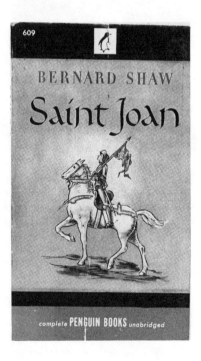

Fig. 5. *Saint Joan*, Penguin Books, Inc., 1946. One of three Shaw editions prepared for the playwright's ninetieth birthday celebration.

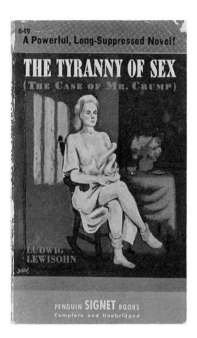

Fig. 6. *The Tyranny of Sex,* retitled paperback version of *The Case of Mr. Crump,* 1948.

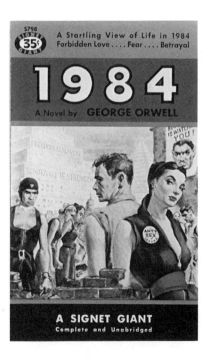

Fig. 7. *1984,* a Signet Giant edition, 1950.

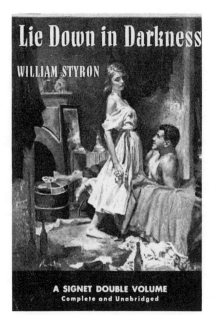

Fig. 8. *Lie Down in Darkness,* a
Signet Double edition, 1952.

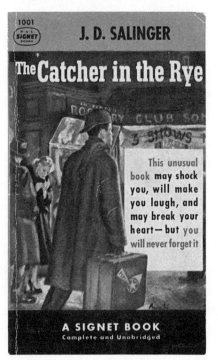

Fig. 9. *The Catcher in the Rye,*
controversial Signet cover, 1953.

Fig. 10.   Delivering "Good Reading for the Millions," 1948. Independent
distributor wholesaler delivery truck belonging to the United News Company
of Philadelphia.

6

Caviar for Short-Order
Readers

The key part of the relationship between the author and the proprietary publisher is their contract of agreement. In theory this document contains all guidelines—legal and otherwise—to carry out successful first publication of a literary work. Within the contract, the author promises to submit an "acceptable" manuscript of a particular nature and length by a certain date. The author also warrants that he will not plagiarize or commit libel. The author's responsibility for required permissions, index preparation, as well as corrections and additions to publication proofs are also specified in the contract. The author further promises that within a specific length of time not to write a competing book. The contract may also require the author to give the publisher first option on publishing his next book. Many authors and agents object to this last feature, the infamous "option clause."[1]

In a proprietary contract with an author, the publisher in turn agrees to issue the publication within a specific length of time and outlines the conditions under which the book will be sold and allowed to go out of print. The contract also assigns copyright and specifies the division of subsidiary income from outside sources such as book clubs, newspaper and magazine excerpts, translations, and paperback publications. Income from film and television adaptation are specified. This division of author royalty, the sales scale on which royalties are measured and paid, and the amount and timed payment of the royalty advance are the fuel of most negotiations between the publisher, the author, and, if the author

1. An option clause can also appear in a reprint publisher's contract requiring the original publisher to submit to the softcover publisher for reprint consideration the next new work by the same author.

is represented by one, the agent.[2] In theory, the royalty advance provides the necessary financial support to allow the writer to complete the book in a reasonable length of time. For many authors, having some royalty up front is also a psychological prop reducing the anxiety of possible failure. With the proprietary publisher making a financial commitment to the work-in-progress, the author has reasonable assurance that his or her efforts will come to fruition.

The quoin of paperback reprint publishing is also a contract; it is negotiated between the proprietary publisher and the reprinter. Like an author contract, this agreement hinges on royalty figures—percentage, scale, and advance. The size of the advance in a reprint contract is most often measured against the author's reputation, the likelihood of the book being adapted for the media, and the sales record (if any at the time) of the hardcover edition. Reprint contracts also specify the retail price at which the paperback edition will sell. A higher softcover retail price means more potential income for the author and original publisher to divide. For instance, in the early days of softcover publishing, a twenty-five-cent book produced only one cent of royalty. (Divided equally between author and proprietary publisher, a 100,000-copy sale produced five hundred dollars in income for the writer.) Royalty increased to almost a cent and a half on a thirty-five-cent book, two cents on a fifty-cent book and three cents on a seventy-five-cent book. Royalty rates were scaled to increase when reprint sales went beyond a certain level. In the late fifties bestselling authors began receiving rates that were slightly higher than standard. Soon some well-known authors also began demanding in their own contracts with proprietary hardcover publishers more favorable deals than the usual fifty-fifty split of paperback income.

In general, bids on a contract between a reprinter and a proprietary publisher are handled in one of three ways. The two publishers can deal with each other directly, negotiating on the terms of the contract. This is usually the case when the softcover publisher is deemed the only or the best candidate for the reprint rights. Or the proprietary publisher can simultaneously submit the same reprint candidate to several paperback publishers. The reprint publisher offering the most favorable terms is usually selected without a great deal of haggling. The third way that bidding can occur is the way most likely to capture newspaper headlines. Auction bidding in one of its several guises most often is employed when the proprietary publisher wants to extract the largest advance possible on a title. Bidding goes back and forth with interested reprint parties until all

---

2. The common literary agent fee is 10 percent of author income; however, within recent years many agents have begun to require a 15 percent portion.

but the highest bidder remains. This method usually is reserved for books with softcover bestseller potential.[3]

In June 1961 Weybright responded to a Doubleday invitation also issued to other paperback publishers to submit a sealed bid for paperback rights to the leading bestseller of that year, Irving Stone's *Agony and the Ecstasy*. In earlier times in one-to-one negotiations, Weybright might have responded with one of his "presentation letters," essays that usually included elaborate praise for the book and touted the skill with which NAL would market it. In this instance, dealing with a hardcover publisher with whom he had done steady business for more than fifteen years, the editor in chief stuck to basics, outlining the key contractual features of a reprint agreement: royalty, amount of advance, release date, conditions of termination, and sales territories.

> We hereby offer an advance of $125,000 against ten percent royalty over a minimum cover price of ninety-five cents. The advance will be paid, as requested by Doubleday, preferably one-third on signing and two-thirds upon NAL publication. We would very much hope for release of the paperbound edition one year after the trade release, but in no event later than the calendar year 1962—and synchronized with a film, if any. I know I need not go into our marketing history with "Big Books," many of which have sold over one million copies at prices of seventy-five cents and above.
>
> We assume that the territories are: the U.S., possessions, Canada and the Philippines exclusively, and the rest of the world except the British Commonwealth of Nations, except Canada nonexclusively, and that the period of the license, although formally stipulated as three years, will be extended automatically until the advance is earned. (27 June 1961)

NAL acquired *The Agony and the Ecstasy*, which went on to become a multimillion-copy softcover bestseller.

Sweeter to obtain than successful bids on books with established hardcover sales records were the bargain prices paid for titles that have had modest hardcover sales but evolved into softcover bestsellers as when NAL acquired from Macmillan on speculation Ian Fleming's James Bond novel, *From Russia, with Love*. Below are excerpts from editor Walter Freeman's 1957 reader's report on this Bond thriller, one of the early titles in the

---

3. The process of bidding on and obtaining paperback bestsellers is described in detail in Whiteside.

series. Up to this time Fleming's Bond adventures had been reprinted by Pocket Books and Popular Library. Their sales were modest.

> This has all the ingredients of an English thriller and doesn't have the dull spots that mar most such books. The principal flaw is that Bond does not appear until 1/4 of the book is finished. But this may be advisable as he is killed in the final chapter. This is done in such a way as to imply that Bond is good and dead but that he could be revived—the poison might be stale or something. . . .
>
> This is one of those corking good yarns that everyone who reads will be able to improve upon, or think so. However, it is the most entertaining book of its type that I have read in a long time. The psychological overtones resemble those of *Death Is a Cold, Keen Edge.* I think the book is worth a bid of $3,000. (10 June 1957)

As revealed in the editor in chief's negotiations with Silas (Si) Peavy of Macmillan for *From Russia, with Love,* Weybright's enthusiasm exceeded Freeman's. A *Time* magazine feature article on Fleming of 5 May 1958 described him as "Mickey Spillane in gentleman's clothing." It could not have dulled Weybright's eagerness. However, the absence of a Canadian market for a Signet reprint directly influenced his initial low bid of four thousand dollars. Fleming's proprietary publisher, Jonathan Cape, was British. As the United States hardcover publisher, Macmillan was only permitted to negotiate American reprint rights, not the Canadian paperback selling rights that would commonly go to NAL if the proprietor was American. Yet it was also not unknown for Weybright in similar situations to employ extravagant praise to distract from the fact that his initial offer was modest.

> We very, very much want to reprint this remarkable and exciting book. I wish I could make a more ambitious offer of an advance against royalties than $4,000—but that seems to be the limit that is prudent in view of the unavailability of the Canadian and open markets. This would, however, be a 35¢ book, with royalties at 1.4¢ to 150,000 copies and 2.1¢ thereafter, which means that if it really got running, the accruals could be substantial. It certainly has the ingredients of a lot of proven literary properties—ranging from Koestler, Graham Greene and Eric Ambler and a plot that is as fantastically astonishing as anything by Mickey Spillane.
>
> I can assure you of a first-class presentation and promotion if

we should be fortunate enough to have the reprint under the Signet imprint. (13 June 1957)

Some months after putting out *From Russia, with Love,* the first Signet Bond, and with a second, *Dr. No,* in the works, there was a controlled urgency within the company to contract for other Fleming titles. Truman Talley picked up the negotiations with Peavy at Macmillan.

We want to continue with *Goldfinger.* We believe $5,000 to be a fair advance for it, and we'll do our reprint at 35¢ not less than a year, of course, from your publication date.

From Russia, with Love has been out with us eight months; early indications are that its sales are not much beyond average. Our hopes are that with *Dr. No* James Bond will take off. Yet it's hard to tell; Ian Fleming's caviar aspects may have, thus far, put off short-order readers.

The $5,000 advance is high for a thriller, particularly when we would have to do without Canada. But our price again would be 35¢ and the higher royalty would be in effect. When resolved, Si, I would like to discuss with you some of the earlier titles; if there are any moribund in reprint perhaps we can work out a new plan. (5 May 1959)

Talley went on to acquire four "moribund" titles for what would also turn out to be bargain prices. The following year, as rumors of television series were spreading, both Weybright and Talley negotiated with Fleming's new United States hardcover publisher, Viking, for three future Bond books. A combined asking price of twenty-five thousand dollars for the three had been established by Weybright. But Kurt Enoch was dubious. He cautioned Weybright (in a memo dictated only a few days after the NAL merger was approved by Times-Mirror stockholders) that Fleming sales records did not warrant this high a bid.

I understand from Mac [Truman Talley] that you ok'd an increase of the royalty guarantee to be paid for the three new Fleming novels to $25,000—the additional $5,000 payable in case of a TV series—I assume that you have not seen the sales and cost records of the three Fleming novels already published by us, on the basis of which I already was very dubious about the advisability of offering a guarantee of $20,000.

I personally like Fleming's books very much, and this liking is obviously shared by quite a few people; however, in spite of

116

substantially greater efforts to get Fleming established than on most of our other thriller writers, we have not yet been able to break the barrier of average sales. We seem to be facing a similar situation as we found with Simenon. The sales round-ups of our fieldmen, which you have seen, are not encouraging either, and the fact that Pocket Books gave up the property also seems to indicate their discouragement. Last but not least, we don't have Canada.

All this does not mean that I have given up hope nor do I discount the possibility that under the Viking imprint and possibly with a TV promotion, we might be more successful in the future. It only means that I consider the gamble which we are taking with $25,000 as excessive and unrelated to the facts before us. As you know, I am all for going way out on a limb on important properties (important not only sales-wise but also prestige-wise) but in order to be able to do that I think we should accept the possibility of losing properties of lesser consequence if the royalty advances would in all probability eliminate the chance of a reasonable profit—particularly at a time when we have to fight to keep enough display pockets available for our important books. However, done is done and I do not suggest to renege, but I propose that we demand a license to last for five years after publication of the last of the three titles in order to have a chance of reissues without new regulations. We should also make a full-fledged TV *series* the condition for the additional $5,000. (12 April 1960)

Enoch gave affront when he expressed his assumption that Weybright had not examined Fleming sales records. Years later, in the bitterness of separation from NAL and the Times-Mirror Company, Weybright cited this Enoch memo as a prime example of his partner's publishing shortsightedness.

In February 1961, after Weybright's decision had prevailed, Truman Talley wrote to Viking concerning the newest Fleming book, an anthology, *For Your Eyes Only*. Talley's bid letter to Viking subsidiary rights director Charles G. Bolte is interesting not only for the optional proposal to supply a larger advance in return for rights to two yet unwritten Flemings, but also for its observations on the relationship between prices and fiction categories and the effect of possible movie and television adaptations on sales.

Our investment on recent "new ones" has been high for a category of book that seldom exceeds sales of 150,000 copies in paperbound. We now indicate our willingness to continue with a high advance and offer Viking $5,000 for *For Your Eyes Only*—or $20,000 pooled for it and the next two full length novels.

Mr. Fleming's books should continue to be priced at thirty-five cents rather than at fifty cents in our market. I suppose that this seems a relatively small matter, but it makes a great deal of difference as concerns advances and royalties. For a long time twenty-five cents has been the ceiling price for mysteries and thrillers, high caliber and low. Only recently have a few well-known authors been able to carry a thirty-five-cent price. In the attempt to enlarge readership and recognition of the "Fleming" name, it would be unwise, perhaps damaging, to attempt a fifty-cent cover price at this time.

A television series would be wonderful—if it's a wonderful television series. We have had enough experience with movie and TV tie-ins to have learned the simple truth. They help when they're outstanding; they do nothing when—for reasons beyond the control of the author and the subject matter—they don't come off. (1 February 1961)

The first real breakthrough on Ian Fleming sales, however, was not generated by television, but by Washington, D.C. In the spring of 1961 *Life* revealed that *From Russia, with Love* was one of President John F. Kennedy's ten favorite titles and sparked an immediate and sustained boost in sales that even the most optimistic Fleming supporters in the company could not have predicted.[4]

At the start of the sixties the top newsstand price for a mass market paperback was seventy-five cents. These editions were usually "complete and unabridged" reprints of thick hardcover bestsellers. Because paper costs made up such a large proportion of a softcover's manufacturing costs, length became a factor in determining the amount of an advance, especially when applied to a book not expected to be an immediate bestseller. As today, the public was more amenable to paying a higher price for a book if its size and reputation seemed to warrant the greater cost. Obviously, lower priced books produce less revenue than higher priced paperbacks when sales are equal. With this in the background, Truman Talley addressed Bennett Cerf about a reprint of Robert Penn Warren's *Wilderness*, eventually issued in Signet at sixty cents.

4. By the close of 1961, Fleming had become softcover publishing's leading author of suspense fiction. At the time of his death in 1964, Fleming's books accounted for 40 percent of the company's total receipts. NAL had by then replaced Viking as the author's hardcover as well as softcover publisher in the United States.

The problem for us on *Wilderness* comes down to a matter of length. This is a relatively short novel for Robert Penn Warren, and our best estimates are that the reprint edition must be priced at 50¢—or at most 60¢—rather than the 75¢ price longer books can command today. This bears, naturally, on the matter of advance.

After discussion among the departments we are most willing to go to a $10,000 advance, but reluctant to go beyond. A considerable part of the $10,000 seems likely to end up as an overpayment though that would bother us less on a Robert Penn Warren than it would on most novels. (26 September 1961)

Cerf was unmoved, however, and the company ended up paying a $15,000 advance for *Wilderness*.

The category of literature being considered frequently determined the amount of advance offered. Nonfiction generally garnered less from a reprinter than fiction. In the forties and fifties, writers of detective fiction usually commanded higher advances than romance fiction or science fiction authors, for instance. In 1956, when $100,000 advances for bestselling fiction were making headlines, NAL claimed to set a record for a paperback advance on a dramatic work when it advanced only thirteen thousand dollars for the filmscript of *My Fair Lady*.[5] In 1953, after having reprinted four Rosamond Marshall novels, NAL rejected *The Dollmaster*. Some insight into advances on historical romance fiction is given in Truman Talley's rejection letter to William Jarrett of Prentice-Hall.

Nevertheless we are going to turn it down for Signet reprint. It's a long story, but it boils down to this: with the glut over the last two years of all manner of historicals in paper editions, a Marshall property in reprint has had to settle for a good deal less in sales than in the first days of *Kitty* and *Duchess Hotspur* [both appeared in mass market paperback reprint in 1947]. Today, a four or five hundred thousand copy sale would be an optimistic figure for *The Dollmaster* in reprint—partly due to the many historicals now

---

5.   One indication of the growth of advances in the years covered by this survey is to summarize one of the few financial records found in the NYU files. In 1961 the average NAL advance was $4,850. Mentor Book's average was a good deal less, $3,215. Genre fiction was lower still: mysteries averaged $2,550; westerns $2,714; science fiction $2,700. The highest advances were awarded to general fiction titles in the Signet series: 189 titles recorded an average of $7,744. Seventeen of these titles were lead titles with softcover bestseller potential; they ranged between $15,000 and $125,000 (*The Agony and the Ecstasy*). If these seventeen were taken out of the Signet general fiction total, the average for this category dropped to $5,134.

available and partly due to the over-production and high returns that are now plaguing the whole small book field.

Our hunch is that you may be able to get five to eight thousand dollars from another paper-bound house, one less committed to a large number of future titles, and thus able to overpay slightly for a name and a very readable book. If it will help your purposes, Victor has asked me to tell you that you can use NAL as a carom-shot on the matter of an advance and to tell whichever other paper-bound house whom you want to submit the manuscript to that you are not quite pleased with what we were offering, and can the other do better, etc. (5 October 1953)

Very early in the company's history, Weybright had to shop around for the best bargains he could strike. Then an advance of even a couple of thousand dollars was a serious strain on tenuous financial resources. Only a few months on the job, he boasted to Enoch about one successful two-book negotiation with hardcover publisher, Coward-McCann. "It takes a bit of doing to get a mystery for less than $2,000, which is Dell's standard rate. Only the desire to do long-term business with Penguin persuades publishers to let us have first-class mysteries at less than the Dell figure" (28 May 1946).

As seen in earlier chapters, when bidding on a book Weybright often argued successfully that his company was the most "bookish" of the soft-cover reprinters. He stressed that they were not one-shot publishers, that is, NAL did not issue a book for a single splash on the newsstands, never to distribute it again. With some justification, he could boast that Signets and Mentors stayed in print, earning royalties for author and original publisher, long after the competition had withdrawn theirs. Therefore Weybright would reason that although NAL's initial advance might not be as high as that of some competitors, over the long run his company would produce royalty income exceeding that of other reprinters. This approach worked particularly well in dealings that centered on literary writers. A report that Weybright made on William Faulkner sales to Robert K. Hass of Random House highlights this strategy.

We are very pleased with Faulkner's reception by the mass audience. *Sanctuary* is doing a good, steady, perennial business, with 148,000 net copies sold in the six-month royalty period ending December 31. The more spontaneous reception of *The Wild Palms* has already resulted in two modest reprintings of 50,000 each of *Sanctuary* in 1948, and we have every hope that this momentum will continue. I believe our statement of policy in the circular letter to publishers will repay study by every publisher with a genuine literary property of long term value for the reprint market. We are the very opposite of one-shot publishers. (11 February 1948)

In 1959 NAL was again negotiating with Random House over a critically acclaimed writer. This time it was William Styron whose first novel, *Lie Down in Darkness*, was reprinted as a Signet seven years earlier. Having just scanned a Random House prepublication copy of *Set This House on Fire*, Truman Talley speedily informed Weybright. "I cannot see that the reception will not be favorable and extensive. And the new novel looks like the first novel since Salinger to penetrate into the colleges. Essentially, this is a 'must' book for us. We must be prepared to pay $25,000 or $30,000 for it—much as that seems this early in the game. Later, Cerf will want $50,000 to $75,000" (22 December 1959). NAL eventually acquired the book for a thirty-five-thousand-dollar advance, paid in installments, a practice common in most prepublication royalty arrangements: ten thousand dollars was advanced on signing, ten thousand dollars on hardcover publication, and fifteen thousand dollars when the Signet edition appeared.

To develop a long-range publishing program for a particular title, a reprinter must license the book for an extended period of time. In the formative years of paperback publishing, a three-year period was common, though some paperback publishers had clauses in their contracts allowing them to automatically extend licensing following a fresh reissue of a title. As noted in earlier chapters, the newly emerging trade paperback series of the fifties competed with mass market imprints for rights. Further, and perhaps even more disturbing to mass market publishers, the new trade series encouraged proprietary hardcover publishers to terminate by cancellation or nonrenewal softcover reprint rights, and begin reissuing previously licensed titles in their own trade paperback series. With concern, Victor Weybright summarized this developing situation for Roger Straus, Jr. "Three years is providing too brief a license period for reprint. There are many books . . . which can be 'rested' and then re-distributed to much better advantage. . . . These constant terminations are a stimulus to [our] undertaking of originals, fiction as well as non-fiction, in which we have a period of copyright and world-selling rights. They are purchased with an author's advance of under $2,000, and we later receive substantial (publishing) advances from British and French publishers. Thought you ought to know" (6 April 1955).

At the time of initial negotiation, however, the date on which the reprinter can issue his softcover edition is usually of much more concern to the parties involved than termination clauses. Victor Weybright highlighted some considerations in setting release date—bestseller placement, film adaptation, and book club acquisitions—in his unsuccessful attempt to obtain Allen Drury's *Advise and Consent* from Mina Turner, subsidiary rights director at Doubleday.

> If the book is selling steadily, and remains on the *Times* best-seller list and the film is not released until 1962, then we are willing to conform with your latest possible date stipulated for reprint. However, in view of the heavy investment, and the small profit margin, we would expect Doubleday to cooperate in giving us an opportunity not to publish the book at a loss, but to consider the establishment of a paperbound release date of the 75¢ edition when the book reaches the lower four positions on the *Times* best-seller list. Book clubs may not compete with trade editions, but the Readers' Digest Condensed Book Club definitely has an adverse effect on paperbound editions in the mass market. We have to be mindful of the fact that 1962 will be a mid-term in a new administration in Washington and that the topical aspects of Mr. Drury's dramatic novel may be superseded by other issues, with a new and younger figure in the White House. (13 November 1959)

Early in its history, the company was reluctant to enter any kind of bidding wars, auction block, or otherwise. When it did have to compete head-to-head, its up-front cash advance offer was generally very modest. In 1947, for instance, Weybright's rationale for a low bid on Arthur Koestler's *Darkness at Noon* proved successful in convincing Macmillan to release this classic to them.

> We were delighted to learn that, at long last, you are open to proposals on *Darkness at Noon*. Confirming my telephone conversation of today, we would offer an advance guarantee of $2,000. We hope that this modest beginning would prove adequate for the actual sales potential of Koestler in the Penguin imprint. We have been disinclined to enter the astronomical bidding which has sometimes occurred in our reprint field; Caldwell's *God's Little Acre*, for example, which is less than nine months old, is almost in the two-million copy class and was secured on an advance guarantee of only $1,000. (6 April 1947)

A year and a half later, however, Weybright weighed taking part in an auction-block type of bid then conducted by Guy Henle of Vanguard

Press. Henle offered mass market publishers twelve spicy works by Donald Henderson Clarke. The books had successful hardcover reprint histories in Doubleday's Triangle edition, a Grosset & Dunlap competitor. Weybright asked his partner, Kurt Enoch, to consider.

A.   Under no circumstances should we publish the books under our imprint or have them identified with our corporate name. With two possible exceptions, the books are unmitigated trash.

B.   But if we could strike a bargain with Fawcett to sponsor the books, without paying any additional royalty to them, I shouldn't object to our manufacturing books in the cheapest possible way. This would require a quick deal with Fawcett and special consent of Vanguard. Guy Henle did not seem pleased by the suggestion of a proposal for a special series under a separate imprint; although I think I dispelled his notion that a new imprint would harm sales by giving him figures on *Hotspur*.[6] (2 September 1948)

NAL's uncertainty about the property plus the difficulties the company had recently experienced with other multiple book arrangements, seems to have prompted too low a bid. The Clarke titles went to Avon, which published them throughout the late forties and early fifties. The list included *The Impatient Virgin,* which in time became a minor paperback bestseller.[7]

In early 1953 uncertainty again entered into reprint negotiations Weybright was conducting. Viking, somewhat to his dismay, was soliciting simultaneous competitive bids for the first time in its history. Also at this time, Weybright and Enoch were deeply enmeshed in censorship cases with their reprints. They seemed to be getting little support in the court battles from their hardcover brethren. The following is an excerpt from the initial Viking bid solicitation, signed by Viking editor Keith Jennison, for Oakley Hall's *Corpus of Joe Bailey.*

Viking will publish this novel with great enthusiasm on April 10 and due to the intense interest already shown by the reprint

6. A year earlier the company had created a new imprint, Eagle Books, with the apparent intention of issuing just this type of risqué fiction. Only three titles were issued under the imprint. One was Rosamond Marshall's *Duchess Hotspur.*

7. For purposes similar perhaps to those of NAL, Avon created its own hot imprint, Novel Library, in which two of the Clarke books appeared. These were issued by the "Diversey Publishing Company," the name of the street in Chicago on which W. F. Hall, the principal manufacturer of both Avon and NAL books, was located.

publishers in this title we have decided to release it for offers before publication.

We should tell you frankly that we are submitting it simultaneously to the largest reprint publishers because we are convinced that it is one of the most valuable properties of the year.

We hope that your estimate of the book will match our own. If your reading schedules permit may we have an opinion from you on or before February 18th? (30 January 1953)

At the bottom of Viking's invitation to bid, Weybright scribbled a comment that was probably shared with his partner, Enoch, "a new policy, which is based on sensation at a price." The heat of discovering Viking engaged in multiple submissions along with the pressures of censorship undoubtedly framed Weybright's reply to the Viking solicitation and encouraged him to try to turn tables on his old antagonist, Viking's Marshall A. Best.

I received yesterday, and read last night, *Corpus of Joe Bailey* by Oakley Hall. I also read Keith Jennison's letter announcing a departure from your prevailing policy with respect to reprint negotiations on this book. That is, that you are submitting it simultaneously to the largest reprint publishers because you are convinced that it is one of the most valuable properties of the year.

I agree with you. NAL would like to publish the book, in reprint, as a Signet double, at 50¢—a price that lists it somewhat above the general reach of the teenagers who Mr. Gathings [Chairman of the House of Representatives' Investigating Committee on Current Pornographic Materials] believes are being contaminated by most modern fiction which is reprinted. However, unless trade book publishers resolve to face the issue of grass fire censorship, pre-censorship, NODL boycott, etc., the *Corpus of Joe Bailey* may be pretty cold by the time it is released for reprint.

Moreover, I hope that Keith's letter does not mean that you are putting Oakley Hall on the auction block—to be knocked down to the highest bidder, whose bid will not be based upon critical acclaim or literary recognition generally, but upon the degree to which he may construe the content as sensational. . . . In short we are reprinters. I emphasize this point because of some recent experience with publishers who have seemed more concerned with their role in dispensing of subsidiary rights than with their responsibilities as publishers.

If you will look at *Publishers Weekly* for last week, where the number of titles issued by all publishing houses, including reprinters, is listed, you will note that New American Library issued 80 titles in 1952. Twelve of them were Mentors and quite a few others were non-fiction, poetry, or conventional westerns. This means that approximately 50 titles—I haven't taken the time to analyze in detail—were Signets. These carefully selected approximately fifty Signets added up to greater volume than that of any other paper bound house, in new units sold or in dollar volume. What I am leading up to is that, if you want to see Oakley Hall reach the adult audience beyond the book shops, in a dignified way and in distinguished company with greater revenue for you and the author, New American Library would seem best suited to give this young novelist his best presentation to the so-called mass audience. (5 February 1953)

Viking apparently took some note of Weybright's displeasure at the bidding procedures by extending the deadline for reactions. But on March 11 the editor in chief, wrote again. With a mixture of self-righteousness and self-confidence, Weybright informed Viking's Keith Jennison that NAL would not submit a final bid. Citing "grounds of taste, not legal obscenity" as reasons for terminating their interest in *Corpus of Joe Bailey,* he continued to decry the absence of industry support in defending censor's attacks and concluded, "I reluctantly bequeath the responsibility for *Joe Bailey* to my competitors."

When Weybright was genuinely committed to capturing a literary property for reprint he made early and repeated but usually tactful queries to the proprietary publishers, attempting to open up one-to-one negotiations and avoid competitive bidding. His correspondence with Scribner's on Dante Arfelli's *The Unwanted* clearly shows his determination to succeed in a competitive bidding environment even after one-to-one negotiation was rejected by the hardcover publisher. This earnestness dramatically contrasts with the sluggish bidding for *Corpus of Joe Bailey.* Early in the summer of 1952, when Weybright first wrote to Whitney Darrow, Sr. about the Arfelli book, it is apparent that Scribner's had not yet decided how to handle reprint rights to their English language translation. As noted earlier, Scribner's was tied to the reprint programs of both Grosset and Bantam. Without naming any royalty figures, Weybright argued that Scribner's had an almost moral obligation to let NAL have the book. His letter is a classic example of blending commercial and cultural concerns in the paperbound reprint marketplace.

At this early stage I want to go on record as unqualifiedly enthusiastic about Arfelli. Here is why: before it was commonly recognized that the post-war times were producing most interesting new writing in Europe, we had license to reprint the works of such authors as Carlo Levi, Alberto Moravia, Vasco Pratolini, and others. We have helped these Italian writers attract readers in the mass market that, otherwise, they would never have reached. Now that others have observed the success of our boldness in reprinting the major contemporary Italian novelists, I dare say that you will receive a number of inquiries about Dante Arfelli. Even if you do receive inquiries and offers, I want you to know that we will match any such offers and that, when *The Unwanted* is made available for reprint, we shall give it an effort in our market that no one else can possibly match. That is the unique advantage that Kurt Enoch and I, as proprietors of our firm, can give to an unique literary property—the unfaltering enthusiasm and impulse of top management (not unlike the independent atmosphere which pervades the Scribner organization). I have faith in the universal appeal of these outstanding writers, and I think you will agree that the editorial faith is an asset in the practical business of merchandising anything as intangible as an imaginative work of fiction. (27 June 1951)

A month and a half later, when Darrow pressed him for an advance figure, Weybright offered a relatively modest thirty-five hundred dollars along with the comment that "I rather deplore all these fancy bids that are going around these days, sometimes to the temporary advantage of trade publishers and authors, but frequently setting a pace which cannot be maintained through earnings, and therefore ultimately creating problems."

Darrow, learning that Weybright was about to leave New York on an extended trip, countered the following day.

We can arrange for reprint rights on Arfelli's *The Unwanted* before publication and we certainly will wait at least a little while thereafter. I have made a note that you suggest $3,500 advance against royalties. You say, however, that this is not a "final offer." If you want to make any other offer which will be final, can't you do it tomorrow so I will have it in my files in case we should make a decision before you return in the middle of September? I don't think I will take it up before that time, but in a case when one makes an offer we consider that as final and have to act accordingly. I cannot receive a definite offer from one person and tell another his offer is below this or isn't sufficient. This is only fair dealing and it is the way we would act with you if conditions were reversed. (14 August 1951)

126

It appears that Weybright stayed with his original bid but on his return found a letter from Darrow confirming that Scribner's had several other reprinters interested in the book. Darrow then asked if NAL was standing by its original thirty-five-hundred-dollar advance. With the situation now altered—other publishers on record as interested in the book—Weybright's hope of convincing Scribner's to let him have it at a bargain price was thwarted. Still anxious to obtain the book, he upped the advance to eight thousand dollars lamenting: "Although—on August 13, when I wrote you I made a conservative advance guarantee and deplored the rather fancy bidding which is prevailing in reprint circles these days, I now find that I have to make a substantial bid, at your request, rather than negotiate" (1 October 1951). But Weybright then asked Darrow if "you can conceivably stretch your policy to consider us as matching the best offer now in hand." Again mixing "luster and lucre," Weybright concluded this letter to Darrow with an extended rationale for NAL's moral claim to the translation in two paragraphs designed to give his company a psychological edge in the bidding competition.

On Arfelli, as on any of the fiction of superior quality now being written—and especially by the Italian school of novelists—I think we can offer you more than an advance guarantee indicates. First of all, a list that includes most of the important Italian writers, so that Arfelli can be promoted to an extent not possible if he were an isolated foreign author on our reprint list. Second, a frame of reference that is acknowledged as the highest quality literary list of any reprint house. And, third, the sales volume and merchandising dynamics that will carry Arfelli in reprint to recognition and review that, I am sure, cannot be matched in any other reprint organization. I mention these points as supplementing the concrete offer— since it is our experience that advance guarantees are much less important than the ability to earn accruals.

We have more than 10 books on our list with advance guarantees of less than $2,000. Yet each has been followed by sales considerably over a million copies. On one, the advance guarantee was only $750—the sales over 2 million copies. It is our preference, as it is the preference of every trade publisher, to deal continuously and energetically with each author and to demonstrate through accruals the ultimate sales potential of the book. Unfortunately, the competitive situation of today doesn't always permit you to allow us to make such a demonstration, as I had hoped when I wrote to you in June. (1 October 1951)

At this point Scribner's appears to have been convinced. The translation of *The Unwanted* was issued as a Signet in January 1953.

NAL's best-known contest for a Scribner reprint property centered around James Jones' *From Here to Eternity*. A 1951 bestseller, Scribner's offered it for softcover reprint late in the summer of 1952. There was to be one set of sealed bids and no further negotiation. Perhaps Darrow, who was again conducting the bidding, was determined not to have a repeat of the awkward and drawn-out Arfelli affair. Weybright was in France at the time; he received this message from Enoch about the book.

> We had decided in our last discussion to offer $75,000. In the meantime I have become doubtful that that figure will take it and I'm wondering whether we shouldn't revise it upwards. It is my feeling that the intangible value of having this book on our list, thus getting at least a moral option on Jones' future writing (which is supposed to be rather promising), would make it worth publishing without profit or at a not too heavy loss. From that point of view a guarantee of $100,000 (or $101,000 to exceed a similar competitive offer) seems to be feasible. According to the figures given above we would break even with a $100,000 guarantee on a sale of 500,000 to 600,000 copies at 75 cents or at 850,000 copies based on a combination of 350,000 copies at 75 cents and 500,000 at 50 cents. (4 September 1952)

Weybright immediately wrote back to Enoch, the man ultimately responsible for marketing within the organization. "*Jones:* we must have the book. It's a big item in editorial competition—and your figures convince me that we'll make money, eventually, even against a $101,000 bid accepted. With the momentum of the titles we have for the coming year, we must *sell-sell-sell;* and that eventually will tell the tale" (8 September 1952).

At this time NAL had lined up a Jones short story "None Sing So Wildly" as the featured piece for the second issue of *New World Writing*. To counter Scribner's sealed-bidding policy further, Enoch and Truman "Mac" Talley worked out some further strategy that Enoch revealed to Weybright who was still abroad. "Mac is going to try—and I have very little hope of success—to get some dope on competitive offers. As soon as we are sure that it will be impossible to get any dope on that, I will send out our offer—probably sometime this week, at the latest next week. Mac will then try to find out when offers are submitted to Jones (which seems to be the Scribner's intention). As soon as we know that, Mac will go to Chicago, with a side trip to Jones, in order to have a chance to influence him. This, of course, will be done very diplomatically" (15 September

1952). The clandestine trip to the Midwest was apparently deemed either unwise or unnecessary, however. NAL acquired the book for a record-setting $101,000 advance. This contract was subject to continued speculation within the publishing industry as the book was published in September 1953. Many believed that NAL would never make a profit on the title. However, an initial printing of 520,915 copies at a cover price of seventy-five cents was immediately followed with several back-to-press orders. In a letter to critic Robert Cantwell, written only two months after publication, Weybright figured that the break-even point on *From Here to Eternity* would be reached at 2.2 million, a figure considerably higher than earlier company estimates. By February 1955, twelve printings, totaling 2.7 million copies, were recorded. There is little question that the book made money for author and publisher alike and broke down the fear of large advance royalty guarantees. Book industry skepticism over the wisdom of big advance payments was further reduced in 1955. Fawcett, which had just terminated its national distributorship of NAL books, signed a highly publicized reprint contract with Harcourt, Brace. With great flourish, Fawcett introduced its new Crest reprint line by purposefully topping by a hair NAL's record payment to Scribner's: a $101,505 advance for James Gould Cozzens' *By Love Possessed*.

As the James Jones case points out, it was generally necessary to be cautious if not secretive about the size of the bid being submitted. But timing was equally important to successful bidding. In early 1952 NAL had heard rumors about a Louis Armstrong autobiography in the works at Prentice-Hall. Recognizing that a big splash by the Ethel Waters' autobiography (*His Eye Is on the Sparrow*) that Bantam was then preparing would cause advances to climb significantly for similar books, Truman Talley wrote to Weybright and Enoch. "I think we ought to make up some sort of contract as soon as possible—before Pocket Books sees it and before Bantam has a chance to bring out the Waters book later on this spring: a contract wherein we would pay around $3,000 now, on signing, and around $7,000 on completion, and an NAL okay of the final manuscript. Thus, we risk, safely, $3,000 for a $20,000 book, dangling a $7,000 carrot before Prentice-Hall who like to see a lot of money in their quarterly accounts" (4 February 1952). The following week Weybright sent in a bid and in the familiar "presentation" format provided Leonard Harris at Prentice-Hall a summary of NAL's record of publishing black writers.

Not only is our volume of sales—at home and abroad—far greater than any of our competitors, but it is achieved on a selective program of many fewer titles per year. Our momentum on best-sellers of unique quality, in every category, cannot be matched.

We have one other unique asset of special relevance to Prentice-Hall in the ultimate disposition of reprint rights on Louis Armstrong. That is our outstanding position in the field of literature by Negroes and about the Negro in America. Five years ago, with the publication of James Weldon Johnson's *Autobiography of an Ex-Colored Man,* we launched a special effort to distribute our books, and especially those of racial interest, in the Negro communities of American cities. . . . We publish such books as *The Street,* books by Richard Wright, Willard Motley, Chester Himes and such books as *Strange Fruit,* and encourage major wholesalers to add book specialists to their staff for Harlem, South Chicago and the colored sections of scores of cities, North and South. This represents an enormous plus to the normal market for a book such as Louis Armstrong's autobiography. (15 February 1952)

A Signet edition of the Armstrong autobiography, *Satchmo,* was published in 1955 and was an active title on the NAL backlist for many years afterwards.

Contractual terms with another black author, Richard Wright, was of concern to Truman Talley in 1958 shortly after the delivery of the writer's latest work, *The Long Dream.* While NAL had reprinted four earlier Wright books in Signet, this new work appeared to Talley to be noticeably weaker than the others. Talley's written assessment includes mention of an acquisition strategy and contractual clause, "pooling," an often hotly debated feature of literary contracts, by which the author or, in the case of a reprint contract, the author and the original trade publisher have royalties on a new work combined with those of one or more earlier works. Pooling several works seems most frequently to occur when a young writer is getting established. A book publisher may insert a pooling clause in a contract after issuing the first book of the writer at a loss. This usually means that the royalties earned on the book's sales do not match the advance that the publisher originally paid out to the author. Finding the author's succeeding work equally as attractive as the first (if not more attractive than the first), the publisher may, for instance, offer to publish the second and pay out all or a certain percentage of the second book's royalties when they have exceeded the advance of the first. Pooling ensures that the author's work gets into print and allows the publisher to reaffirm its faith in the writer and reduce its risk of losing money on him or her in the future.

In a reprint contract, both the author and the original publisher must agree to the pooling clause. However, with *The Long Dream* Richard Wright had changed proprietary publishers. This marooned NAL's chance to take a calculated risk on the weak new work through pooling. Talley proposed, instead, reissuing earlier Wright works still under reprint contract with Harper & Brothers, in particular, *Black Boy*.

But some books have 'surface electricity,' and this one [*The Long Dream*] does not. A 320 to 340 page fifty-center, its sales for us look to be no higher than in the 100- to 150,000 class. The difficulty is added to by the fact that this is a Doubleday book, with no chance to pool royalties with the Harper titles. The difficulty is added to further by the fact that if we take on this new novel, we will continue to bypass limited reissues on one or the other of our long-out-of-print *Black Boy* and *Native Son*.
A reissue of *Black Boy* . . . will sell *at least* as well in reprint as this new novel. Also, it's a semi-classic that will salvage out where *The Long Dream*, like our other unsuccessful *The Outsider*, will not. *Black Boy* has a large unearned advance ($17,270 unearned *pooled* with *Native Son*), by now written off. This aspect, together with the margin involved in a 192-page fifty-center, would make a limited reissue a particularly profitable one. (10 October 1958)

Talley's recommendations eventually prevailed: *The Long Dream* did not become a new Signet, but *Black Boy* was reissued as a Signet Classic.
A pooling clause was generally not popular with proprietary publishers. This was especially true when the succeeding work by an author was noticeably stronger than the earlier work. Some trade book publishers instituted policies that forbade signing reprint agreements with pooling clauses included. Yet pooling was used with some frequency in the early days of paperback publishing when reprinters were anxious to build their lists by obtaining rights to several different titles of a well-known author at one time. These works were usually a mix of old and new titles with contrasting reprint income potential. A pooling clause in a multiple book contract allows the profit made on the stronger titles to offset predicted losses of the weaker. One of NAL's most ambitious pooling contracts centered on James Farrell. In an arrangement with Vanguard, NAL agreed to advance eighty thousand dollars to Farrell, payable in half-year installments. This money was a drawing account against titles already in print, titles under contract to be printed, and seven future works. At least twenty titles were reserved for NAL reprint under this pool cover. Vanguard was prohibited from terminating the contract before the eighty thousand dollars was accrued in royalties. Nor could it arrange reprint contracts with any other paperback house for new Farrell titles. The key prize in this bunch was the *Studs Lonigan* trilogy, then recognized as an American classic.

This pooling arrangement, however, eventually contributed to the bitterness Farrell felt toward the reprinter in the early twilight of his career. In 1958 NAL returned to Vanguard reprint publication control of a large number of Farrell titles. Not selling up to expectations, they contributed little to the reduction of the half-year advances. This appears to have been a very stressful period in Farrell's life. His difficulties writing also strained his relationship with his publishers, hard and soft. In 1959 when Farrell proposed a new Signet collection of short stories, the best Weybright was willing to offer was an advance of twenty-five hundred dollars. A bitter note of protest to NAL received this sobering Weybright response. "If you would like to refund, say $50,000 on unearned royalties, we would gladly up the advance on the short stories to $5,000. Otherwise, the deal must proceed as agreed upon. I really think, Jim, that you have no right to be so abusive toward a publisher who thinks so highly of you and your work" (16 November 1959). By 1964, however, of the nearly twenty Farrell titles that Weybright and Enoch published since 1946, only *Studs Lonigan* remained on the NAL list.

7

Irish Whiskey for
the Cardinal

The postwar awakening of local censoring groups in the United States paralleled the rise and expansion of mass market paperback publishing. These groups were generally community or religious organizations with some kind of national affiliation. They were often aided by various governmental bodies, ranging from municipal police departments to the Congress of the United States. During the late forties and the fifties, right-wing organizations mounted strong anticommunist attacks while other groups, especially those connected with the Roman Catholic Church, waged battles against literature they perceived to have strong sexual content. Half-jokingly, publishers claimed that to put out the Bible they needed an endorsement from Eisenhower's conservative Secretary of State, John Foster Dulles.

During this period NAL probably had more censored authors on its list than any other American publisher.[1] Weybright, Enoch, and others on the company's editorial and marketing staffs devoted much energy responding to the constant attacks. At one point the American Book Publishers Council's specialist on book censorship problems, Theodore Waller, was hired as a company officer to aid in the combat. Early in his tenure at NAL, Weybright became directly involved in censorship battles. In two highly publicized and separate trials in March 1949, he testified in Boston on behalf of Caldwell's *God's Little Acre* and James M. Cain's

---

1. Among the authors published by NAL who experienced frequent censorship were James Baldwin, James Cain, Erskine Caldwell, Ralph Ellison, James T. Farrell, William Faulkner, Chester Himes, William Bradford Huie, D. H. Lawrence, Margaret Mead, Norman Mailer, Henry Miller, J. D. Salinger, Lillian Smith, Mickey Spillane, and Kathleen Winsor.

Serenade, both Signet bestsellers. In the trial of the latter book, he was joined by Alfred A. Knopf. Eventually both cases went to the Massachusetts Supreme Court, which ruled in favor of *Serenade* but declared *God's Little Acre* obscene. Weybright recorded this as the only censorship case that the company ever lost. As such, it was frequently used as a frame of reference by Weybright to classify the source and gauge the intensity of censorial challenges to other Signet and Mentor titles.

Early in 1951 the company was more concerned about the political nature of some Caldwell writing. As Senator Joseph McCarthy was capturing headlines with his Senate investigations of Communist influences in the United States government, Caldwell was pressuring NAL to add his novel *All Night Long* to his string of Signet reprints. Written immediately after Caldwell as a reporter left the World War II Russian front, this book was originally published by Duell, Sloan & Pearce in 1942. It was very sympathetic to our Soviet allies. Kurt Enoch's letter to Caldwell, following Weybright's initial rejection, confirms that the two company heads complemented each other in handling sensitive issues with important authors. But what is more important, pitting culture against commerce, it reveals how the hysteria of the times directly influenced the company's unwillingness to publish politically sensitive material even when written by a bestselling author.

Although I am sure that you know whether you get a letter from Victor or myself it is always the expression of the opinion of both of us, I would like to stress this point with reference to his letter of January 8th. I have been around in the field quite a bit recently and am in continuous close contact with Fawcett and many wholesale distributors, here and abroad. I can only repeat what Victor expressed in his letter, that the reissue of *All Night Long* at the present time might be fatal for the sales of your books. This does not imply at all, as Victor said in his letter, any criticism on our part of the validity of the book and its implications at the time it was written and published. Times have changed; we are facing today an entirely different ideological and political situation which has necessitated drastic revisions of our points of view and attitudes. So I hope you will understand our advice and accept it. (9 January 1951)

Later in the fifties when much of the Red Scare had subsided, however, NAL was open to reprinting the novel provided that a film supporting the commercial risk and shielding it from criticism was in the offing. Weybright reveals these factors in a letter to Clarence Paget of Pan Books, publishers of Caldwell paperbacks in England.

This very dormant film option, is for a novel originally entitled *All Night Long*, dealing with the German-Russian front during the late war. It was written after Caldwell had covered the Russian front for *PM*, the now defunct New York evening newspaper, once owned by Marshall Field, and somewhat left of center politically. We have never reprinted the novel, though we have it on option, largely because it seems so very pro-Soviet, and might be misconstrued, thereby harming the entire Caldwell property. If a film is made by MGM, we should of course take the plunge. (19 May 1958)

Neither the film nor the Signet paperback edition of *All Night Long* ever appeared.

On at least two occasions Caldwell was invited to writers conferences behind the Iron Curtain. In both cases he solicited NAL for advice on accepting, and in each instance NAL was unenthusiastic. In 1955 Weybright wrote that "New American Library would never intrude on the life of writers to the extent of advising whether or not they should visit the Soviet Union. . . . Our relationship as publishers must be to an author's work." However, he adds a few lines later that he "would personally not accept an invitation since it might be construed as approval of the Soviet Union" but that Caldwell, being a writer, might be seen in a different light. Caldwell evidently decided not to go.

Publishers like NAL, at the height of the McCarthy investigations, were especially sensitive to charges of political bias in either direction. Personally, Weybright strongly supported Adali Stevenson's presidential candidacies. However, nowhere in the files could I find an instance where his political convictions influenced his editorial judgment.

In 1951 John Dos Passos, a contributor to the original Mentor edition of the anthology and book list *Good Reading*, charged that the recommended readings of the first edition were heavily directed toward "the party line." *Good Reading* was, however, prepared by the Committee on College Reading of the National Council of Teachers of English. Weybright must have been well pleased by the response of the collection's general editor, Atwood H. Townsend, who wrote directly to Dos Passos.

Our present list is spotted here and there with party-line books. That results from the fact that the present list was compiled early in 1947 when "one world," including a friendly Russia, seemed still a tenable hope, and when some of the authors involved had not yet been identified as party-line affiliates. I can assure you that the new list, to be published January 1952, will correct what appears an error in judgment by 1951 but was, I think, a reasonably fair balance in terms of the 1947 situation. . . . I am certain that you will find the new list, not exactly what you would choose, nor what I would choose personally, nor what any other individual would choose, but a cooperative democratic consensus that results in a "balanced diet" slanted neither to the Right nor to the Left. I am sure that you will also find the material well balanced between basic books of "serious thinking" and popular contemporaries' reflections of "fashionable attitudes." We need both in *Good Reading* if we are not to frighten away those whom we are trying to lure into reading solid stuff.

Two points should be noted. If our "balanced diet" is to be comprehensive and representative, then we have to list (which does not imply recommendation) a few spokesmen for the extreme Left: Marx, Lenin, etc.—properly labeled, of course. There will be an approximately equal number of spokesmen for the extreme Right, mostly Catholic. (18 July 1951)

In 1961 the specter of right-wing censorship continued to haunt the company. For NAL its presence was amplified by the channel through which the criticism was transmitted, the Times-Mirror Company that had only recently acquired the softcover publisher. Times-Mirror's chief holding was the *Los Angeles Times* newspaper, best known at the time as an influential voice for conservative causes. At this time NAL was deeply committed to and had worldwide, softcover distribution rights, for a projected multi-volume set of cultural and scientific histories sponsored by UNESCO. These volumes were being cooperatively published in various languages throughout the world. Weybright saw the project as one of major importance, one that would add luster to the company's reputation. He was somewhat rattled, however, when a series of attacks originated on the West Coast were forwarded to him by the same Times-Mirror executives who had purchased the company one year earlier. In a pair of letters to Robert M. Allan Jr., Weybright defended the UNESCO books that were eventually issued as the Mentor series, "Readings in the History of Mankind." "This is a project which Times-Mirror should be proud of and not retreat an inch. It is non-political, non-ideological and will be published first in hardcover by Harper & Brothers in the U.S.A. and by Allen and Unwin, Ltd. in Great Britain, prior to worldwide circulation of the Mentor series of volumes in the English language. "We have followed this project with interest from its inception, and I can assure you that it has never been even remotely a 'pink' project" (17 May 1961). The following week the editor in chief again defended the series with Allan by citing the authorities who were contributors and adding his financial projection for the series.

It has always been difficult to answer in detail the onslaught of the extreme left and the extreme right. A vast complex of scholars have contributed to the preparation of this extraordinary publishing project. However, the controls rested with the chief and secretary of the commission, Professor de Berredo Carniero and Dr. Guy Metraux respectively—both of whom are solid and non-ideological scholars. Sir Julian Huxley, well-renowned scientist, was the orig-inal sponsor of the World History project. He is the brother of Aldous Huxley, who is now, I believe, a resident of Los Angeles, despite the fact that his house recently burned down in one of the canyon fires. I have personally read all of the first draft of the history— some 3 million words—and have not discovered any hidden or semantic distortions. . . .

Off the record, I predict an average sale, of our total 20 volumes (projected), within five years, of 300,000 copies each for a total of 6 million unit sales, with a gross profit after production and royalties of at least 20¢ each or $1,200,000 minimum.

If the Communists, who don't like the project any more than the John Birch Society does, try to smash the prospects of the books in schools and colleges, I am told by friendly teachers and librarians that the net effect will be to enhance adoptions and educational recommendations of the series. (23 May 1961)

Later in the year, Times-Mirror's Philip Chandler passed on a newspaper clipping from the Montrose (California) *Ledger*. It was still another attack on the series composed by conservative critic, Florence Fowler Lyons. Weybright responded to Chandler.

The project was not "atheistic-commie" inspired, and the five-sixths of the manuscript which I have read certainly doesn't reflect any Communist ideology. . . . The work of all the scholars involved in the series is carefully reviewed, checked, and brought into objective compliance with the purpose of the series, by Guy Metraux, a celebrated Swiss scholar (with an American wife) who is a brother of Albert Metraux, the renowned archeologist who has done pioneer work on Easter Island. I also have absolute confidence in Dr. Veronese, Director General of the UNESCO, and the final authority in the project, who is a devout Catholic and very close to the Vatican, an insurance that there will be no concealed ideology in the project.

If Florence Fowler Lyons wants to prevent the reading of the series in the schools of the United States, it is her privilege to try to do so, but I certainly can't devote much time or energy in trying to inform a person so obviously addicted to smearing innuendos. . . . [Weybright then repeated the financial projections for the series which are outlined in his letter to Robert M. Allan, Jr. quoted above.]

I realize that it would be a catastrophe to make any money, let alone a substantial sum, out of a project that was even remotely harmful to the American system of capitalistic society at its best. I don't think it is asking too much to let Florence Fowler Lyons and her group know that the Times-Mirror Company has confidence in the integrity and objectives of New American Library—and let it go at that. (16 October 1961)

It appears that NAL continued its involvement in the international project without any direct opposition from the Times-Mirror Company. Reflection on these exchanges, however, leaves room for speculation on how much weight Weybright's financial calculations restrained the Times-Mirror executives.

Until he won a Nobel Prize in 1950, William Faulkner was a noteworthy target of independent wholesale distributors, the prime distribution mechanism through which softcover titles reached their public. These independent distributors—often themselves the initial prey of local censoring crusades—objected to what they perceived as racist and racy dialogue in some Faulkner fiction. Their concerns were usually filtered through NAL's national distributor, Fawcett, which, in turn, passed them on to NAL's sales department. The replies that follow in part reflect the education of a publisher, in this case, Victor Weybright. The first deals with Faulkner's *Sanctuary*; Weybright's reaction was directed at Edward E. Lewis of Fawcett. His letter was written in spring 1947, a year before NAL separated itself from Penguin and not very long after Fawcett became the national distributor for the paperback publisher. The letter has a resolute, directly argumentative tone absent in similar messages drafted later in his career.

I can't believe that you have read *Sanctuary*, for if you had, you will readily have perceived that the book is no more anti-Semitic than the *New York Times* if the *Times* were to quote, as it has done, passages from a racist speech. You should know that Faulkner's

138

trade publisher, from whom we secured rights, is a predominantly Jewish firm—Random House. I haven't referred your letter to Bennett Cerf and his associates for comment because, as I said, they would only reply that you hadn't read the book, that you had picked up a quotation from a character in the book, without even referring to the reply to the tirade made on page 158.

I shouldn't like to think that, because of a lack of understanding of a great American author and his best-known work, you or any wholesaler would question Penguin's editorial judgment or show any lack of enthusiasm in the promotion or sale of the distinguished literary property. You, and any wholesaler whose attention you call to the allegedly offensive passage in *Sanctuary*, should know that Faulkner, like Caldwell, writes of the South with biting realism, and in doing so reveals the degradation and bigotry which thrive on ignorance in the backward areas which, alas, have not yet enjoyed all the advantages of education and tolerance.

I'm frankly astonished that a man of your experience in the book world would misrepresent an author's work to the extent of completely reversing the author's intention. . . .

Actually, Penguin feels that Faulkner should enjoy a special promotion through the trade, and several days ago you assured me that a special effort would be made to acquaint the trade with the sales potential of *Sanctuary* as a great American novel. (18 April 1947)

In less than a year Lewis again forwarded new objections to Faulkner, qualms originally raised by a particular local distributor, "Mr. Mallory." Weybright's response this time was less confrontational. His last paragraph in fact reveals the reprinter as self-censoring gatekeeper in his attempts to reach the mass market through the independent wholesale distribution chain.

I can understand Mr. Mallory's feeling about low literature—but I hope you won't consider *The Wild Palms* by William Faulkner in that category. . . . [Weybright then quotes from the *New York Times*' review of *The Wild Palms*, "I believe Faulkner to be the finest author writing in America today."]

In our selection of titles we are guided by two considerations: first, literary quality and importance; second, acceptance of a book by the mass audience. It is true that many of our best-selling books have dealt with human relations in which sex has been a motivating force. However, we have never published, and never will publish, a book which panders to the public by erotic vulgarity. We rejected two books currently on the newsstands under the imprint of a competitor because they lacked the literary quality upon which we insist, and in both cases we knew that references to sex in the books would put them on the bestseller list.

It all depends on what one knows of literature and literary standards. *Strange Fruit* is a good book, universally acclaimed by critics; some other books that we could mention, published by our competitors are trash. No one can deny that sex is one of the most interesting subjects in the world. The Rockefeller Foundation, one of the most respectable institutions in existence, has sponsored the Kinsey Report on *The Sexual Behavior in the Human Male*. Hundreds of thousands of copies have been published by a medical publisher and sold at $6.50. In early spring, with the blessing of outstanding physiologists, psychologists, doctors, churchmen and lawyers, we hope to produce a volume revealing the most important implications of that book. I hope that you will make it clear to Mr. Mallory that there is no comparison between such a project and pure unadulterated and corny dirt. Look over the list of people noted for pornographic publications and see how many items such as Tawney's *Christianity and the Rise of Capitalism* or *Sweden: The Middle Way* will be on their lists. . . .

I can't understand how anyone handling a great volume of current publications can have his attention called to specific instances in our books which, at first glance, might seem low. It is the frame of reference which gives a clue to the subject. There are dubious pages in the Bible, if read out of context. *The Kinsey Report*, if read for the wrong reasons, could appear naughty despite the sponsorship of Rockefeller and the University of Indiana. The courts tried to hound *God's Little Acre* into oblivion. . . .

At the risk of losing Faulkner as an author, we have now substituted dashes for several words which appear in the first edition. This goes against the grain, and could almost be construed as breaching our contract to publish the book without any change or abridgment. If it's good enough for the *New York Times*, it's good enough for me—but since that isn't good enough for a few people, I have taken the risk of deleting a few words in all printings after the first edition. This in itself is full of risk since it tends to concede that the book, as originally published, was a dirty book. That I will not admit even though I have made the concession. (7 February 1948)

Shortly after completing this memo, Weybright sent a call for support to Clifford Foster of the American Civil Liberties Union, an organization that in the past had aided in the defense of NAL authors. Included in this letter was a catalog of cities, some of which are today considered among the most liberal in the United States, whose independent distributors refused to sell either the expurgated or the unexpurgated editions of *The Wild Palms*.

This afternoon I telephoned you about action which has been taken locally against this book by law enforcement agencies of cities and, in some cases, by magazine wholesalers who object to certain words in the book. . . .

We are mindful of the effectiveness of ACLU action in the case of *God's Little Acre* which we first published just two years ago, and in the case of the Reynal & Hitchcock edition of *Strange Fruit* by Lillian Smith which we are publishing this month—using "f---" instead of the four letter word. We believe that it would be a contribution to the freedom of expression if the ACLU could mobilize its local machinery in all of the communities where *The Wild Palms* has been suppressed.

We have reprinted Faulkner's *Sanctuary* through arrangements with Random House, as well as *The Wild Palms*, and contemplate issuing a number of other Faulkner works. What concerns us at the moment is not merely the embarrassment and loss of trade good will involved in action against this book, but the manifestation of a trend against the free circulation and wide currency of the writings of a responsible author. We have taken out the offending words on pages 31 and 54 in subsequent editions of *The Wild Palms*—not because we want to, but because of the threat that our books will either be boycotted and banned in many important cities, which we cannot afford on either moral or financial grounds. . . . There is no need at this time to take any action concerning *Strange Fruit* since our modification of the four-letter word may result in the book being acceptable everywhere except in Boston. I gather that Boston is hopeless.

Listed below are the following agencies which would not distribute *Wild Palms* because of a ban by police. They include: Los Angeles; New Britain, Connecticut; New London, Connecticut; Washington, D.C.; Des Moines, Iowa; New Bedford, Massachusetts; Springfield, Massachusetts; Akron, Ohio; Pittston, Pennsylvania; and Pawtucket, R.I.

The B list is those who rejected the first edition but will accept the second edition: Meriden, Connecticut; New Haven, Connecticut; Pittsfield, Massachusetts; Pittsburgh, Pennsylvania; and Massillon, Ohio.

The next section are agencies which "banned the distribution of *Wild Palms:*" Hartford, Connecticut; Boston, Massachusetts; Lynn, Massachusetts; Cleveland, Ohio; Newport, Rhode Island; Providence, Rhode Island; Milwaukee, Wisconsin; and finally there is one undecided about it and that's Cincinnati, Ohio. (11 March 1948)

Possibly no aspect of publishing is marked by as much uncertainty and equivocation as the attempt by a publisher to prophesy the standards that the police and the courts apply to literature that contains explicitly sexual or erotic passages. In 1952 Kurt Enoch, who tended to be more conservative in his evaluations than Weybright, addressed his partner about Chandler Brossard's *Who Walk in Darkness*. In his memo Enoch referred to a specially appointed investigating committee of the House of Representatives, the Gathings Committee, which was then examining the sale of pornographic materials in the United States.

The new Brossard book can and should wait until you come back. Roger [Straus] has signed it up in the meantime but agreed not to make any deals before you return. I read the manuscript over the weekend and it is now circulating among the editors. As it is I don't like it at all. It is brilliantly written, but with no substance and message, and with long weird passages which must frustrate the reader. Besides, it is a handbook for crime and decadence without any attempt to give a reason for drawing this picture or any indication what conclusion the author wants the reader to draw from it. In short, decadence for the sake of decadence which would be just the food the Gathings Committee is looking for. I can see this book as the work of avant garde for a specific hardcover audience, but I don't believe that the mass audience would feel that the brilliance of writing, fantastic sex scenes in a catalog of crime, mixed with a lot of weird dreams and visions, would be proper compensation for the lack of story content or purpose. (15 September 1952)

Despite Enoch's concerns, Weybright supported publication of the Brossard book for some of the same reasons that troubled Enoch; it was issued as a Signet two years later.

Weybright had twice rejected Christopher Isherwood's *Goodbye to Berlin* for reprint because of certain racial overtones. However, by late 1951 the editor in chief believed the book could be reprinted because of changes in wholesaler attitudes. He so informed Isherwood's hardcover publisher, James Laughlin of New Directions.

I'm very glad that, on re-reading *Goodbye to Berlin*, I am completely persuaded to reprint it as you suggested, and I hereby suggest an advance guarantee against royalties of $3,000. As you will recall, twice in the past I have seriously considered it. But it isn't until now that I have felt that there was sufficient historical perspective for us to avoid difficulty with a number of wholesalers who, being predominently Jewish, have in the past taken great exception to books which contained anti-Semitic remarks, even though such remarks were made by the most reprehensible Nazis. Indeed, only two years ago a number of wholesalers were boycotting our Faulkner reprint of *Sanctuary* because of a very minor colloquy in the book that was construed as anti-Semitic.
I mentioned this to Isherwood the other evening. He thoroughly understood, and he also understood why now the climate of opinion offers less of a risk. (8 November 1951)

Meyer Levin, author of the Signet *The Young Lovers*, frequently corresponded with Weybright about NAL titles he found objectionable because of their portrayal of Jews. In the spring of 1953 Levin vowed to alert the Anti-Defamation League of B'nai B'rith to Harry Grey's *Hoods* which had just appeared as a Signet.[2] In response Weybright summarized the history and attitude of his publishing company as it related to controversial literature, an interesting mixture of idealism and commercialism that rested side by side in the heart of the company, accounting for much of its success in the fifties.

I am sorry that you regard *The Hoods*, or any other book reprinted by New American Library, as a candidate for special attention of the Anti-Defamation League. It is an interesting fictionalized memoir by an authentic hood of a day and age that is past—and it

2. Levin, husband of Tereska Torres, whose Gold Medal *Women's Barracks* was vigorously attacked by the Gathings investigating committee for its sexual content, had in earlier correspondence singled out Harold Robbins' *A Stone for Danny Fisher* (Pocket Books), Irving Shulman's *The Amboy Dukes* (Avon), and Budd Schulberg's *What Makes Sammy Run* (Bantam) as offensive to Jews.

never occurred to me when I first read it, or subsequently, that it could be possibly construed as a fixitive of the image of the Jew in modern American literature. Anymore, for example, than Ed Reid's *Mafia*, which we are reprinting through arrangements with Random House could do a disservice to Italian-Americans and members of the Italian community in the United States. We have been exposed to a good many pressure groups as publishers—mainly by censorious Roman Catholic groups —and this is only the third occasion that I can recall any question of our giving wide currency to material which has been considered objectionable from a Jewish point of view. The first was in the case of Graham Greene's early thrillers, originally published by Viking; the second was in the case of *Sanctuary* by William Faulkner, originally published by Random House.

Partly because of Kurt Enoch's integrity as a distinguished Jew, who was driven out of Germany and ultimately out of Europe by the Nazis, and partly because of the honest selectivity of our entire list, New American Library has won special praise from prominent Jews and Jewish groups from the very outset of our publishing program. Likewise, and for the same relevant reasons, from Negro individuals and organizations. Indeed, several years ago our sales department prevailed upon me to abandon the publication of a book for which I had contracted with Doubleday: Conrad's *The Nigger of the Narcissus*. Even when Walter White of the NAACP agreed to write a foreword condoning the title, I finally gave in to the pressures of our own sales department and swapped that Conrad title for *Heart of Darkness* to avoid any possible misconception of the attitudes of New American Library on the delicate question of the use of the word "nigger," even in a semi-classical frame of reference.

And I mention all this so that you will know that, as an editor, I am extremely sensitive to questions of human dignity and the avoidance of even an accidental contribution to any sort of racial or religious prejudice. (18 May 1953)

Perhaps the most difficult and certainly the most insidious to defend against were the censorship advocates, like those connected with the Roman Catholic Church, which used its political clout to pressure for conformity to conservative moral values. In 1955 both politics and sex were company concerns while it was weighing publication of Norman Mailer's third book, *The Deer Park*. Rinehart, hardcover publisher of Mailer's first two novels, had declined to issue his third. It was taken up by Putnam. Weighing whether to negotiate for a reprint of *The Deer Park*, Enoch asked the advice of NAL's chief counsel and corporate shareholder, Rudolf Littauer. The lawyer replied:

Since the book, as rewritten, is said to be "frankly sexual in its preoccupation" and, therefore, may cause censorship trouble, may I be permitted to advise caution.

I refer to an editorial in last week's *Life* entitled, "Wanted: An American Novel," which is also attached. I do not agree with its contents and I hope that Victor and you will continue to publish tough, bitter and satirical novels whether or not they are liked by the monsignors, the *Morning Stars* or the Eisenhowers. But with regard to Mailer, judging from his earlier books and from what Miss Kirkus says, the *Life* editorial may have a point. If you published it, in our present day, the determination of the legality of the work might be influenced by a consideration of Mailer's hostility to our society. (12 September 1955)

Despite Littauer's hedging, NAL issued the book in 1957.

The unholy combination—politics, sex, and religion—is the subject of review in a Weybright letter to James Baldwin's hardcover publisher, George Joel of Dial Press. NAL was about to publish Baldwin's nonapologetic portrayal of homosexuality, *Giovanni's Room*.

Herewith the reprint license agreement, which I hope is in order. We are pleased and proud to have this book and author in prospect and already are looking forward to his new novel on a more "natural theme" for his extraordinary talent. . . . We know already that it will probably be refused by the wholesaler in Detroit, and possibly in Chicago, not to mention a few less consequential market areas. I can recall only two spots in the galleys where a change in language or sentence would be greatly appreciated by us, exposed as we are to a double standard applied to literature by the Catholic church and its political allies. (8 August 1956)

Both Weybright and editor Walter Freeman supported Signet publication of Chester Himes' *Primitive*. However, its controversial nature led the company to cut the initial print order. The domestic market was not the only sales source affected by nonconventional literature, as Weybright explains to Himes. "The print order was cut from the usual because the book was not considered acceptable by chainstores, and too risky for

145

Canadian customs censorship, and inadmissable in other market areas, such as South Africa, most Army Post Exchanges, etc. Because the book was brief, we shall probably not lose money, but we won't make much, if anything. As you know, Walter and I both liked it; but it does have certain commercial handicaps because of its nature" (16 April 1956).

In the summer of 1948 Weybright asked publisher Roger Straus, Jr. for time to weigh the new manuscript *Maelstrom* written by future Watergate figure E. Howard Hunt.

Can we have sixty days to study Howard Hunt, get market as well as literary opinions on his new book—and to test the reaction of a few friends on passages in the book which, although not likely to create difficulties for your trade edition, might get us involved with local censorship—particularly the lesbian and flagellation scenes. Right now we are so involved with local censorship in Philadelphia, Boston, and Sioux City, etc., that we probably are being over cautious; yet I know that we could sell more copies of Hunt, if we decided that he fit our list, than any of our competitors. (28 July 1948)

Perhaps the most logical if not courageous strategy for the publisher weighing a controversial book is to request that the author remove the offending passages. "Can the flagellation be tempered," Weybright finally inquired directly of E. Howard Hunt, ". . . so that censors cannot point to the passage as a demonstration which might corrupt the young or demented?" Hunt evidently did temper the "flagellation." NAL issued the book as *Dark Encounter* in 1950.

In 1946 the company published the first softcover edition of *Lady Chatterly's Lover* in an expurgated form. It issued two succeeding Signet editions, the last of which was still on the market when Grove Press successfully sponsored an unexpurgated edition in 1959, overturning a Post Office ban in a highly publicized court case. At the time of the decision, NAL claimed to have sold a million and a half copies of its estate-authorized, expurgated edition. Following the court decision it, along with Grove as well as Pyramid and Pocket Books, rushed into print an uncut version. These actions did little to enhance the often questionable image of paperback publishing in the eyes of the American public.

Some expurgations can appear more surreptitiously without knowledge of the author or of his or her hardcover publisher. In 1953 NAL was working with United Artists on joint promotion of the book and film *I, the Jury*. United Artists was anxious to see a softcover edition of the Spillane book appear in Australia before releasing the film there. The book, whose

Commonwealth distribution rights were held by British publisher Arthur Baker, could not get through Australian customs. Weybright, writing from London to Kurt Enoch in New York, revealed that he had urged Baker to issue an expurgated, if unauthorized, Australian edition. "I told him to edit without referring back to Mickey, since Mickey would never approve of touching a word of the book. He will try to do what we have done with a few Caldwell titles, such as *God's Little Acre*, in Canada, plus a little bowdlerizing. . . . This should be kept confidential, and United Artists should be told that the British publisher is trying to clear the title for internal production in Australia" (9 September 1953).

As we have seen in the cases of Faulkner and others, censorship or even its threat can draw a dollar line of definition for a publisher that pits business sense against literary authenticity. With a popular writer like Mickey Spillane, the pragmatics of profit making seem in 1953 to have easily outweighed any qualms about textual expurgation particularly in foreign markets.

In 1958 a portion of the first Signet printing of *My Fair Lady* was offered to the Teenage Book Club (Scholastic Books) for distribution to secondary schools. In the following excerpt, the president of the book club, William D. Boutwell, asked for some "editing" of this initial printing.

We've all had a chance to look at the full text of *My Fair Lady* and are eager to have it for TAB. There are a few items in the text which might give us some trouble, even though we expect to mark the book "M" for mature readers. . . .

There were two or three other uses of the word "God." Some of them are okay because of the context, but we would appreciate it if those instances in which "God's sake" is used could be changed. There are groups in this country, as you know, that protest every time the word "God" is used as profanity.

In the last line of "Ascot Races" I would suggest that the same device be used as in Freddie's repetition of his line, that is "Move your bloomin' . . . "

Although the word "damn" is used regularly, it is so essential to the show that we will take our chances and patiently answer the complaints.

P.S. Our minimum sales estimate for *My Fair Lady* is 50,000 but we think it might go to 75,000 or perhaps more. (26 May 1958)

Three years later Simon & Schuster surveyed NAL interest in a softcover edition of a book on deSade by Guy Endore that they themselves were weighing. Since its contents were to some degree sensational, Weybright proposed that the hardcover publisher not only make necessary alterations, "exercise their full filtration machinery," but also protect the paperback edition should it be attacked by censors and its sales restricted. Such a request for "warranty" from a hardcover publisher could not have been conceived of ten years earlier when mass market paperback publishing was struggling for the recognition and good will of major trade book publishers.

> But we all know that editorial discipline is going to be essential if the book is to be generally purveyed by Simon & Schuster and ultimately in paper by NAL. I don't mean to imply that we want to inhibit the constructive intention of the book— i.e. to reveal the remarkable contribution which deSade made to the understanding of human nature, mentally and physically—but to limit the language and the instances to those generally permissable in general literature. I am not thinking about possible legal or illegal attempts at censorship, but of the esteem of our two houses.
>
> Because of the nature of the book, and the predictable literalism of the content, and assuming that NAL will not have control over the editorial development of the book, I think we should be protected by a firm warranty that would cover not only legal expenses but also the possible contingency of prevention of inter-state distribution of the book in reprint. We don't anticipate this, but we can predict two pigs in a poke;
>
> a) Endore's insistence upon very practical Sadisms and b) the mood of censorship efforts at the federal level.
>
> All this may sound quibbling. Please don't take it as a dilution of enthusiasm. On the contrary, I have confidence enough in the taste and integrity of Simon & Schuster to have very little fear of you doing a book which would be deemed inappropriate under present law for paperback distribution at a price, say of 75¢, well above the impulse spending level of adolescents.
>
> I am not worried so much about deSade as I am about the NODL; and I am not worried about the NODL if Simon & Schuster really exercise their full filtration machinery on the book. (16 October 1961)

As described in *The New Catholic Encyclopedia*, the National Office for Decent Literature (NODL) was founded in 1938 by Catholic bishops "to set in motion the moral forces of the entire country . . . against the lascivious type of literature which threatens moral, social and national life." For approximately twenty-five years, it was the most active and vocal of United States censoring groups, frequently including NAL reprints on its blacklist. In the following letter to Theodore Waller, then employed at the American Book Publishers Council, Weybright cited one of many instances of this time when religious censoring and government policies directly influenced softcover distribution.

> Two of our large post-exchange distributors, *The Stars and Stripes* in Germany and *The Army Times* in England, are now being influenced by the NODL and the Gathings Committee. We have just been informed that *The Stars and Stripes*, because of pressure from chaplains, are canceling their orders for a number of paper-bound book titles including two of NAL's—*Act of Passion* by Georges Simenon and *We Fished All Night* by Willard Motley. *The Army Times*, also because of chaplain activity, have canceled orders for *Act of Passion* by Georges Simenon, *The Unwanted*, by Dante Arfelli and *Let It Come Down* by Paul Bowles. . . . This is another censorship matter which should be called to the attention of the anti-censorship committee, and I would like to discuss it with you as soon as possible. (2 February 1953)

An early Weybright strategy to deflect some of the NODL attacks was to sponsor, under the more widely distributed Signet imprint, books favorably reviewed by conservative Catholics. This scheme was revealed in a review of NAL activities sent to Professor Eduard C. Lindeman of Columbia University, adviser to NAL and shaper of the Mentor list.

> Don't chide me!—but I have just signed up *Human Destiny* as a Signet, not a Mentor, simply so our list reflects a more diversified cross section of outstanding contemporary literature in every field. We had a heated contest with Doubleday's Perma Books for the title. We were determined not to let Perma use the book as a non-fiction leader in their growing challenge to the paperbound field in certain sectors of the market place. Confidentially, of course, the book will afford a certain amount of protective coloration when the hierarchy studies our program with censorship in mind.[3] (24 May 1949)

3. Doubleday's Anchor Books series, started in 1953, has been cited by publishing historians as the first significant trade paperback series. However, trade book publisher Doubleday sponsored the relatively short-lived Permabooks imprint. It began in 1948 and was a competitor of NAL's Mentor and Signet editions. It was sold to Pocket Books in 1954.

Weybright himself was a member of an Episcopal church in New York but admitted, in response to a fund-raising appeal in memory of NAL author, A. Powell Davies, "I must confess that intellectually I am much more a *Unitarian*" (5 December 1957). NAL occasionally reprinted publications of the Beacon Press, the controversial publishing arm of the Unitarian Church. "The Unitarians love us, and we love them," Weybright once boasted to Beacon editor Melvin Arnold. Beacon was the publisher of Paul Blanchard's stinging attack on the Roman Catholic Church's influence in the United States, *American Freedom and Catholic Power*. Weybright continued, "By the way, has Paul Blanchard ever taken a good look at the NODL? It would provide him with an interesting example of Catholic pressure and strategy, so innocent on the surface, but cunningly calculated to affect education and culture and to dilute the First Amendment" (18 May 1953). Yet Weybright's catholic interests and tastes encouraged friendship with and advice from prominent Catholic liberals such as John Courtney Murray and Anne Fremantle. In the early sixties he began the Omega imprint, Mentor-like titles that rivaled Doubleday's successful Image trade paperback series (started in 1954) in attracting Catholic intellectuals, both writers and readers.

Weybright's patience with what he viewed as the intolerance and hypocrisy of the leadership within the Catholic Church was frequently taxed. In the mid-fifties fellow publisher (and author of numerous softcover westerns) Charles N. Heckelmann of Popular Library received a full measure of Weybright's anger after writing to solicit a corporate contribution to Brotherhood Week.

I'm all for Brotherhood Week, and a great admirer of the wonderful work which the National Council of Christians and Jews have done, but frankly I don't see any reason why civilized book publishers need to be organized in favor of objectives which are obvious to us all.

Personally and professionally you can consider us committed to Brotherhood.

I would like to point out, however, that I am not tolerant enough to condone some of the objectives expressed in the advertisement enclosed by the Supreme Councils of the Knights of Columbus. It is neither democratic nor consistent with the objectives of Brotherhood Week for the Catholic church to legislate Catholic doctrine to the public laws concerning birth control, freedom of expression, etc. (I know you will not consider my objections based on prejudice against Catholics or the freedom of Catholics to stipulate the nature of their own institution.)

Would you, for instance, join in an effort to permit the exhibition of Louis de Chemont's *Martin Luther* in Quebec where it is now officially banned? We now have forty-two books on the NODL list, their distribution prevented by local pressures in a number of communities.

I would not want to see Brotherhood Week every day of the year used as a gag to open criticism of some of these Catholic inspired tactics. (10 December 1955)

Criticism from one's established publishing peers was predictable as mass market publishing evolved in the late forties and fifties into the freewheeling segment of the book industry. As they generated record-setting sales, softcover title selection and cover designs both spawned the ire and jealousy of the publishing establishment. When NAL was singled out, the bestsellers of Mickey Spillane were the most obvious and convenient targets. In November of 1951, for instance, while sharing an elevator ride in their common office building, Alfred A. Knopf verbally castigated Weybright for publishing Spillane. Weybright afterwords penned a lengthy defense composed of a pastiche of culture and commerce arguments.

Here's the first Mickey Spillane, *I, The Jury*—19th printing— and the latest, *The Big Kill*, our first printing of which is slightly over 2.5 million. He was brought to Dutton by a printing salesman, and I leapt at the reprint rights (for a modest advance of $750, against royalties on *I, The Jury*, which now has sold considerably over 2 million). Among Mickey's fans are two Supreme Court justices, Arthur Krock, two Lieutenants General, and a cross-section of eminent people, including practically all of the old fans of Hammett and Chandler. He is not a pornographic author, but a projection of the hard-boiled school into the writing arena formerly staked out by western pulp writers, comic strip extravagandists, and Walt Disney in the cinema. Like Chandler, his first reviews have been contemptuous and jealous expressions by mystery writers who have failed. Like Chandler, he is about to be interpreted to the intelligensia by Charles Rolo.[4]

A writer who outsells Erle Stanley Gardner is certainly going to make William Morrow [the hardcover publisher] sore—just as a reprinter (I am speaking of ourselves) who outstrips Pocket Books

---

4. In 1952, to counter some of the written criticism of Spillane, Weybright published Charles Rolo's scholarly review "Simenon and Spillane: Metaphysics of Murder for the Millions" in NAL's first issue of *New World Writing* (1952).

and Bantam by a considerable margin on net sales is apt to make Pocket Books, in particular, sore—and, indeed, has led them to vilify Mickey Spillane and his reprinters. I hadn't realized—and I shall keep in confidence—the fact that the Duttons are now a target for Spillane criticism.

Perhaps the best clue one can offer to the particular vibration of Spillane is the fact that he is an ardent Jehovah's Witness and when not at his typewriter is ringing door bells with the message of that mysterious creed.

Simultaneous with the release of *The Big Kill* in November (along with the new distribution of one million copies of Spillane's four previous books) we are reprinting Conant's *On Understanding Science*, Faulkner's *Soldiers' Pay*, Engstrand's *The Invaders*, and Simenon's *The Heart of a Man*. I offer this as evidence of the variety and quality that our reprints bring to the mass market. We are publishers, not panderers, and our inspiration, which we are frequently proud to acknowledge, derives no small part from your example. I am glad you publish Jim Cain, and that we reprint him. I am disappointed that you don't still publish Chandler and that we don't reprint him. I am sorry that Cleve Adams, whose *Contraband* is selling very well, died in your hands before we had a chance to promote him in a big way in our market.

This is just a re-hash of what I would have said if I had been going up the street with you after our little chat in the elevator. (23 November 1951)

Weybright, however, recognized attacks from fellow publishers were to be expected and might even be understood as a barometer of one's success as a publisher. After acquiring in a bidding contest Harry Grey's fictional "exposé" *The Hoods*, Weybright warned Enoch: "Our competitors, who failed to get the book, will undoubtedly try to precipitate some censorship on either sex or criminal grounds. In my opinion, we should prepare well in advance for any such contingency. Perhaps it would be a good investment to have the book read by a friendly criminologist, or a psychologist could write a letter to wholesalers on the eve of distribution" (5 August 1952).

Criticism from liberal journalists whose magazines were not in competition with NAL cut more deeply. In the November 1954 issue of the *Saturday Review* an article entitled "The Booming Busts of Paperbacks" was accompanied by four cartoon parodies of contemporary, mass market paperback covers. One of the four satirized was Thorstein Veblen's classic, *The Theory of the Leisure Class*. NAL had published a softcover Mentor edition wrapped with a sedate cover design. Weybright was incensed over the cover parody. He immediately demanded a retraction from his friend and *Saturday Review* editor Norman Cousins. The 27 November retraction praised Mentor books, but it also questioned whether the price to be paid for having the imprint, that is, the publication of books like those of Mickey Spillane, was worth it. With an advance copy of the retraction in hand, Weybright predictably replied: "In your November 27th edition you served yourself a dish of crow all right, but the size was one inch by one and a half. When we have to eat crow we like to do it graciously and in generous portions. We are very sorry you did not do the same." After several further acrimonious exchanges, early the following year, Cousins and Weybright apparently met and resolved their dispute.

As outlined in chapter 4, Victor Weybright brought to NAL a personal and professional background weighed with a wide variety of social and political experiences providing him with a realistic understanding of the root causes of book censorship. Further, despite the constant threats, direct or indirect, that censoring individuals or agencies made to the company's book distribution plans, NAL seems never to have been endangered economically by them. And the period of the most intense censorship—the early fifties—matches the company's emergence as a fiscally sound and profitable business. This raises the question, which unfortunately is not answered by the archival documents, of whether censorship might not have had an overall positive rather than negative effect on NAL's growth. Through the publicity and notoriety they inspired, did censors actually increase the sales of titles they aimed to drive from the marketplace? It is clear that NAL believed this to be the case with a few books whose censoring attracted nationwide attention. Sales of a book "banned in Boston" seem to have increased dramatically sales in the rest of the country. In 1956 when Cardinal Spellman attacked Tennessee Williams' *Baby Doll*, which had just appeared as a film, newspapers across the nation relayed the Cardinal's warning that those who went to see it "commit sin." Weybright, who had published the *Baby Doll* film script to coincide with the movie's premiere, wrote to London publisher Frederic Warburg with glee. "I thought you'd be interested in the *Baby Doll* fanfare. Note the clippings. The film opens tonight. We really ought to send the Cardinal a case of Irish whiskey for Christmas" (18 December 1956).

8

"Allowance for the Vagaries of Hollywood"

Hardcover reprinter Grosset & Dunlap may have been among the first American book publishers to directly call book and film connections to readers' attention by announcing movie tie-ins on its dust jackets. Five of the first eleven titles that Pocket Books issued in 1939 to inaugurate the so-called paperback revolution had or would soon have celluloid cousins. Early contacts between softcover publishers and film producers were usually initiated by the reprinter whose retail sales outlets—smoke shops, drugstores, and newsstands—were often adjacent to downtown movie theaters. Film promotion was found on bookmarks and fliers inserted between the softcovers. Movie stills—first black-and-white and later color—illustrated front and back covers and were tipped into the book's text. Back covers also contained film summaries. Banners on front covers urged, "Read the book, see the movie."

To complement new big screen and technicolor film technologies, movie producers of the fifties looked for stories that were equally expansive. Very often these were book-length novels. Film companies had offices in New York to scout for story material and script writers. Hardcover publishers, principal proprietors of most of the book-length fiction suitable for film adaptation had, of course, regularly submitted their newly published novels hoping to attract film company option and eventual production. By the late fifties film companies found it advantageous to encourage the transformation of original screenplays into book form. These converted scripts increased ticket sales, and their royalties provided additional income for the film producers. It was not uncommon for all three parties—hardcover publisher, paperback reprinter, and film producer—to enter into joint arrangements sometimes built around nothing more than a story

154

concept. To encourage these joint ventures and also line up fresh writing talent, the major paperback publishers made frequent trips to the West Coast, to set up tie-in deals and to scout for new writers. Paperback publishers became part of the Hollywood community when they began hiring West Coast representatives and, finally, set up permanent Hollywood offices.

Throughout the fifties NAL garnered its share of tie-ins with major Hollywood films. Each arrangement seemed to develop in a slightly different way from earlier tie-ins or to present new problems for the publisher. In May 1951 Kurt Enoch's assistant, Hilda Livingston, attended a preview of *A Place in the Sun*. Livingston reported back to Weybright and Enoch. The soon-to-be highly acclaimed film was based on Dreiser's *American Tragedy*, which had been published in a condensed Signet edition two years earlier.

It is an extremely moving, well acted, and adult version of the book. Unfortunately the title has been changed, the characters' names have been changed, and the action takes place in the present rather than at the turn of the century. . . . Paramount is exceptionally eager for a book tie-in; censorship might motivate this interest, I suspect. They are aware of our promotion difficulties in view of the deviations in title, etc. I have asked them if they would be prepared to pay for the cost of making and wrapping a new jacket around our 96,000 copies, and they will let me know on Thursday whether or not they are interested.

This picture is a splendid opportunity to move some of our stock—if we can get Paramount to absorb the cost of working out an effective tie-in on the jacket.[1] (21 May 1951)

In contrast with today, arranging tie-ins after film production appears to have been common throughout the first half of the fifties. Perhaps even more surprising was the cavalier attitude some hardcover publishers took to the disposition of paperback reprint rights when a major film was planned for their property. Marie Wilkerson, assistant to the president of G. P. Putnam, wrote to Marc Jaffe about *Battle Cry*, Leon Uris' 1953 bestseller. "Since I returned, I found that the movie of *Battle Cry* will open in Baltimore on November 10th. The book is still selling along very well, and we are not anxious to dispose of reprint rights. However, I realize that if anyone is to do a movie edition, they would have to begin making plans.

1. It appears from the correspondence files that a deal with Paramount Pictures was not worked out. There is no record of a dust-jacketed reissue of the Signet *An American Tragedy*.

I promise to let all the interested parties know simultaneously, which I am doing today. I look forward to hearing from you as to your interest in the book at this time" (24 June 1954).[2] Contracts for softcover film editions allowed release of a tie-in edition when the film premiered or, if the film production was not immediate, allowed first reprint publication at a particular point after first hardcover publication. Putnam was of course seeking bids on *Battle Cry* well after their hardcover release, leaving little advance time for the reprinter to design a softcover edition and prepare a movie tie-in marketing campaign.

By the mid-fifties NAL seems quite sensitive to the complexities of film cooperation and adaptation. In December 1956, Victor Weybright bragged to Bennett Cerf in the midst of their negotiations over the Terence Rattigan play *Separate Tables* (then under film option), "I am especially pleased to have *Separate Tables* in prospect because—no kidding—we really have a very matey relationship with the Hecht-Hill-Lancaster boys." A few weeks later Weybright described to Harry Maule of Random House the reasoning behind the dollar figures for his separate bids on Rattigan's *Separate Tables* and *Sleeping Prince*, figures that were based on his past dealings with Hollywood producers.

> When I discussed the two Rattigan plays with Bennett, with a $5,000 advance on *Separate Tables*, and a $3,000 advance on *The Sleeping Prince*, the disparity in advances was the outcome of a lot of experience in such matters. As you know, Hecht-Lancaster is making the *Separate Tables* film; they also backed the New York stage version. They will therefore, without any doubt, make a big promotion, as they always do, supplemented by the extremely dynamic activities of United Artists as their distributor. One cannot predict, on the other hand, the extent of the promotion on *The Sleeping Prince*. It has been independently produced by the Monroe-Olivier interests in England, and [Laurence] Olivier is now completing the editing of the film. The title will be changed. Warner Brothers will distribute. At times, on independent productions, Warner Brothers goes all-out in its exploitation campaign; sometimes not. Hence, our more cautious approach, which Bennett fully understood after we discussed it.
>
> Nothing would give us more pleasure than for Marilyn Monroe to carry *The Sleeping Prince* film into really substantial sales as [Ingrid] Bergman seems to be doing with *Anastasia*. It is a pleasant little soap opera that we are selling like hotcakes in our edition at

2. The book eventually went to Bantam where it became one of their bestselling titles.

the moment (and the advance on which was only $1,000 because we got in on the ground floor merely on the rumor that Bergman and Yul Brenner were going to make a big thing out of it). (3 January 1957)

Shortly, *The Sleeping Prince* title change that Weybright refers to presented its own problems for the company. Apparently because of the indifferent reception *The Sleeping Prince* received on Broadway, the movie title was changed to *The Prince and the Showgirl*. The producers further insisted that any book tied to the film make no mention of the play. NAL, however, was required by FTC regulations to do just that in the theatrical edition it had contracted to reprint. As a result NAL was forced to go back to Random House and renegotiate the contract. As revised it permitted NAL to publish the script of the movie as opposed to the play script. This then allowed NAL to duplicate the movie title and not mention the original play. Fortunately for all concerned, the playwright was unlikely to protest. Terence Rattigan also wrote the film script for *The Prince and the Showgirl*.

Even outside of FTC concerns, title changes and textual adaptations were constant problems for reprints with theatrical and Hollywood connections. Arrangements got more than just a bit convoluted, as exhibited in this letter from Arthur H. Thornhill Sr. of Little, Brown to NAL editor Walter Freeman about an H. E. Bates novel. "Lawrence Pollinger [Bates' English agent] has written saying that Bates doesn't like the idea of changing the title of your edition of *The Darling Buds of May* to *The Mating Season*. He thinks that the movie may not bear much resemblance to the novel. On the other hand, the play based on the novel has been sold to Robin Fox Productions. If it is successful and gets on in New York under the original title, he thinks this would be helpful to NAL" (3 October 1958).[3]

A similar title problem arose with the Signet tie-in to a Faulkner film, as Truman Talley notes in his query to Lee Wright of Random House.

I learned in Los Angeles last week from both Jerry Wald and Dick St. Johns that their Faulkner movie, utilizing the trial in *Requiem for a Nun* as the film's narrative thread would have flashbacks to *Sanctuary* and that the film itself would be given the title *Sanctuary*.

By agreement with Random House NAL is to reissue *Requiem for a Nun* before this coming September, such reissue to extend our agreement on the book for an additional three years.

With all due allowance for the vagaries of Hollywood it would

3. NAL retained the original title and issued *The Darling Buds of May* in 1959.

seem clear that the motion picture will not be finished and released until sometime in 1961—possibly the fall.

What, quite simply, can NAL and Random House work out? Ideally, of course, we'd like to be able to reissue the two books again in our recent joint edition. It seems clear we cannot properly reissue *Requiem for a Nun* by itself and change the title to *Sanctuary!* The film sounds like a big one, with every chance for the kind of newsstand sale that we enjoyed on *The Long Hot Summer*. (1 July 1960)

NAL gained Random House approval to continue publishing both titles in one edition. This was the third Faulkner project that involved Random, NAL, and producer Jerry Wald. Presenting William Faulkner to "the millions" was challenging, but when film companies become involved with the production, it could become hazardous.

Faulkner film adaptations drew readers who would not normally have been attracted to the writer, readers who might have earlier been dissuaded by the author's reputation and arduous writing style. Prose presentation to a mass reading public was magnified greatly, however, when the film production bore little or no resemblance to the book of the same name. This was clearly the case with *The Long Hot Summer*, the first of the Signet tie-in editions with the Faulkner films. The film premiered in April 1958. Despite Talley's boast above of "newsstand success" for *The Long Hot Summer*, reader reaction to the Signet edition, excerpted from Faulkner's *Hamlet*, was vitriolic; for example:

I recently read Signet book no. S1501— *The Long Hot Summer*, by William Faulkner. There are scenes on both the front and back cover and four pages in the body of the book taken from the 20th Century Fox motion picture of the same title. The stars in the picture are named three times in conjunction with these pictures.

Yet, you know perfectly well that not one single incident in the whole book has the slightest relation to any scene in the movie. This book was released simultaneously with the movie, I believe. I also believe the inclusion of the scenes depicted is only a gimmick to hoodwink people who have seen the movie into buying the book, on the (natural) assumption that they bear some relationship to each other. As such I think it's a dirty trick. (5 May 1958)

This reader response to the same edition must have been both clear to and evocative for the company that also issued so much hard-boiled fiction. "My boss, my brother, several of my neighbors and others all have been disappointed and misled by the wrong impression this cover and contents give as to the story being about 'The Long Hot Summer.' . . . We as a unanimous committee all feel that the people who chose William Faulkner as Nobel Prize-winning author should all have their heads examined. He stinks! (24 July 1958)

A surprising number of readers wrote in praise of the film but condemned the book. Conceding reader criticism, a typical Talley reply could only weakly outline the problem of tie-ins from the reprinter's perspective. "Your well-taken letter deserves a reply, even if—as in this instance—there is no argument. This particular "movie tie-in" turned out to be the most extreme case thus far of a problem that will plague us again, I fear. First, at what point is a movie "based" on a book no longer really relevant; second, and more practically, are we going to neglect contracting for possible movie titles due to the fact we seldom see the movie itself until a week or two before its release? It's a problem—our problem—very properly" (20 May 1958).

The problem of balancing "luster and lucre" was never clearer than when the publisher was bidding on books on which a film likely would be based.The temptation to ignore a book's faults are great when visions of bestseller sales rise backwards from the western horizon. For a reprinter these visions often had color added by a starry-eyed hardcover publisher. An extreme example was this 1953 promotion letter sent to NAL editor J. Bradley Cumings from William Jarrett, publisher of Sasha Siemel's *Tigrero!*.

This is just a note to emphasize what I reported to you on the phone yesterday about *Tigrero!*. Twentieth Century Fox bought the screen rights at one of the fanciest prices any studio has offered for a book property in recent years. [In the margin of this letter "$35,000" was written.] Further, they are about to announce the appointment of one of the coast's more prominent and high-priced writers to prepare the film version. So we're pretty well assured that this will be a big job and that they will be pouring lots of $$$ into the promotion later on.

We have *not* made the decision as yet on reprint rights, Brad, and though you have already said "no," we feel that this new information may revive interest. Bear in mind, too, that we have gone back to press three times already—the book isn't officially launched until the 26th. That shows how much the book dealers across the country feel about it.

And to illustrate how this kind of story can capture the public fancy, take a look at this week's issue of *Life*—we are mighty pleased with their treatment of *Tigrero!* and are certain that it will help a great deal in getting it off to a good start. I understand that the forthcoming *Argosy* article will be one of their best—indeed our cup runneth over.

We realize you put serious thought into the first decision, Brad, but we honestly feel that *Tigrero!* is now BIG—let me know what the reaction is at your shop and perhaps we can rejuvenate this one. At any rate, we'll throw this open on a bidding basis to make sure everyone has an opportunity to cast their vote. (23 October 1953)

Cumings appears to have supported acquisition at one time; Weybright and Enoch did not. Apparently the book never made it to the screen, but it was reprinted by Ace Books four years later.

In the mid-fifties NAL initiated fresh contact with western writer Frank Gruber, who was enjoying success in Hollywood as studios were taking up options on his books and hiring him to do screenplays. NAL had published several of his titles in the late forties and early fifties, but Gruber had been almost exclusively a Bantam author since then. Before throwing a new lure to the author, Marc Jaffe shaded in some recent background about the writer in a memo to Victor Weybright.

Bantam paid $5,000 for *Buffalo Grass*, which Alan Ladd is doing for Warner Brothers, and I believe an equal amount for *Lonesome River*, which has also been sold to the movies. If we want to take Gruber on—and I certainly think we should—we'll have to pay premium prices. But I think he's worth it, and I think that we can also promise him the number one spot on our list (for the time being, at least).

We turned down Gruber westerns some years ago, as a little on the crude and mechanical side. He's a real pro who knows how to put a story together, but his novels still lack the solid atmosphere that characterizes the work of such people as Short and Haycox. I doubt that Frank will ever make the *Saturday Evening Post*, and he doesn't always get good reviews—but, except when he gets far off the trail, he can always tell a rattling good story. (12 February 1957)

A decision was immediately made to go ahead and approach Gruber, and two days later Jaffe penned a valentine smacking of the same West Coast hype that introduced *Tigrero!* to the NAL editors.

We want to do business with you!

We have a healthy western list, one that is growing healthier all the time, and I think that your name would add considerable luster to it. We don't make a general practice of rating our authors. I can say, however, that if we are able to strike a satisfactory bargain on *Town Tamer* and succeeding books, we will push your name and books to the hilt.

If you have been observing our balliwick lately, you will have seen that we have been extremely active and successful with our movie tie-ins; *Baby Doll, Anastasia* and *Tea and Sympathy* are but a few which have been both distinguished and profitable. I think we can do the same sort of thing with the *Town Tamer*. If by some chance there would not be a movie tie-in on one of your westerns, we would nevertheless be able to package it in a big way and promote it strongly to our wholesalers and dealers. With two or perhaps even three books a year under our imprint, I feel confident that we can push you right to the top. (14 February 1957)

Gruber's reply to this loose tender revealed the heady atmosphere in which West Coast writers worked. After describing some of his recent work for an NBC television series and mentioning that Gary Cooper's producer was interested in doing *Town Tamer*, Gruber related some very recent happenings.

Two weeks ago, out of the clear sky, I got a telephone call from an actor I have never met, but with whom I'd rather do a picture than any other actor in this business; he has been #1 as far as I am concerned. Gregory Peck. Peck said that he missed my last two books, as he had read them too late to make offers. He especially liked *Bitter Sage* and *Buffalo Grass*. He said he wanted first crack at my next one. We had lunch and I suggested a springboard for which he went. Agents came in and I sweated it out for two weeks, but two days ago we closed the deal—for my next book after *Town Tamer*, for which I haven't written one line! I have made deals in the past fifteen months, with Alan Ladd, Gary Cooper and Gregory Peck. Also one with a producer, Nicky Nayfack. With Gregory Peck I am taking a big gamble. He wanted to make an all-cash deal, but I decided to take a plunge and we finally worked out a small cash down payment and a piece of the picture. If the picture is a real hit—as most of his pictures have been—I stand to make a tremendous amount. A modest success, and still a good amount. Only an outright flop can hurt me and that is virtually impossible. Even the stinker, *Moby Dick*, has done over five million domestic to date and will eventually go closer to ten million. A number of Peck's pictures have grossed 10, 11 and 12 million. Should I be lucky enough to have a ten-million picture I would stand to make over $300,000. (22 March 1957)

Weybright soon met with Gruber in Hollywood but was unable to work out a publication arrangement. Two older Gruber titles, first reprinted as Signets in the late forties, were reissued two years later, however.

Marc Jaffe's evaluation of William Brinkley's *Don't Go Near the Water* was both qualified and cautious. In recommending purchase he rationalized that the book, not yet published but being sought after by four Hollywood studios, could be obtained as a loss leader. "In spite of my negative reaction to the book as such, I have a feeling that the book can't help but do pretty good on the newsstands, what with the high-pressure promotion that will go along with the trade edition and the movie. In my opinion this is a half-a-million copy net seller. This is not a book, I feel, that we can count on making money on, but if we can break even with a high advance on the kind of sale I refer to above I think it is worth a big pitch" (17 February 1956). Weybright was less restrained and quickly pressed the proprietary publisher, Random House, for a decision. He offered a sizable advance of fifty thousand dollars plus a very favorable royalty rate: 10 percent of the 50 percent cover price or five cents a copy. In bidding on the book with Bennett Cerf and the author's agent, Weybright further pointed out his offer presented "enormous opportunity for accruals if book and film reach expectations." He then briefly outlined how his terms translated into projected sales. "For example, a million copies would earn the guarantee. Two million would mean $50,000 additional accruals; three million an additional $50,000 accruals. We have sold 3 million copies of a number of our more popular books. If everybody is right, this should match that figure. I hope you'll regard this as one of those 'box office cut' deals that seem to be the vogue with movies these days, greatly to the advantage of the author" (20 February 1956). The hardcover edition of the book became the leading seller of 1956. Neither the film nor the Signet softcover version, both released the following year, met with comparable success, perhaps bearing out Jaffe's more cautious evaluation. Weybright's assessment for a member of his editorial staff of Richard Condon's *The Manchurian Candidate* was on target, however. Both book editions and the film garnered critical and financial success. "The fact that the book is dedicated to Max Blumstein leads me to believe that ultimately it will be taken by the movies. We must certainly have this book, and I hope that McGraw-Hill will accept our offer of $5000 with a $7500 escalator in the event of the movie. Condon is far ahead of his performance in *The Oldest Profession* in this book. I believe he has a considerable future, way beyond a cult, and that he definitely must be an NAL man from here on in" (1 June 1959).

In the late fifties Weybright came to a working agreement with Ted Loeff and Charles B. Bloch who had formed a scouting operation in Hollywood, Literary Projects. Loeff put up most of the money to set up the agency, and he did most of the legwork. The partnership soon dissolved with Bloch becoming a very successful West Coast representative for Bantam. Loeff continued to look after NAL interests. A 1960 memorandum of agreement drawn up to clarify relations between the two companies shows that for NAL's part Weybright was responsible for all important decisions between the two firms. Literary Projects' chief responsibilities were to turn up West Coast writers and writing projects, not necessarily with film potential, that could be developed or converted into salable books. It was free to work with Hollywood agents and producers but could not appear to be stealing authors tied to important New York trade publishing houses. Weybright's letter to Alan C. Collins of the Curtis Brown literary agency described the operation more concretely, relating it to the Irving Wallace deal made earlier in the year.

> Literary Projects Company is an organization operated by Ted Loeff and Charles Bloch in Beverly Hills, exclusively on behalf of publishing projects for New American Library. It is not a literary agency; on the contrary it operates entirely through agency and other basic channels. Perhaps the enclosed clipping from the *New York Times* will give you an idea of a recent project, which of course was handled by Mr. Paul Reynolds, agent for Irving Wallace. New American Library financed Mr. Wallace on two books—with an advance of $25,000—so that he could develop as a book author rather than as an assigned dramatist in the film and TV industry, at which he was making some $75,000 per annum. I took a chance, and now his novel has gone to Zanuck for $175,000 plus $150,000 penalty if no film is made or 5% of the world gross, which cannot conceivably come to less than $300,000. We have developed a number of other projects which we have placed with a wide variety of trade publishers, including Doubleday; Coward-McCann; McGraw-Hill; Little, Brown; etc. In every case the trade publisher gets his full fifty percent share of subsidiary income. What New American Library gets is a good book, for ultimate publication in our paperbound format, usually with world rights, which in turn we place with London publishers. . . . I mention this so that you will know there is nothing unconventional about the operation

163

of Literary Projects Company except that—on authors who are totally uncommitted by option or inference—New American Library becomes the primary contractor and holder of publishing rights. If we pay an advance of $10,000, half that amount goes to the trade publisher in the usual way.

I am certain that you are aware of our interest in keeping authors not only alive but solvent and at work on books. Literary Projects Company is our reconnaissance organization on the West Coast, where a lot of roving and talented authors have become lost to literature through their attachment to the television and film industry. As time runs on, they become interested in their genuinely creative literary careers.

Occasionally, major projects arise out of a body of material crying for the attention of a creative writer; occasionally it comes from the brains of the film industry which, these days, likes to use a major book as the foundation for recognition of an ultimate film. (9 September 1959)

One individual dominated the dealings that Weybright had with Hollywood in the late fifties and early sixties. Jerry Wald, model for Budd Schulberg's Sammy Glick in *What Makes Sammy Run*, was an executive producer at Columbia Pictures when *From Here to Eternity* was released in 1953. Perhaps it was through this picture that he and Weybright first made acquaintance. Drawn to the movie adaptation of modern American fiction, Wald left behind at his untimely death in 1962 an association with a string of films based on works by Faulkner, Hemingway, James Cain, James Jones, and Tennessee Williams as well as those by Rona Jaffe and Grace Metalious. At the close of 1957, a year during which he produced films based on *An Affair to Remember*, *No Down Payment*, and *Peyton Place*, Wald summarized for Weybright the value of a paperback tie-in edition.

I am sincere, Victor, when I say that the paper-back manufacturers can do more for a picture than hard-backs because their circulation is limited. Am I right in assuming there are less than 1,000 bookstores of the Martindale type throughout the country? If I am, then I would like to compare this figure with the outlets for the paperbacks, which will be 100,000 or more. How many outlets would there be in the world? The point I would like to make is that the paper-back manufacturer brings the book to the public: where they travel, where they shop, where they eat, etc. If you will send me all such information, our department out here is ready and willing to go to work on it, and it will, of course, result in mutual benefits. (31 December 1957)

At this time NAL was cooperating with Wald on the promotion of the Faulkner adaptations, *The Long Hot Summer* and *The Sound and the Fury*. But the company needed the producer's help in wrestling softcover rights for the latter from Random House as we learn from this Weybright dictation to his secretary. "Please remind me immediately, upon my return, to speak to Bennett Cerf about *The Sound and the Fury* and its simultaneous release with the Jerry Wald film. If, on account of his Oscar activities, Jerry Wald doesn't get hold of Bennett to urge a release to Signet, of the book, I can telephone Wald and ask him to do so. He promised to do it. At the moment, as chairman of the Oscar Award activities, Wald probably will not have time to cope until the ceremonies are concluded. Please give this priority on the list of things I must do upon my return" (24 March 1958).

At the turn of the decade, using Ted Loeff and Literary Projects as a frequent intermediary, Wald and Weybright sketched out a series of separate book-film story concepts that they referred to as the "American Scene" project. It was Wald's responsibility, through a subsidiary that he set up, Wald Publishing Company, to develop a detailed story outline for each book in the series and to find a writer to complete each. Weybright, in turn, would place each with a hardcover publisher and later issue each one in a Signet paperback. If the book was successful, Wald would then arrange film production. Andrew Tully, through a contract with Wald Publishing, agreed to write one of the books in the series. In order to do this he had to be released from a "next book" option clause by Simon & Schuster. Wald was technically the proprietary publisher of the novel that eventually became *Capitol Hill*. NAL became softcover reprinter and was responsible for lining up an established trade book publisher to do the hardcover edition. Simon & Schuster, given assurances that a film would be forthcoming and promised a percentage of the film sale, agreed to do the hardcover. Weybright reviewed these contractual convolutions in a letter to Wald associate Richard St. Johns.

I believe the deal is now ready for wrap up. For your guidance in organizing Wald Publishing Company's contract with the author, I am enclosing a copy of our agreement with Wald Publishing Company. Obviously you will not want to have it signed until the entire deal is ready for simultaneous—more or less—closing.

We went to $8,000—$5,000 to be paid on signing. S&S will go to $6,000, in consideration of 5% of the film sale (not 5% of the picture) including both the Wald and Tully film sale. Since

Jerry doesn't have to invest anything except his idea and since S&S will give this project a terrific boost, I recommend that S&S terms be met. In fact I have included them in our agreement so that we can assign to S&S all of their publishing rights, their share in subsidiary revenue—reprint and book club, etc.—and also waive their option with Tully on this particular book.

Not many major hard-cover publishers would be so cooperative as S&S has proven. (20 May 1960)

About this same time Wald summarized for Weybright his vision of their cooperative ventures and their mutual benefits. "I always like to work with someone with whom I can bounce ideas off on, as from such an interchange an enlargement of ideas is bound to result, and when you work in a climate of enthusiasm and excitement the material becomes deeper and more perceptive, which is necessary to put together exciting books. The primary mission of my association with you and Ted Loeff is to build our books into best sellers. The pictures will eventually take care of themselves. I hope I will be able to come up with as many blockbuster book projects for you as Ted has" (17 May 1960). Wald's "enthusiasm and excitement," however, created problems for the editor, particularly when the producer, through Wald Publishing Company, began to sign up writers to carry out these projects. Wald frequently approached writers who, like Tully, had active option arrangements with established New York publishers. When this occurred, it often created problems within the book industry for Weybright who was known to be associated with Wald. In spite of NAL's major shift toward proprietary publishing, reprints of hardcover texts continued to represent the bulk of NAL monthly releases, and the company depended on the good relations of the major trade publishers for reprint properties. In 1960 when Weybright cautioned Wald on the protocols of book publishing, Wald responded quickly. "Frankly, Victor, I really do not have the time or the know-how as to who to contact regarding each of my ideas for novels. I can do the most amount of good in the inception of the idea, ideas for pre-selling, promoting and creating a climate of excitement and enthusiasm about the various projects. Beyond this I depend on you and your valuable organization to carry the ball" (25 May 1960). However, by midsummer Weybright apparently believed it necessary to detail some clandestine working procedures to reduce trade publisher tension and elude some of the sort of criticism then being directed at the perceived creation of Irving Wallace's *Chapman Report*. The book was then under attack by the East Coast press for having been cooked up by Victor Weybright (see chapter 10).

There are certain points that, though they sound negative, are vital to the full critical and sales reception of books which you control. . . . May I list them?

1. Publicity prior to placement of hardcover rights, which links a book to a film source, is harmful among critics, literary snobs and a considerable sector of the traditional book trade. After a hardcover publisher has accepted a book, as Simon & Schuster has done with Tully, advance publicity is good, so long as it stresses film interest rather than film control by Wald Publishing Company.

2. General publicity on Wald Publishing Company's connection with the book prior to hardcover publication can be harmful (reviewers may sharpen knives on the subject of "pre-fabricated fiction"). After the reviews are out, no harm really is done—but it is much more to the point to publicize Jerry Wald's interest in the property as inspired or suggested by you, without too much reference to Wald Publishing Company, which could get a lot of unnecessary adverse criticism (as Literary Projects Company has gotten in *Publishers Weekly* and in various professional publishing forms).

3. NAL's role should not be publicized until after the hardcover title is well established. It simply gives certain book sellers an alibi to drag their feet, saying that they can't stock and promote a book that is already announced as an imminent paperbound.

Some of these points are rather inhibitory, at first glance, but I know you can cope with them by various subterfuges. For example you can say that you have seen an outline or a manuscript and immediately got involved with the project, or you can say that you know the author and have suggested that he write the book, etc. Simply to avoid an innuendo that Hollywood is swinging the Grand Seigneurs of book publishing by the tail, I have to do the same thing myself. For example, we control *The Chapman Report, Diamond Head, The Walls of Jolo,* and a number of other books that have been discreetly placed with hardcover. These all came through Ted Loeff. Nevertheless, Ted and NAL lean over backward to keep out of the picture while a book is being launched. We've all run the gamut of criticism and realize it can be harmful to the development of a best seller. (27 July 1960)

Within a week of sending the letter to the volatile producer, a second, more soothing note, drafted in West Coast vernacular, rushed westward from Weybright. "Just a little fan letter to let you know how magnificent we all think *Sons and Lovers* is as a film. Also, how nice it was to see you, even though all too briefly, on Oscar Levant's show. . . . If you get East before August 18th, do get in touch if you possibly can. I go abroad on that date, itinerary enclosed, just in case you should be passing through London on your way to Italy, where the newspapers announce that you are soon bound. . . . I think our organization, editorial and otherwise, is now very well alerted on all the book projects that are finalized" (3 August 1960).

None of the projects developed jointly by Weybright, Loeff, and Wald appear to have bloomed completely. Perhaps the premature death of the producer eliminated full exploitation of the books lined up for the "American Scene" series. Some of the manuscripts did find a Signet imprint, however, including the Tully novel. The evaluation of a tinsel-touched manuscript solely on its intrinsic merits may indeed be impossible for any commercial book publishing organization to undertake either then or now. These Hollywood alliances are dramatic examples of how mass market editorial selection considerations were weighed on the culture-commerce scale. Slanted by hype and exploitation, the balance invariably tilts toward the commercial end.

9

"Good Reading for the Millions"[1]

The sales success of early mass market softcover publishing rested on a base of approximately eight hundred local wholesale periodical distributors. Along with national newspapers and magazines, these independent distributors supplied, on a consignment basis, the 100,000 or so newsstand, drugstore, and variety store outlets that sold paperback books. They accounted for well over 80 percent of all retail sales.[1] Paperback publishers used "national distributors" like Fawcett Publications to sell their monthly lists of softcover books to the independent distributors. With percentages based on past sales records, most independent distributors agreed to service a certain number of display pockets for each major publisher's books in the retail outlets they supplied. These local wholesalers generally had little say about or concern for the individual titles that filled these pockets.

Through the national distributors such as Fawcett, each softcover publisher kept a watchful eye on the imprint display proportions within each independent distributor's territory. Then, as today, survival in the paperback book industry depended on each imprint gaining as much retail display area as possible, the general theory being that the more titles seen, the more titles sold. One simple and direct strategy was to produce as large a number of book titles each month as one could afford. Sheer title quantity alone could produce more display pockets for a publisher and, therefore, greater sales. However, it also could generate the return of large quantities

---

1. With the dramatic growth in recent years of retail book chains, today's domestic mass market book sales divide roughly in half with 50 percent sold to one of the four hundred or so wholesale distributors spread around the country and 50 percent sold directly to retail booksellers.

of unsold books that historically have been death knell of weaker imprints. A second strategy was to produce fewer titles but through judicious selection, attractive design, and appropriate promotion make them attractive enough to command adequate display. More than any other softcover publisher of the late forties and fifties, NAL seems to have succeeded best at employing this second strategy—a marketing plan that relied on the quality or the appearance of quality of individual titles to capture the sufficient retail display space required for successful sale. Commanding adequate rack space was then and is today the minimum task of any mass market publisher's distribution effort.

Through the late fifties paperback displays were generally arranged by publisher imprint rather than by subject category, the rationale being that imprint arrangements were easier for the publisher to police and the wholesaler to restock. Softcover publishers therefore tried to maintain strong design identities. NAL, for instance, had color bands on the top and bottom of Signet and Mentor front and back covers. Artistically they served as frames for its cover illustration; practically they made identification and inventory easier. On several occasions other publishers, here and abroad, used NAL format designs on their own publications. NAL usually tried to discourage, often with threats of legal action, this packaging plagiarism.

When Hillman Periodicals incurred NAL's displeasure by issuing Erskine Caldwell's early novel *The Bastard*, it produced for their new Novel Selections book imprint a close copy of NAL's successful Signet design. The discovery of this design had one humorous aspect as Weybright observed to Caldwell's agent, James Oliver Brown, "The Hillman people succeeded so well in imitating a Signet book, complete with our own distinctive top band, that the printer sent the enclosed cover proofs to us—naturally!"

As the fifties progressed, many of the smaller softcover publishers went out of business, unable to compete with the major companies at the retail level. Larger companies, like NAL, became even more dominant as they vied with each other for the top position on the paperback sales chart. Retail displays grew steadily. Title arrangement by publisher imprint, however, was no longer permissable: a self-service oriented public demanded book arrangements by subject and genre rather than by publisher. Independent distributor wholesalers no longer became the automatic recipients of predetermined numbers and quantities of titles. Local independent distributors began to select for themselves from each softcover publisher's monthly list titles and quantities they were willing to display at retail outlets that they serviced. Increasingly, softcover publishers sold directly to larger retail outlets, so-called legitimate bookstores, bypassing both the national distributors and the independent distributor wholesalers. Publishers generally set up separate sales staffs to accommodate these "direct sales."

Marketing a book to an independent distributor wholesaler or directly to a retailer and ultimately to the buying public is accomplished by sales, publicity, advertising, and design staffs, which for the most part, shape the image the title is expected to project on display. In recent years the media, especially radio and television, have made the task of presenting leading softcover titles to their buyers more sophisticated and expensive. Compared with today's techniques, marketing a softcover title in paperback publishing's formative years was simple and often primitive.Furthermore, large mass market reprint sales of well-known hardcover bestsellers were not likely to overtly impress the proprietary publishers. The original publisher could claim with justification that its initial sales and promotion efforts laid the ground work for the success of the follow-up paper edition. Therefore, it was a particularly tempting challenge for a reprint publisher, especially in the infant days of mass market publishing, to take a book that had not achieved renown in hardcover and turn it into a paperback bestseller.

Harry Grey's *The Hoods* apparently had a lackluster hardcover sales record, but based on the success that NAL was having with Mickey Spillane titles in the early fifties, it seemed ideal for the mass market. With *The Hoods* as a featured title when finally released as a Signet the following year, Weybright proposed to Enoch a sales promotion campaign that was quite extensive for its time.

I suggest that plans get under way for a special drive—and special presentation—of *The Hoods*. This is the book that everyone wanted, and that NAL got for a sizable guarantee. At the time when it was released by Crown, Crown was very involved with *Washington Confidential*. As a result it was neglected. At last, the *Times* has given it a very flattering review—a review which should be exploited to the hilt in due course.

The Hoods should lend itself to a lot of trade fanfare—and considerable build-up. Among the possibilities: 1. a Spillane endorsement on the cover. Spillane could be quoted along the general line that if you think he's tough you ought to read this authentic tale of the New York hoods. 2. A memorable and uniquely recognizable cover should be worked up well in advance—that will lend itself to blow-up posters, etc. 3. Fawcett might be willing,—in *True*—to work up a thriller article on the sensational gangsters of the Hoods—with some references to *The Hoods*, and the fantastic author, Harry Grey. Who is—who was—Harry Grey?

If *True* will not play ball, perhaps some other man's magazine—
even *Argosy*—might see the advantages of a little mutual log-rolling.
4. *The Hoods* will be a Giant [35¢ edition]. With enough
support and presentation and publicity in general trade build-up,
including a Spillane endorsement, it is a lively candidate, if the
Fawcetts will cooperate—for a considerably larger distribution than
any previous Giant in the paper-bound field. (5 August 1952)

Like most aspects of book marketing, even book advertising was relatively rudimentary at this time. In a 1957 memo to the two NAL partners,
the company's promotion specialist, Jay Tower, listed only eleven daily
newspapers worthy of receiving advertising for an important movie tie-in;
only three papers west of the Mississippi were considered.[2] However,
joint book and film promotions were becoming more common, aided by
advertising contributions from the film studios involved with the production or distribution. For *The Chapman Report*, a West Coast publicist hired
by NAL outlined a twenty-six-part promotion campaign that combined
more or less traditional book promotion activities with more Hollywood
inspired activities such as "getting three very sexy actresses to pose for a
picture reading *The Chapman Report* with shocked looks on their faces."
Perhaps the most farfetched proposal recommended: "Let's put a copy of
The Chapman Report in a jug, drop it in the ocean and see where it lands.
We include a note saying that the finder will get an all-expense trip to
Hollywood, visit around the Twentieth-Fox lot, tickets to the premiere of
the film, etc. We could advertise it as 'Sex around the World' or 'How
Long Does It Take Sex to Go around the World?' " Predating by twenty-
five years the commercialism of the 1984 Los Angeles Olympics, he finally
suggested:

And speaking of the convention, the Democrats convene in Los
Angeles next month. On their heels will be several hundred
newspaper men and television commentators. We should not
overlook the possibility of doing something in regards to this
convention. One idea which I really am sure will create controversy
and copy would be to get a sample election ballot and print over it
"Don't Vote Until You Read *The Chapman Report*." Hire several
young kids to stand outside the Sports Arena in downtown LA

2. She named the *New York Herald Tribune, Washington Post, Los Angeles Examiner,
Chicago Tribune, Cleveland News, Boston Herald Traveler, San Francisco Chronicle, Milwaukee
Journal, Detroit News,* and *St. Louis Globe-Democrat* as well as the *New York Times* Sunday and
daily editions.

where the convention will be held and hand out these pamphlets to the delegates as they arrive, spread them around the major hotels where they are staying and even slip them under the doors. Many will think it's a political report of some kind. The newspaper men will jump on the story and it could really take off like a rocket. (19 April 1960)

Timing the release of a potential blockbuster paperback was, as noted in chapter 6, the subject of calculation and speculation at the time of reprint negotiations. In mid-1957 Norman Mailer's *The Deer Park* was being weighed for release. The author himself was becoming concerned about the timing and publishing promotion that would accompany the softcover edition. With paternalistic self-assuredness, Weybright reviewed some of the publication factors with Walter J. Minton who had recently succeeded his father as president of G. P. Putnam, proprietary publisher of *The Deer Park* acquired by NAL six months earlier.[3]

I gather from your telephone conversation that Norman [Mailer] wants assurances that we will undertake all-out promotion and special display of *The Deer Park* before he will consent to our fifty cent Signet reprint appearing earlier than October, 1957. I can give you this assurance, and if I understand you rightly, this means that we may issue our reprint in December, 1956 or thereafter i.e. earlier than October, 1957.

I would like to schedule the book for February, 1957. We had it on our schedule for December, but for lack of authorization had to delay it, since we are determined not to release *The Deer Park* simultaneously with any other title which would detract from it in our sales campaign. In January, for example, we have already organized a very special sales and promotion campaign on Anne Morrow Lindbergh's *Gift from the Sea*. Hence, February.

One reason we wanted to schedule our release in December was that in that month we were putting out a large reissue, nationally, of Norman's *The Naked and the Dead*. We had hoped to make it Mailer Month. As you have probably been told, we sold over a million and a half copies of *The Naked and the Dead*, and expect to sell hundreds of thousands more with some help,

3. Ten years after Minton became head of Putnam, he acquired a mass market company of his own, Berkley, and subsequently added several other mass market imprints, including Ace and Jove.

ultimately, from the promotion of the motion picture which is now reported as actually about to get under way.

We cannot permit an author to stipulate our method of promotion—anymore than an author such as Norman would permit us to stipulate how and what he should write—we can promise special promotion, publicity, and special display of *The Deer Park* in every sort of retail outlet which will cooperate. This means that in cities such as New York and Los Angeles, for example, we shall provide and push special displays of *The Deer Park* in special cardboard racks as well as on the regular book display racks. The real test of a book's sales, however, as Norman should be the first to realize, is how many people really want to read what's inside the book. (*The Naked and the Dead* certainly proved that.) No amount of artificial promotion and display can sell a book that people don't want. Ask Pocket Books about *Bridey Murphy* which in spite of all their exploitation is selling very poorly in many areas. All the merchandising tricks and devices which Norman has referred to in connection with *Gray Flannel Suit* or *79 Park Avenue* were initiated by New American Library. It should hardly be necessary for us to affirm our intention of doing better than Pocket Books. After all, we launched the fifty cent price in the mass market—with *The Naked and the Dead, Knock on Any Door, Forever Amber*, and *The Young Lions*, all of which went beyond the million mark. We launched the seventy-five cent price and have put *From Here to Eternity*—which benefited from the Columbia Picture promotion—to the three million mark, at seventy-five cents.

I should like to point out that despite our sale of over a million and a half copies of *The Naked and the Dead*, Rinehart sales rose when we released our reprint. Moreover, our lawyer succeeded in breaking down the censorship ban against the book in Canada, which resulted not only in our selling the book there in our edition, but in the sale of a great many copies of the Rinehart edition.

. . . We do have a number of other authors, including Erskine Caldwell, Tennessee Williams, and Anne Lindbergh, who also worked closely with us and their trade publishers in fixing the reprint schedules. We can't renege on other commitments at this date. This is not really to your or Norman's disadvantage—since *The Deer Park* will enjoy the Signet momentum in the marketplace created by a strong list of which he is definitely the strongest element in the season ahead. (8 August 1956)

Following a book's publication, the most common concern or com-

174

plaint of authors was their book's lack of availability. Many writers, impressed by the dazzling sales figures of Spillane and Caldwell, became disillusioned when their local, hometown source for paperbacks failed to display or restock their new title. And even Caldwell, who was as widely sold as any softcover writer in the world, constantly questioned the efficacy of NAL distribution. With an author as profitable and visible as Caldwell, it was crucial for the company to have its books widely and constantly available. After one such Caldwell criticism in 1948, Kurt Enoch shot a memo to NAL's national distributor, Fawcett, "However, if things go on this way, where we can't even keep up an adequate distribution in Caldwell's hometown, we not only continue to lose considerable sales but are risking the loss of Caldwell's confidence in our efficiency and consequently our publishing rights on the best selling property anybody can have." When author Larston Farrar expressed fears of a conspiracy of local wholesale distributors to keep his book off display racks, Weybright assured him. "There is no evidence, direct or indirect, that any wholesaler deliberately withheld *Washington Lowdown* from sale at any time. Whatever his personal feelings, no wholesaler is going to cut himself off from potential revenue. It is our experience, in fact, that wholesalers usually have no personal feelings about any book, pro or con. They simply 'move' them in response to the needs of their territories pushed from behind by our national distributor and ourselves" (3 April 1957).

Part of the limited availability problem lies in the very nature of the wholesale distribution system. Geared to distribute national periodicals and newspapers, it forces softcover publishers to issue books on monthly magazine distribution schedules. Actual visibility on display racks in variety stores and supermarkets averages much less than thirty days; only best-selling titles command display space for more than a few weeks. In a letter to NAL editor Walter Freeman, author Henry Miller revealed his understanding of this distribution system: "As I got the picture, the new editions crowd out the old before the latter have a real chance to sell. Or, to put it another way, there is not enough space on the racks. The reader can, of course, write direct for a book he can't find. But few bother, I suppose. (Most never even notice the paragraph at the bottom, in fine print, suggesting this procedure.) Even my intelligent friends never think of this alternative. They write and ask me if I can dig up any. Or, they say—' Too bad, Henry, we can't find any in this town. All sold out ' " (25 May 1956). A year later, after publication of both Miller's *A Devil in Paradise* and *Nights of Love and Laughter*, Weybright responded to a similar Miller assessment.

I often lie awake at night thinking of the distribution jungle. After a good solid period of visibility in all sorts of outlets, the more bookish books are not abandoned but moved into restricted display in the big outlets with a large number of display pockets—book shops in major department stores, heavy traffic downtown types of shops, and major airports and bus depots. I should say that they dwindle from the original 75,000 outlets, to 10,000, and ultimately to something like 1,500 (the latter being just about double the number of bookshops, genuine bookshops, in the nation). When a book ceases moving, the process begins; but it is still available in select outlets, and on order. For some reason known only to God, some of the best books sometimes prove disappointing; and yet they often respond, later, to re-distribution of returned copies. (19 April 1957)

Another way mass market houses encouraged longer running sales was through reissuing fresh editions, often with new covers. (Truman Talley once summarized this backlist strategy for another concerned author by observing that "titles, including successful ones, have to be rested when the velocity of sales slows down.") When Frederic Melcher, the distinguished editor of *Publishers Weekly*, raised concerns similar to those of Miller, Kurt Enoch, directly responsible for marketing within the company, concluded his defense of the lunar-based system:

There is one additional point which is overlooked most of the time by the critics of our industry. It is the undeniable fact that a great number of books are now available only in paperbound reprints. Even if we are not yet able to keep them on display permanently everywhere, they will appear for an extended period of time at least once and, in the case of more important books, again periodically (by way of reissues) in every one of the approximately 100,000 newsstands. They are therefore exposed to an audience which can never be reached by the traditional book selling practices. What this means for our cultural, educational and overall development of readers, I don't have to tell you, nor do I have to emphasize here the enormous increase of distribution the works of particular authors have gained by these methods. (30 November 1954)

Book returns in the mass market paperback distribution system created an even larger problem for the softcover publishers and eventually for authors and others who shared subsidiary royalties. Paperback books, like hardcover trade books, are sold on a returnable basis.[4] As the industry expanded after World War II, so did the size and percentages of book returns. For some companies these grew from less than 2 percent to a figure that today may average around 50 percent of the total first printing. When publishers failed to accurately project returns, royalty statements, even for authors as popular as Erskine Caldwell, could unwittingly assign royalty overpayments. This occurred if the statement weighed only the number of books sold to distributors as opposed to the number actually sold to readers, that is, if it did not take possible future returns into account. In 1950, however, this pitfall of paperback distribution was unfamiliar to many hardcover publishers. It was summarized by NAL accountant Milton Rosenblitt for the comptroller of Duell, Sloan & Pearce.

The difference between the number of copies printed and sold consists of the inventory still in our warehouse and the inventories in the field (at wholesalers and dealers). On December 31st we had close to a million copies of Caldwell books in our warehouse, a substantial part of which had been printed in advance to have enough copies available for special reorder drives scheduled for January and February. The balance consists of field inventory in the warehouses of over 800 magazine wholesalers and on display or stocked by 100,000 odd dealers. All of these books are returnable. The field inventory figures are based on inventory reports supplied by the wholesalers to our national distributor and, after checking, by him to us. They represent as accurate as possible a statement of unsold books at the end of the royalty accounting. (29 March 1950)

Unjustified royalty projections or overpayments were most disconcerting to authors who based their own projections of future earnings on first printings and early sales. Succeeding royalty statements could show new sales income offset by large returns. The reprinter's own balance sheet could be seriously affected when forwarded royalty payments later were negated by large wholesaler returns. These overpayments were rarely if ever returned to the reprinter. This was one reason why, with an author who had more than one title represented on the company list, the company sought to negotiate future contracts that pooled the author's earnings on

4. In the late fifties and early sixties, publishers began accepting from distributors the stripped front covers of their volumes in lieu of the whole book. This wasteful and widely criticized practice continues today and is the subject of much of the criticism directed at the mass market industry over the last quarter century.

all titles on the publisher's list rather than make payments based on individual title earnings. (See also chapter 6.) Pooling allows the publisher to balance out in any one payment period the plus sales on some titles with the negative sales of heavily returned titles.

One of the few books with a continuous sales history in the editorial files was Lillian Smith's controversial *Strange Fruit*. It was first reprinted by NAL in 1948. Its sales history, while not typical of all Signet books, does indicate something of the pattern and quantities of sales of a strong backlist title in the formative years of the company. The book's first printing was 555,340, and after two additional printings in 1948, 931,473 copies were issued for the year. Returns for the year equaled only 19,760 for a net sale (gross sales minus returns) of 911,713 for its first year as a Signet. (Reprintings in 1948 and 1949, five in all, averaged between 100,000 and 150,000 each.) In 1949, 268,216 copies were sold and returns were even smaller totaling 14,257. However, the following year 535 more books were returned than were sold. And in 1951 and 1952 combined net sales totaled only 4,000 copies. In 1953 an eighth printing and a freshly designed edition were ordered; 172,850 copies of this reissue were manufactured. Gross sales for 1953 totaled 184,344, indicating that copies of older printings were still available and being sold. Returns in 1953 were 1,040 for a 183,634 net sale. This dramatic turnaround in sales demonstrates, among other things, the power of freshly designed paperback reissues in the marketplace. Sales of *Strange Fruit* declined steadily after 1953 and no further printings appeared through mid-1959. At this point 1,547,203 copies of *Strange Fruit* had been sold in softcover and only 146,908 returned for a net sale of slightly under 1.5 million copies. (Returns for the first half of 1959 produced a net sale of minus 75 copies.) Still another newly designed reissue appeared in the latter half of 1959. While its sales figures were not recorded in the NAL archival files, the reissue does seem to confirm the company's faith in the power of freshly covered editions of previously issued titles.[5]

Each paperback title must sell itself at least twice in its life—with the

---

5. It appears from the scattered printing and sales records that Signet reprintings, as opposed to reissues, of established authors such as James Cain, Erskine Caldwell, and William Faulkner were made in fifty-thousand-copy quantities. Because of their more selective and limited distribution, first Mentor printings were much smaller than initial Signet printings. These seem to have averaged between thirty-five thousand and fifty thousand copies.

Mass market publishers today are seldom reluctant to share initial printing, new printing, and reissue figures with the public. However, much to the chagrin of independent industry statisticians, net sales figures are seldom made publicly available. Returns—the difficulties they present in controlling and accounting—explain in great part mass market publishers' reticence at releasing net sales figures.

middleman (i.e., the independent wholesaler or the retail bookseller) who puts the book on retail display and with the ultimate buyer-reader. Since it is usually impractical if not impossible for either the middleman or the buyer-reader to have more than a superficial familiarity with the book, publishers rely on the book's cover design to interest purchasers. Perhaps publishing company personnel direct more attention to cover design and art work than to any other aspect of a paperback publication. The cover is the reference point around which marketing plans evolve. Along with its goal of attracting buyers, the cover also helps define the text.[6] However in doing so, cover design can interpret a work and intentionally or unintentionally mislead potential buyers.

Cover designs played an important part in the early history of NAL, serving as a major factor in its separation from its parent, Penguin Books, Ltd. Pictorial covers were introduced on American Penguin books during World War II when Allen Lane's London supervision of the company was weakest. They were defended by the managers of the American branch as necessary for success in the magazine and newspaper marketplace in which they were competing with flashy and slick-papered periodicals. In contrast, English Penguins displayed the conservative, typographical covers Lane preferred. Lane's opposition to illustrated covers added to the tension that already existed in 1947 between himself on the one hand and Enoch and Weybright on the other. Shortly after the Penguin separation, NAL initiated fresh cover designs with Signet cover illustration that fell somewhere between the exaggerated pulp and the idealized slick magazine styles of its competitors. Later imitated by virtually all of the mass market publishers, these realistic and often somber portrayals of city and rural life initiated the "paperback look" of commercial art.[7]

Besides the front cover illustration, a wrapper design contains the title of the book, the name of the author, and publishing imprint as well as some promotional blurbs about the text and/or its writer. The back cover contains additional blurbs, often quotes from reviews, which further indicate what the book is about. For approximately its first ten years, NAL

6. For a detailed explanation of the creation and function of the paperback cover, one should consult Schreuders or Bonn, *Under Cover.*

7. "Signet had found the exact midpoint of American culture, and had staked out its position there. Whatever contradiction existed between high and low, between literature and exploitation, were to be welded together in a single image. It is the blending of opposite points of view that gives the Signet covers their vitality. At first glance the art work seems part of the usual trashy paperback syndrome. But when you look at it again, the setting comes into focus, the faces are seen to have ambiguous expressions, the instant reading pulp cover has given way to something unsettled and quietly disturbing. The composition is objective, and therefore powerful. It is also designed to sustain a multitude of interpretations, to offer something different to each point of view" (O'Brien 62).

also included some brief biographical information about and a photograph of the author, a practice not followed by other softcover publishers. Some authors saw this general design as particularly well suited to their personal, long-range literary goals. In a brief memo to Enoch's assistant, Hilda Livingston, Weybright passed along a Norman Mailer request forwarded by the author's representative and prominent civil liberties lawyer, Charles Rembar. "Cy Rembar reports that Mailer would like a large photograph of himself on the back cover of *The Deer Park* to establish reader-relationship with him as a personality. I told Cy that it was also important to refer to the book and also to *The Naked and the Dead*, and that it would be useful if Mailer brought in his favorite picture to Marc Jaffe" (13 August 1956).

Also standard on the Signet and Mentor back covers was the company's motto, one that troubled Elliott Arnold, author of the Signet, *Everybody Slept Here*, when he addressed Kurt Enoch. "Your slogan 'Good Reading for the Millions' which appears on the back of your book somehow strikes me as being offensive. "It has a patronizing tone, as though you were implying 'Good Reading for the Common People,' or 'Good Reading for the Poor,' or, even, 'Good Reading for the Proletariat.' "I think the whole thing is contained in the word *the*. 'Good Reading for Millions' is alright, to my ears. The other seems to me to set aside a great block of people as *the* millions, and thus *the* lesser people" (5 August 1950). Enoch was in Europe at the time and Weybright replied for him. " You have a point, but, after trying it on a couple dozen guinea pigs, I find that they infer 'Good Reading for the Millions' as a simple contrast to 'Good Reading for the Few '—and they all prefer the rhythm of the phrase with the article before 'Millions.' Since you are the only one who has thus far raised a point, we are sticking to the slogan as is—but we want you to know we considered seriously the suggestion you made" (14 August 1950).

Like the publisher, most writers focused not on the back but on the front cover, weighing how well the design, especially the illustration, portrayed the book's contents and the writer's aims in producing the work. The authors who were easy to work with editorially were also appreciative of front cover results. Isaac Asimov, never restrained in showing appreciation to his publishers, wrote to Truman Talley shortly after receiving a first printing of his *The Currents of Space* about the finished cover. "The advance copy of the Signet edition arrived and struck me (a) dumb with delight and (b) speechless with gratitude for your thoughtfulness in sending them. I sat back and stared at it for ten minutes—the front, the back, the blurbs, the photo. Boy, did I feel *good*. "And Signet puts out such a damn attractive piece of work. I just feel honored to be one of Signet's writers" (10 December 1953). When Mickey Spillane-protégé Earle Basinsky viewed the cover to his second Signet, his reaction was, "Boy, I bet the original cover art is really something!," and asked Marc Jaffe if he could have it for "home loan." Jaffe replied in his best tough-guy editor style. "Glad you like the looks of *Death Is a Cold, Keen Edge* and I trust that several hundred other folks will be pleased enough, likewise to lay out two-bits for the privilege of reading it. . . . I'll try to pry the original artwork away from the production department " (5 November 1956).

Original cover art often ended up in hands outside of the company and its writers. James Avati's illustration for Ralph Ellison's *Invisible Man* was admired by Springfield, Massachusetts, wholesaler Sam Black who had been involved in defending Signet titles from state censors in the early fifties. Weybright saw some tangible benefits to be derived from a publicized bestowal that would also include the author and the cover artist. He described these in a memo to his marketing people.

> What would you think of an advance presentation of Avati's *Invisible Man* cover to Sam Black, who covets it, and who says he would replace an original *Saturday Evening Post* cover with it in his office?
>
> Since some of the contents of this remarkable novel, which won the National Book Award, might frighten certain wholesalers, it would seem to me worth a special effort to identify Sam Black with the book.
>
> What I would propose is to send Avati and Ralph Ellison, the Negro author, accompanied by a Fawcett and an NAL representative, to present the framed cover in time for it to be photographed as a ceremony in order to publicize the book to wholesalers. As you know, Ralph Ellison and his wife are charming, cooperative people, and an expedition to Springfield, Massachusetts with the Ellisons would be no great strain. TMT [Truman M. Talley], who knows the Ellisons well, or AJP [Arabel J. Porter] might go along.
>
> I would very much like to see a man of Black's strong feelings, vigorously and frequently expressed, identified with some bold high-quality literature which by no stretch of the imagination can be described as trash. (13 April 1953)

Throughout the late forties and fifties, the portrayal of sexual themes on paperback covers accounted for much of the marketing success of popular fiction but at the same time fixed on softcover publishing a coarse and earthy image that haunts it even today. As might be expected, authors would be in the forefront with objections to the racy visual interpretations that surrounded their texts. Some, like novelist Carl Bottume, author of

181

Sailor's Choice, were able to take it somewhat in stride as we learn from his note to his NAL editor, Marc Jaffe.

> First of all, let me congratulate you on the arrival of Nina. It is the first time to my knowledge that an editor has named his daughter after one of his author's heroines. Deeply honored.
>
> In the second place, let me thank you for the pre-publication copies. With the cover I believe you have established a new trend. Prior to my book, the girl usually had two protruding breasts, one or the other exposed or both, depending on expected sales. Now some genius on your staff has turned her about and exposed two buttocks. Revolutionary! But where do you go from here? (21 January 1953)

Jaffe's reply was drafted in the same facetious vein. It offered a prediction of future paperback covers, which has undoubtedly been carried out by some softcover publisher, though probably not NAL. "Thanks for your note acknowledging receipt of the two copies of *Sailor's Choice*. We did an extensive study before preparing the cover for the book and our researchers turned up the fact that there is a definite trend toward the appreciation of callipygian attractions. You ask where we go from here. The only direction to go is down, so that some of our future covers undoubtedly will be directed toward the foot fetishists in our audience. "P.S. The daughter is fine and equally honored to bear the name of one of your heroines" (3 February 1953).

Perhaps no author was as bitterly critical of paperback covers as James T. Farrell. Farrell believed that early editions of his works published by NAL and Avon were misrepresented by the covers, citing as an example the 1952 Signet edition of *A World I Never Made*. "It pictures a whorehouse which was never seen on land or sea, with open doors, and two girls, one with a sheet on her and one with thighs more bone than flesh; there is a boy who is a cliché of the newsboy of the 1890s, plus a few other characters, none of whom has anything to do with *A World I Never Made*." In 1959 Farrell, who had been quarreling with his publisher over his royalty advances, offered Weybright some recommendations on what should appear on the cover of a proposed Farrell Signet.

> Walter Freeman tells me that you are publishing *An Old Sweetheart* within six months. I am writing to ask that I get different treatment on the cover and the blurb, and that I see both well in advance of publication. I would prefer not to have any picture at all on the

jacket, and most decidedly do not want anything comparable to the very rotten blurbs I've gotten on my past books.

In the past, my books have been inaccurately described and my work has been reduced to the level of moron reading. This has hurt me very much in my career and is one of the reasons why I have had so much trouble in the last couple of years. It has created a false image of me as a Chicago writer who doesn't know anything. Sex has been referred to in a way that is misleading; violence and fighting have also been over-emphasized and nonsense has been said about the Chicago South Side. I am asking that my books be treated with some dignity and respect.

Such blurbs and pictures do not help the books to succeed, and I am certain that they had much to do with *French Girls Are Vicious* [Signet, 1956] and *A Dangerous Woman* [Signet, 1957] being failures; as a consequence I'll be in hock to you for life.

On what grounds, other than possibly an unconscious wish to degrade me, have my books been given this treatment? I do want whatever books of mine you publish from now on to be treated differently—as well as you treat your classics. (4 November 1959)

Weybright's reply was quick and direct, presenting in the second paragraph an idealized principle in regard to authorship and publishing.

Please, please don't be such a scold! No publisher has ever had more concern for you as a person or your writings as the finest expression of American literature. If we have any unconscious wish concerning you it is to elevate you, not degrade you. I can assure you that *An Old Sweetheart* will have respected and respectable cover and blurb treatment. It is totally unfair to judge the covers of a decade ago in terms of today. Then, we were wooing new and uninitiated book readers. Today, thanks to our aggressive selling of the best books at the lowest price, the habit is established.

We have to be free to publish without interference, just as authors must be free to write without interference.

Don't forget, Jim, that I lived in Chicago in part of your period there, as a resident of Hull-House, and a student of the University, not unfamiliar with the South Side. I bring to your work not only the general perception of an editor, but the first-hand appreciation of your milieu. (9 November 1959)

Three months later Weybright read a clipping from the *San Francisco Chronicle* dated 14 February 1960. Not intended as a valentine to NAL, the piece—an interview with James Farrell—presented, among other things, the writer's observation that "the nation's taste is so deformed by the flood of cheap paperbacks that serious works cannot be sold." Farrell, who by that time had over two dozen titles in paperback, stated further that "lurid-jacketed paperbacks are being overproduced by more than 150 million a year" and as a result are "being dumped abroad, especially in England and Australia, giving these countries a false impression of America." He went on to offer his own mocking solution: "These half-draped women on the covers—they don't know how to dress. If I were a dictator I'd drown them all. And the males, mostly dope addicts, I'd shoot as something not human."

NAL, like most softcover publishers, tried to avoid showing cover designs to authors and original hardcover publishers until the book came off the press. In a letter to NAL's West Coast representative Ted Loeff, Truman Talley summarized this rationale. "There are so many ways to skin a cat promotionally that what we do and what an author thinks ought to be done are seldom quite the same animal. If our jackets are attractive, and most of them are, a published example has that nice feeling of finality about it that will spare you or ourselves getting into lengthy explanations by mail" (20 August 1961).

The heavy-handed, sexually oriented covers of the late forties and early fifties did prompt concern and criticism from outside and inside book publishing. Industry spokesperson and *Publishers Weekly* editor, Frederic Melcher, was among those who believed that sensational cover designs had much more to do with the denunciations rather than the contents of the books themselves. Referring to one of the few successfully prosecuted censoring cases of this time, Melcher summarized his concern to Weybright: "I know that you and [Ian] Ballantine think that I have gone on the prudish side about jacket covers of 25¢ books, but I have this matter of atmosphere in my mind and not my own reading interest. The presentation of any number of jackets which are trying to carry a suggestion even beyond that which is justified by the texts is not good for the immediate situation that faces pocket-book distribution . . . and I am, as you know, definitely interested in the maintenance of the prestige of these books" (25 August 1950).

Some hardcover publishers insisted on cover approval clauses in their reprint contracts with all softcover publishers. Such a clause might simply read, "New American Library shall submit to the Seller jacket design and promotion copy for its approval which shall not unreasonably be withheld." But as Joseph C. Lesser, treasurer at Knopf, explained to Victor Weybright, this type of clause did not seem to be strong enough.

This business of yours is becoming more and more difficult to deal with through no fault of yours, I am sure. Some of the twenty-five cent reprint people had adopted a new gag to sell their books on the basis of sex appeal. On the page opposite the title page of the book they will reprint the "hottest" episode in the book as a kind of come-on. Taken out of context, these episodes are frequently so erotic as to invite prosecution under the obscenity laws, and this manner of setting up the book practically destroys the basis for invoking the rule that a book is to be judged as a whole and that the sexual episodes may not be isolated from the context in ascertaining whether the work violates the law against obscenity.

Although we now insert in our twenty-five cent reprint contracts a provision that we have a right of approval with respect to the contents of the front and back covers of the paper edition, this right of approval will not cover the practice to which I have referred above. Our attorneys have therefore suggested the following clause be inserted in future agreements: "The Proprietor shall have the right of approval of cover design of the reprint edition, of all illustrations therein, and of all textual matter descriptive of, referring to, or taken from the text of the work, which appears either in the front or back cover of the reprint edition or elsewhere in the reprint edition before the first page of the text of the work or after the last page of the text thereof."

The only alternative would be to delete the Seller's guarantee and warranty against any obscenity actions. I'm asking all the twenty-five cent reprint people to accept this clause in future contracts. I hope you will agree, too. (27 November 1951)

Lesser and his colleagues at Knopf believed that without cover and copy approval their company was at greater risk of expensive litigation. Common contractual clauses with reprinters required proprietary publishers taking part in defense against censors. Lesser feared being dragged into a case over a book (issued without incident in hardcover) whose sensational softcover reprint wrapper would draw the attention and ire of censoring groups.

Reader reaction to cover art, as noted earlier, could also be jocular or vitriolic. A few were neither, offering instead a considered analysis of the cover art and its reflection on the text, as was this letter from a professor of art history at Rutgers.

There is one aspect of your publication that could be improved, however, and that is the book cover. In my opinion, for what it's worth, this definitely harms the value of the service you have rendered. *1984* is not really a novel; rather it is a philosophical treatise, a disquisition on the nature of freedom and the nature of power, in novel form. That is what makes it a great book. But from the illustration on the cover, and the by-lines which accompany it, one might believe that it is merely a sensational, run-of-the-mill thriller. I don't think that this does the book any service. Those who buy the book thinking they are going to get a vicarious, erotic stimulus from it will be disappointed. And the by-lines may well discourage serious readers from looking into it; if they haven't heard of it, they will pick it up thinking it is on the Erskine Caldwell level. . . . I feel very strongly that Orwell's is a book that should be as widely known as possible, and wish that the cover were more appropriate. If you intend putting out a second printing in this edition, I hope you will consider the matter of redesigning the cover. (21 October 1950)

The reply he received summarized the basic rebuttal paperback publishers offered when facing criticism of covers that misrepresented the text within. (See fig. 7, p. 109). In a convenient blend of idealism and commercialism that slides around the misrepresentation issue, Hilda Livingston argued that the end, reader entrapment, justified the cover as a means. "I'm delighted with your enthusiasm for the Signet edition of George Orwell's novel, *1984*. The book has been a great success in our edition and undoubtedly a large part of its sale has been caused by people who have never heard of Orwell or his work but were attracted by the illustration on the cover. Although we may disagree on what makes a good book cover I am glad we are united on the importance of bringing Orwell's message to the mass audience" (26 October 1950).

Reissued paperbacks distributed many months or years after the initial softcover edition often carry a fresh front cover design. Changes in cover design tend to give reissues a more contemporary look. They tend to elicit larger orders from wholesalers than those obtained without new cover designs. Cover changes can also signal an attempt to reach an audience different from the first one that the softcover publisher intended to attract with the initial cover. For instance a reissued cover might project the content of a mystery when the book originally carried a cover designed to attract gothic romance readers. A tie-in to a film production was still another opportunity for the cover to reinterpret the work within. Putting a book into a school- and college-oriented series, as NAL did in 1959 when it began Signet Classics, generally means designing more conservative or less representational art work for the reissued publication. This, incidentally, did occur to *1984* when it was reissued as a Signet Classic in the early sixties.

In the first thirty years or so of mass market publishing, softcover reprinters seldom used the art work that originally appeared on the dust jacket of the initial hardcover. Usually more conservative in its approach to complementing the text, dust jackets were seen as appealing to a more book-oriented audience, who often based purchase decisions on reviews and word of mouth.[8] Today, as then, paperback books are sold mainly by display; each is in competition with the titles in its category in the pockets alongside each other. To be successful, each has to call attention to itself—not unlike a poster or billboard.

The more important the book, the more likely that the publisher assigned the cover illustration to the most talented artist available. Throughout most of the fifties, James Avati was considered the best in the industry, and for a good part of this time, he was under exclusive contract with NAL. His painting style, once described by Weybright as Rembrandt-like, was imitated in the cover designs of most of the other paperback houses giving birth to the "paperback look" category of commercial art. In 1950 he undertook what was probably the most important assignment of his career up to that time, illustrating *Knock on Any Door*, the Willard Motley title that inaugurated the Signet Double Volumes. In a letter to Samuel Rapport of Appleton-Century-Crofts, Weybright describes how Avati carried out the illustration assignment after reading the text.

I'm glad you are as enthusiastic about our cover for *Knock on Any Door* as we are. It was done by James Avati, our best cover artist, exclusively working for us in the paperbound field, and the most competent man we have ever known in grasping and rendering the mood as well as the drama of important fiction. He posed his models on a street in New York as near to a Chicago street in atmosphere as he could discover, and worked from his photographs and notes made on the spot. What is equally important, he read the book thoroughly and discussed

8. Since the late seventies, the design of hardcover dust jackets, particularly for popular fiction, seems to have turned around. Many new hardcover jackets display the same design formulas as mass market paperback covers. Much of this has to do with the expansion of chain bookstores and the corresponding greater opportunities offered hardcover books for sale through attractive display to the same audience that is attracted to paperbacks. To many within the book industry, the distinctions today between hardcover and softcover book audiences are very slight.

ideas for a cover before even embarking on his preliminary sketches and posing his models.

Avati works in oil, on cardboard, blocking out his first color sketch—for color—with his live models, and using his reference photographs as he completes his assignment. (17 July 1950)

The original Avati art work for the cover was given to the author. Willard Motley's description of where the painting to his *Knock on Any Door* was first placed must have certainly amused the editor in chief.

Thank you very much for sending on to me the original painting for the Signet cover of my book *Knock on Any Door*. I'm delighted with the cover and the truly fine edition of the book that you have published. . . . I think that both you and the artist will be pleased to know that the painting is hanging temporarily in the tavern next door. The owner asked if he might exhibit it for a while and several people have wanted to buy it from me. The tavern owner has also bought a dozen copies of the Signet edition and is selling them across the bar. This, to me, seems somewhat in keeping with the atmosphere of the book. (31 August 1950)

In the late spring of 1951, Hiram Haydn, then Bobbs-Merrill's New York editor, announced to the book trade the discovery of a major writing talent, William Styron. Supporting Haydn's appraisal were statements from a variety of prominent literary and book industry personalities, including one from George Salter, perhaps the most influential hardcover jacket designer of the mid-twentieth century. Salter, who was preparing the dust jacket for *Lie Down in Darkness* (see fig. 8, p. 110), Styron's first novel, supplied a long quote describing how much the manuscript impressed him. Weybright was quick to acquire the novel for the Signet list. But Bobbs-Merrill and the young author were both concerned about the nature of the paperback cover that NAL would employ. The art work was assigned to Avati. To counter any outside reservations, Weybright took the unusual step of having the cover artist describe to the hardcover publisher his arrangement of the illustration and his own personal enthusiasm for the title. This excerpt, from Avati's letter, sounds like a counterpoint to the Salter endorsement; it was directed at Ross Baker of Bobbs-Merrill.

The enclosed photo was selected and heartily endorsed by all here concerned with, however, the reservation that the character on the bed wear some kind of undershirt. We have discussed other approaches, particularly having some more symbolism with regard to the family's dilemma but felt cold to such treatment. . . . The reader with a lazy mind needs some extra stimulus to get him over some of the parts, and a very earthy enticement to persuade him to enter these tragic premises.

I (now) hope you are pleased with this. Mr. Styron has my sincerest admiration. In this scene of degradation, I find the same emotional values as in *Crime and Punishment*. I have been caught up in this story. I think it's great. (14 August 1952)

The author's reaction to the final cover is recorded in a letter that NAL received from the author's father, William Clark Styron, affirming, if nothing else, that beauty is in the eye of the beholder, if not of the author.

Your kind letter of October 31 and the two copies of my son's novel *Lie Down in Darkness* have been received, and I thank you very much for presenting the copies to me, gratis.

I quote from the first letter that Bill wrote me from Rome: "I've gotten a proof of the jacket of the jumbo economy-sized Signet Double Volume which will appear in November on which a wan, sad, half-clad Peyton is seen on the verge of climbing into bed with one of the most unsavory looking Italians you ever saw—*sic transit gloria literary* but it will sell 250,000 copies and my stock will soar in Peoria."

While parts of my son's observation may be to the point I should like to compliment you people and the artist on how well one phase of the doomed girl's life has been depicted on the cover. It is just as I had imagined the girl and her milk-man would look in the flesh, and I should like for you to pass on to the cover designer my congratulations. (6 November 1952)

Few authors reacted more bitterly to their Signet cover designs than Richard Bissell. After viewing cover proofs of his *Pajama*, the author wrote to Weybright.

I think I had better quit unburdening myself to Hilda Livingston and tell you directly that I am suffering extreme mental torture as a result of seeing the cover you propose to put on *Pajama*. I am not kidding.

In my opinion and the opinion of my wife and associates the characters portrayed can only be described as obscene. Hilda says that perhaps the artist conceived the characters a little differently

189

than I did. That is true. I did not conceive of Sid as a pimp and Babe his whore, or something worse. I resent bitterly, after working to build my reputation as a writer, to be thus tossed into the cesspool with all the smut writers in the country. (18 April 1954)

Weybright immediately responded to Bissell, a writer in whom NAL saw a great future.

Even before your letter of April 18th arrived, we had taken measures . . . to meet your criticism of the *Pajama* cover. The scene remains, but the man has been altered: his hat removed, his tie neatly in place, etc. The girl's sweater has been more modestly fitted. . . .

I can understand the strain under which you are working in your present incarnation as a dramatist, which certainly must account for the sharpening of your critical outlook on the world, including cover artwork. I can assure you that we respect, admire and value your work, and knowingly or subconsciously, would never want to detract from it in any manner of presentation which would harm your standing or sales. It's the nearest thing to Mark Twain since Sam Clemens departed the American scene. (21 April 1954)

In this instance it appears that the flattery and cover revisions were successful. NAL issued two additional Bissell titles after *Pajama*.

For many Americans who grew up as part of the fifties paperback generation, the Signet cover of *The Catcher in the Rye*—Holden Caulfield, suitcase in hand, red hunting cap affixed, on an odyssey down New York's mean streets—is an icon of adolescence (see fig. 9, p. 110). This edition firmly established Salinger as one of the most revered American writers.[9] Perhaps no cover in the history of publishing, however, stirred up more controversy and acrimony. It contributed directly to the permanent division of the author from NAL, the company that did the most to secure his popularity. Weybright completed negotiations with Arthur H. Thornhill, Sr. of Little, Brown for *The Catcher in the Rye* by observing: "It is a special pleasure to enclose herewith signed copies of the reprint agreement on *The Catcher in the Rye* by J. D. Salinger—a book which has given me more sheer pleasure than anything I have read this year. I congratulate you on

---

9. It was reprinted at least seventeen times in eight years, selling close to two million copies.

discovering Salinger and launching him as surely one of the most gifted writers of all the young novelists today" (4 June 1951).

From the outset it appeared that the author had reservations about any illustration that might appear on the Signet edition. At Weybright's invitation, Salinger submitted his own cover concept. Salinger saw a cover built around the scene at New York Central Park's carousel. He did not wish for either Holden Caulfield or his sister to be illustrated since neither was described in the book. Salinger recommended that his protagonist be illustrated sitting in the rain on a park bench. Caulfield would be wearing his red hunting cap and his back would be turned. Weybright at first seemed receptive to the concept: "I'm very grateful indeed to you for your suggestion concerning the cover for the reprint edition of *Catcher in the Rye*. It's a good idea, and James Avati, our best man on covers, is now working on it." The editor in chief's satisfaction is further confirmed with this letter to Thornhill, written the same day as his acknowledgment to Salinger.

> When it came time to tackle the question of a cover for *Catcher* I asked John Woodburn to see if Salinger himself could produce an idea. He did—a charming one. I am enclosing a copy of Salinger's letter. When Avati has completed the art work I shall send a photostat of it, and the attendant blurbs for clearance.
>
> Ordinarily, we would never want to seek, or rely upon, an author's advice on a cover; but we don't want to stray far from the author's desires in this case, since rumor has it that he is very finicky on matters involving his work. (31 March 1952)

Avati reacted sensitively to Salinger's concept but rejected it in this letter to Weybright.

> The cover suggestion of the author, Salinger, for *Catcher in the Rye* appeals strongly to those of us who have read the story. It would compose well, too. Perhaps it might sell. It is impossible to be dogmatic about such things, *but* . . . it seems both too anonymous and too enigmatic for immediate understanding by anyone who has not already met Holden.
>
> Here then is a suggestion on our part. Let us show him coming down Broadway or Forty-second Street expressing his pained reaction to people who LIKE movies, etc. He is very much a definable personality, a foil to the crowd. And the crowd in its varied normality and the theater background, exciting, suggestive, provides lures which will attract a very broad audience of readers.

Mr. Salinger felt that since he had not described Holden in physical detail his face should not appear on the cover. We have always had that problem. It is, in fact, quite frequently the core of our cover thinking, to the extent that it is the resolution of personality as expressed by some graphic device that makes up the cover. We try to find a way of conveying the mood of the book rather than describing some particular scene. Within reasonable limits it has proved true that physical characteristics are of much less importance than reactions expressed. (3 April 1952)

Again, Weybright informs Thornhill.

James Avati has submitted his comment on the Salinger cover with the attached memorandum, which I strongly commend to you for approval on behalf of the author. I still feel, and so does Mr. Avati, that Salinger's suggestion is a charming one—and apt—but I am convinced that the Avati alternative is far superior for a paper-bound book. It's consistent with every intention of the author except, perhaps, the revelation of Holden's physiognomy—and is still a far cry from the usual run of paper-bound art work, and in rendition would reflect the flavor and purpose of the book, without a disturbing element.

As we think about it, we feel more than we did at first that Mr. Salinger's suggestion would look like a cross between the *New Yorker* cover and a juvenile book rather than like a substantial modern novel. It would make an excellent inside illustration, but it fails to express universally recognizable sentiment.

I feel sure that you will cooperate on this matter—which may make a considerable difference in sales—and we, in turn, will comply with your desires as to our schedule for the Signet reprint. (3 April 1952)

Obtaining approval from the author was very difficult and took an extraordinarily long time. In the spring of 1953 Salinger met at the NAL offices with Avati, Weybright, and others about the cover design. After a long, drawn-out session Salinger reluctantly agreed to the Avati concept and illustration.

About this same time NAL was negotiating with Little, Brown for a collection of nine Salinger short stories, all which had appeared in the *New Yorker*. Aware of the company's reluctance to publish short story collections, Truman Talley urged Enoch and Weybright to acquire them, commenting that "they are superb . . . [and] as a collection, the book would grace any publisher's list." Talley reminded them that in the past, in order to retain a prestigious young writer, it had been company practice to reprint the author's short stories as a follow-up to the first novel. (He cited Truman Capote as an example.)[10] By the time the meeting about the cover for *The Catcher in the Rye* took place, NAL had acquired *Nine Stories* as well. Salinger left this meeting believing he had won at least one concession from the reprinter—the short story collection would carry purely a typographical cover. When preparations for production of the short stories began, however, NAL personnel appear to have forgotten the agreement; an illustrated cover was sketched for *Nine Stories*. With a memo to Salinger agent, Ivan von Auw, Marc Jaffe delivered the proposed design. "I'm sending along herewith by messenger a package containing the layout for our proposed cover for *Nine Stories*, and the sample art work which I showed you a week or so ago. Would you forward these to Mr. Salinger? "Undoubtedly you will write him an accompanying letter and I wish you would emphasize the fact that the portraits in the layout are only to indicate placement. The characterization will be completely different by the time we get finished art work (as per the sample)" (2 January 1954). The reaction from the author, as reported in a Marc Jaffe memo to Weybright and Enoch, was predictable.

Yesterday, the rough layout and sample art work which we had pre-pared for *Nine Stories*, by J. D. Salinger, was returned by the author's agent. The agent had written to Salinger asking if he wanted to see this material and Salinger politely declined. He remembered, as a matter of fact, that at a conference in VW's office, when the approval for the cover of *The Catcher in the Rye* was obtained, NAL had agreed to use a typographical jacket on the "next book." This turned out to be *Nine Stories*. Since there was this agreement, it seemed to the author unnecessary to even look at any jacket design containing realistic illustration. The meeting to which Salinger referred was attended by KE, VW, MHJ [Marc H. Jaffe], Arthur Thornhill, Stanley Salmen [a Little, Brown executive], and the author. By coincidence, Salmen was in the Little, Brown office in New York when the communication mentioned above came down from Salinger. He also remembered that we agreed to use a typographical jacket.

All this puts us somewhat on the spot in connection with our promotion of *Nine Stories*. The proposed cover copy has been approved and we must decide immediately whether to go ahead

10. Capote's 1949 Signet reprint of *Other Voices, Other Rooms* was followed by the 1951 reprint of his short story collection *A Tree of Night*.

and do as strong a typographical-design jacket as possible, or try to convince Little, Brown and the author that an illustrative approach is necessary, *in spite* of our earlier agreement. (29 January 1954)

Weybright's reaction appears to have been swift and unsympathetic. It was handwritten on the bottom of Jaffe's memo and apparently forwarded to Enoch. "There is no such general agreement—besides that our illustrations are only supplementary ornaments to the basically typographical cover. We have paid a high royalty guarantee and cannot permit to be handicapped in our sales effort by an *unreasonable* attitude of the author. I suggest KE make a very strong point of this with Little, Brown" (n.d.). This episode over the *Nine Stories* cover apparently ended with a compromise that seems to have favored the author. Their agreement is summarized in a memo from Weybright to Enoch's assistant, Hilda Livingston: "Today in conference with Arthur Thornhill it was agreed that a dramatic typographical cover would be substituted for illustrations or decoration on the present cover—and that if sales were disappointing Little, Brown would make an adjustment in our guarantee on the next Salinger book—a novel which we have under option" (5 February 1954).

Apparently neither NAL nor Salinger's agent, Ivan von Auw, were fully aware of how deeply Salinger resented the cover deliberations. This became dramatically apparent, however, in the summer of 1959 when NAL was anxious to put *The Catcher in the Rye* into its Signet Classics series. After a disturbing discussion with Salinger's agent, Arabel Porter wrote to Arthur H. Thornhill, Sr. at Little, Brown.

We should like to publish a Signet Classic edition of *The Catcher in the Rye* by J. D. Salinger. . . .

I spoke to Ivan von Auw about this, thinking he might elicit from Mr. Salinger some suggestions for a cover for this edition. I gather that Mr. Salinger was not responsive—to put it mildly. I told Mr. Ivan that we would drop the idea, simply continuing the edition we are already selling. But Mr. Ivan encouraged me *not* to abandon the idea. He suggested that if we simply submitted a cover sketch and blurb copy for approval, in the normal way, through you, Mr. Salinger might be amenable. (We are working on three cover suggestions right now, and I shall get them to you by early next week.)

I gather from Mr. von Auw that Salinger does not view with pleasure the thought of a foreword or afterword, even by an esteemed critic. Therefore, we shall definitely plan not to have either. (12 August 1959)

On this same day Porter also reported on some office discussions with NAL's direct sales manager, Maizie Halpern, about the back cover. "Maizie likes the typographical cover, as presented by Bill Gregory [NAL's art director]. She further suggests we use a photo of Salinger on the back. However, TMT reminds me that Salinger refused to permit his photo on earlier paper editions. We could ask again, but perhaps it would be better to handle his countenance in a line drawing as we do with the other Signet Classics" (12 August 1959). The last piece of correspondence in the NAL archival files about Salinger is a terse memo jointly signed by Truman Talley and Peter Gruenthal, Kurt Enoch's son-in-law, who was in charge of NAL's book production department. "Please drop *The Catcher in the Rye* from the February, 1960 list of Signet Classics. This title will probably not reappear on future Signet Classic lists due to unusual author-trade publisher-NAL relationship" (17 August 1959).

NAL continued to sell both *Nine Stories* and *The Catcher in the Rye* (whose seven-year-old, illustrated cover was becoming dated) for approximately two more years. In 1961 Little, Brown published a third Salinger title, *Franny and Zooey*, which stayed on the bestseller lists for two consecutive years. Reportedly at the insistence of Salinger, NAL's contracts for the earlier titles were not renewed. Like his future reprints, the former NAL titles were optioned to Bantam Books, which continues to publish them to this day—with typographical covers designed by J. D. Salinger.

10

"I Am Not Paternalistic, Dear Old Boy"

Throughout the seventeen years of company growth that I focus on, New American Library's relationships with three writers—Erskine Caldwell, Mickey Spillane, and Irving Wallace—demonstrate the degree of influence and range of control a publisher, generally identified as a reprinter of another company's authors, has on a writer's career and publications. With each of these writers, the company attempted to achieve some degree of "exclusivity." NAL's relationship with these three writers argues for closer scrutiny of the exchanges between authors and their softcover publishers, exchanges largely ignored in current gatekeeper examinations of the book industry.

The "blockbuster" sales of the first two writers—Caldwell and Spillane—not only achieved financial stability for the company, enabling it to pay off its substantial loans, but they allowed it to sing a siren promise of substantial future royalties to proprietary publisher, agent, and author. This call did not go unheeded. As a result, reprint arrangements promoted curious intrusions into the traditional relationship between hardcover publishers and their writers. As seen in the earlier chapters, by the close of the fifties the company had itself become heavily committed to proprietary publishing and was beginning to compete directly with trade book publishers for writing talent. The Wallace excerpts in this final chapter amplify this editorial direction and present the bizarre situation of the company being labeled as the contriver as well as the gatekeeper of literary work.

* * *

"There is not now, nor never will be, we feel, any more important item on the NAL agenda than the works of Erskine Caldwell," Victor Weybright observed to Arthur H. Thornhill, Sr. of Little, Brown (12 January 1953). Caldwell's sales successes contributed, albeit unwittingly, to the fortunate separation of the American Penguin imprint from its English parent company. Between the NAL and the American Penguin imprints, more than thirty different Caldwell titles were issued. Caldwell was the paperback industry's first bestselling writer with literary credentials. Sales of his softcover editions of *God's Little Acre* rank among the highest of modern paperback publishing. In the late forties and early fifties, NAL was fond of calling him on its publications and promotion material, "the world's bestselling writer."[1]

During his twenty-year tenure with the company, Weybright gave no other author under his care more personal attention. Most was given enthusiastically, even when Caldwell sales declined and then leveled out in the latter half of the fifties and in the sixties. In 1953 Weybright wrote that there was a "natural affinity between Erskine Caldwell and Kurt and myself, as working partners in a common interest." Primary in that common interest were economic concerns, which Weybright described to Little, Brown's Arthur H. Thornhill, Sr. "No one can touch him [Caldwell] for literary earnings from paper-bound reprints. It is very easy for Pocket Books to talk about 50 million copies of Erle Stanley Gardner. They are including the war-time figures, pre-1945. Skinny [Erskine Caldwell] is top man in the marketplace today. His sales since 1945 exceed Erle Stanley Gardner's, and when the final tally is made Caldwell's works will far surpass 50 million copies of Gardner now being advertised by Pocket Books" (12 November 1953).

But there was more than just a mutual interest in large sales and making money that tied "Skinny" Caldwell to Weybright. Weybright, who first introduced the author to his fourth wife, Virginia, summarized their affinity in a radio introduction he delivered in 1957 to accompany a Caldwell reading of his short story "Where the Girls Were Different ": "Erskine Caldwell and I are contemporaries, born in the same year, 1903. We shared somewhat similar experiences in our early lives. We each come from rustic upland South, from comparatively simple and pious backgrounds, and we each studied a while at the University of Pennsylvania. Erskine Caldwell became a writer, one of the great American authors of the first half of the twentieth century. By good chance—indeed by a great deal of calculation and negotiation—I became Erskine Caldwell's reprint publisher " (n.d.).

The NAL records show direct and personal correspondence between

1. By the close of 1960 NAL had issued almost 60 million copies of various Caldwell titles in Signet. It had also arranged for the foreign publication of 278 different editions in twenty-nine different countries.

the publisher and the author began as early as 1947. By 1949 an agreement had been signed stating that no matter who published Caldwell in hardcover, NAL would be his exclusive softcover publisher.[2] This was not a proprietary arrangement but appears to have simply tried to ensure that all Caldwell paperback editions would bear an NAL imprint. As a frequent recipient of carbon copies of author-agent and author-hardcover publisher correspondence, Weybright, throughout his tenure at NAL, often served as a referee for problems and issues that arose between these other gatekeepers and the writer. In effect, beginning in the late forties, Weybright and NAL controlled the publication of almost all Caldwell literary properties despite their not being proprietors.[3]

Caldwell's confidence and trust in NAL and in Weybright was partially based on the vigor with which the paperback publisher defended Caldwell's works from the attacks of censors, including the encouragement and support the company gave to the eight hundred wholesale distributors, often the primary targets for censoring groups, to continue distributing the writer's controversial books. In the 1953 letter to Arthur H. Thornhill, Sr. quoted above, Weybright outlined for Little, Brown (then about to become Caldwell's latest hardcover and proprietary publisher) NAL's strategy on Caldwell censorship. The editor in chief also revealed his belief—a theory that appears at other places in the NAL correspondence as well—that much of the criticism was inspired by rival paperback imprints.

When we first undertook Caldwell's works for reprint, we realized that it would require the utmost courage and statesmanship to uphold Caldwell against attack, suppression and censorship. We did not anticipate, however, that the nastiest whispering campaign against Caldwell would come from our eminent competitors who, now that we've built up Caldwell as the most important literary property in reprint, would like to pinch him off for themselves. . . .

When we took on Caldwell's works for reprint, we did not passively and negatively simply wait to defend his work, when and where attacked. We spent more time and money than any other

2. Caldwell was published by a number of hardcover houses during his writing career. In the late forties, NAL dealt with Duell, Sloan & Pearce. Throughout most of the fifties, he was published by Little, Brown, but at the end of the decade, he moved to Farrar, Straus. Succeeding Maxim Lieber in 1951, Caldwell's agent through most of the fifties and into the sixties was James Oliver Brown. Brown was assisted by John Van Bibber.

3. A 9 November 1960 Weybright memo informs NAL executive staff that Caldwell's *Jenny by Nature* "is under direct control of New American Library and arrangements are being completed for Farrar, Straus & Cudahy to bring out the prior hardcover simultaneously with Heinemann in England, with as much fresh promotion as possible."

paper reprint publisher has ever spent on a single property, to acquaint wholesalers with Caldwell's genuinely wholesome American personality, and to establish his writing as significant enough to withstand the attacks of censors. We endeavored to establish Erskine Caldwell's part of the folkways of the new generation of readers, most of whom are accustomed to slick magazines, not widely acquainted with the bolder content of books.

I don't think that anyone at Duell, Sloan & Pearce [Caldwell's previous hardcover publishers] would deny that we did more than they to prevent the complete suppression of Caldwell's works and accomplish their wide distribution in inexpensive form. (12 January 1953)

As with Mickey Spillane, NAL's other early author whose books sold multimillions of copies, NAL frequently fought off the publishing overtures Fawcett Publications made to Erskine Caldwell. In the late forties Caldwell submitted to Duell, Sloan & Pearce a manuscript with a Maine setting. One of Caldwell's first book-length attempts, it had been rejected by Scribner's years earlier. At this time Duell, Sloan & Pearce was also hesitant to be its initial sponsor. Fawcett, whose distribution wing had help make Caldwell "the world's bestselling author," learned about the manuscript and approached Caldwell with an offer to issue it in their new Gold Medal imprint. In the spring of 1950 Weybright reminded Caldwell that no matter what Duell, Sloan & Pearce decided, NAL had first paperback option on the work. *A Lamp for Nightfall* eventually appeared in a Duell, Sloan, & Pearce hardcover imprint in 1952 and two years later in a Signet softcover. In 1955 Fawcett was replaced as NAL's national distributor. At midyear Weybright learned that NAL's rival was again romancing Caldwell, offering to publish his latest novel, *Gretta*, as a Gold Medal paperback. In a terse letter to his editorial counterpart at Fawcett, Ralph Daigh, Weybright emphatically reaffirmed that "Mr. Caldwell is under exclusive contract with NAL for the publication of all his work in paperbound form, and is hence not free to enter into any other agreements." Little, Brown issued a hardcover edition that same year; *Gretta* was published as a Signet reprint the following year.

To NAL's dismay, however, Fawcett had gotten Caldwell to endorse a pair of Gold Medal titles and had then used the testimonials as cover blurbs. When Weybright finally objected, the author ceased the approbations. In 1958, however, Fawcett's Ralph Daigh approached John Van Bibber, who was an associate of Caldwell's agent, James Oliver Brown. Daigh proposed that Caldwell become a Fawcett "editorial adviser" for a retainer of one hundred dollars per week. "The result would be a small number of publications issued annually by Fawcett which would be in a series tentatively entitled "Erskine Caldwell Selects." Daigh further explained:

This legend would be prominent on the cover and most likely at the top over the book title.

The author's name would appear under the book title clearly and legibly but presumably not in as large type as was used for Mr. Caldwell's name.

Somewhere else in the volume, either on the fly leaf or on the back of the cover, would be an explanation that Mr. Caldwell has selected this book for publication, or even worked with the author on its revision, and that he believed it a good book in its field, worthy of reading.[4] (27 December 1957)

An initial verbal Fawcett offer had already been made directly to Caldwell. He appears to have wanted to accept it. At this time the sales of his books had declined. Caldwell was justifiably concerned, however, about NAL's reaction to the Fawcett offering, but he concluded in a letter to his agent that "the present offer is a financial one, and I must consider it as I would any other commercial offer in my field." Once Weybright became aware of the situation his reaction, also directed at Van Bibber, was swift and indignant.

I was shocked to receive Friday afternoon, the carbon copy of Erskine Caldwell's letter to you concerning Roscoe Fawcett 's overture. This is a violation of the code of responsible publishers. It shows Fawcett's pernicious tendency to capitalize on another fellow's success, rather than compete straightforwardly by developing distinctive literary properties of their own. If you think this is a strong statement, I would be glad to enlighten you further.

So far as Skinny is concerned I think his decision is a moral one, not a commerical one.

We shall have to rely on James Brown Associates, as a reputable literary agency, to advise Skinny on the ethics of the proposed project, and I trust that you will keep us informed of

---

4. In September 1955 after examining a Caldwell cover endorsement for a Dell anthology, *Local Color*, Weybright wrote to Caldwell: "I have just noted your August correspondence with Kurt about *Local Color* in which First Editions gives you top billing over the author. I think the typographers at Dell, at least on the cover, did rather stretch themselves in the exploitation of the biggest name on the Signet list."

developments. I shall not, at this time, comment further. I think you all know how valiantly and single-mindly we have functioned not only as Caldwell's paperbound publisher, but as his personal and professional friend, with his best interest always at heart. The paperbound field, unlike hardcover publishing, is fiercely competitive—but in all the years that I have been identified with this field, I have never encountered a more reprehensible gesture than that which Skinny describes on the part of Fawcett. (30 December 1957)

Within the week, supplying neither a moral nor a commercial reason, Caldwell had backed out of the project. In a note to Van Bibber he simply concluded, "From my own part, I must say that the proposal in written form would call for me to do a bigger chore than I could agree to do."

NAL's exclusivity as Caldwell's softcover publisher was also threatened by another softcover publisher. In 1953 NAL discovered that they did not have control of the reprint rights to two very early Caldwell novels, *The Bastard* and *Poor Fool*. The reasons for this are not clear from the NAL files at New York University but probably stem from the fact that both books were first issued in hardcover by fairly obscure publishers no longer in business. Weybright had not seen either until *The Bastard* was issued that year in a new paperback book imprint, " Novel Selections," published by Hillman Periodicals. Its cover format was designed to be similar to Caldwell's Signet books (see chapter 9). *Poor Fool* was scheduled by Hillman to soon follow in softcover. Because Hillman was a new imprint and a minor paperback publisher, the retail outlets open to Hillman books were limited and could not match those available to the major softcover logos like Signet. Not surprisingly, however, NAL was sufficiently piqued by the situation to try retaliation against the upstart imprint. Both Caldwell novels were apparently erotic enough for NAL to suggest to local wholesalers that they would be leaving themselves open for attacks by censoring groups if they distributed the Hillman books. This was a complete reversal of roles for the company that had in the past accused their rivals of similar sabbatoge while defending Caldwell works in censorship encounters across the country. NAL censorship attempts were only mildly successful since it appears that both Hillman editions were reissued soon afterward. Caldwell, however, could not have been happy with NAL's tactics. He apparently elicited from Weybright a promise to publish both *The Bastard* and *Poor Fool* sometime in the future. Three years later, in 1956, Marc Jaffe was asked to review them. In a memo to Weybright and Enoch, he concluded:

These are, in my opinion, wholly defensible as literary creations. If they had been published in the past, in one or another of the volumes of collected works, they would not have excited any special attention. . . . In any case, the question of to publish or not to publish is a tactical one which has little to do with literary judgment or taste. The safest thing all around would undoubtedly be to try to hold these books off the market for an indefinite period of time. But if for one reason or another we are forced to a positive commitment I feel the publication is justified. (11 April 1956)

Two years later both were bundled with a short Caldwell piece, "The Sacrilege of Alan Kent." The three were issued under the accurate if awkward and concealing title of the shortest work, *The Sacrilege of Alan Kent: A Novella with Two Complete Novels*.

NAL's feudal control extended not only over Caldwell's novels but also over his short stories. In 1947, shortly after the company began reprinting Caldwell, Pocket Books issued *The Pocket Book of Erskine Caldwell Short Stories*. Five years later, NAL, well established as the author's reprinter, weighed a comprehensive edition of all Caldwell short stories, including those published in the 1947 Pocket Books edition. To clear rights to these previously published stories and to prevent Pocket Books from further reissues, Weybright queried Caldwell's agent, James Oliver Brown, "Is there any way that Pocket Books can be restrained from interfering with the full exclusivity of the *Complete Stories*?" Governance even extended to reprints of Caldwell short stories in hardcover publisher anthologies. Doubleday sought permission to reprint in a collection edited by Louis Untermeyer a Caldwell short story that had earlier appeared in a Signet anthology. Weybright laid out the conditions and restrictions under which permission would be granted.

> We don't want to interfere with the use of Erskine Caldwell's short stories in a comprehensive anthology, but on the other hand we can't afford to permit other publishers of inexpensive reprint editions to exploit the Caldwell name and thereby interfere with our Caldwell program. Therefore, we grant permission for the Untermeyer volume to be licensed for reprint by Doubleday provided that Caldwell's name or reference to his stories does not appear on the cover of the paperbound reprint or that his name is not used in press releases or promotion to distributors. (28 May 1956)

In the latter half of the fifties, the company's correspondence with Caldwell contains less information about new writing and more about the concerns and distractions that lure successful authors away from the typewriter. Speech and travel itineraries abound. Weybright was always generous with providing introductions to interesting and influential people and would make plans to cross paths with his roving writer when each ventured abroad. And news of a visit by Caldwell to New York invariably elicited a response such as Caldwell received in December of 1951 from the editor in chief: "Kurt is scheduled for a foreign sales trip sometime in March; so let's plan, soon, a firm date so that we can have a quorum present to discuss the publishing side of our private lives." The two also consulted on a variety of honors and awards that were proposed for the writer. These ranged from an invitation to join the Euphemian Literary Society of Erskine College in South Carolina, a school Caldwell once attended, to honorary degrees from Ivy League schools. At different times Weybright worked on obtaining honorary doctorates for the writer and at one point set sights on an award considerably higher. In 1957, Weybright told Caldwell: "Don't build up hopes, but in my opinion there is a good prospect, ultimately, if we can revive basic literary and critical appreciation, of a Nobel Prize. God knows, in my book you have written rings around Sinclair Lewis and Pearl Buck, and certainly matched the importance of Faulkner."

As noted in chapter 4, Weybright was fond of comparing many of his Signet authors to classic novelists. In a letter to Arthur H. Thornhill, Sr. of Little, Brown, he described *God's Little Acre* as "a great modern classic which, in my opinion, ranks with the work of Dickens, Balzac and not very far from Cervantes." Perhaps a bit more realistically, Caldwell is described in a letter to Albert Bradley, chairman of the board of General Motors, as "the Chevrolet of American literature. That is what Mark Twain was too; and Dickens in England." Yet by the mid-fifties, Weybright appears to have believed that the best of Caldwell had already been published and that future novels were unlikely to capture the enormous mass audience of a *Tobacco Road* or *God's Little Acre*. This view is supported by his candid comment in June of 1954 to London publisher Peter Guttman. Made in the midst of sticky contractual negotiations, Weybright observed that "it is very unreasonable for him or Jim Brown [James Oliver Brown] to get the idea that we are the Ford Foundation instead of New American Library ... [for] it now appears that his future work is not likely to match in popularity and importance the earlier titles." (This assessment was shared with the author in a less direct but more concrete way as he discovered that his NAL advances on new novels were declining. For instance in 1957 *Certain Women* received twelve thousand dollars; the following year *Claudelle English* warranted only ten thousand dollars.)

In 1960 Weybright was an informed observer to another Caldwell contractual arrangement, this one between the author and his agent. James

Oliver Brown estimated that he was now losing money—as much as five thousand dollars a year—on Caldwell who appears to have demanded much more than routine agent representation and contractual guidance. Brown found that these added services, supportable in earlier years when Caldwell was receiving large advances and enjoying multimillion copy sales, were no longer affordable when the royalties for all NAL sales were averaging only around seven thousand dollars. Weybright, who attributed the decline of public interest in Caldwell rural settings to the urbanization of the United States, continued, however, to issue new Caldwell titles including a freshly edited volume of Caldwell short fiction, *Georgia Boy*, in a Signet Classics edition. Weybright justified this new publication in a memo to Kurt Enoch by citing both potential poaching from other publishers and the company's historical relationship with the author. "Despite the fact that Caldwell short stories have not proven nearly so successful as his novels, we have had to make a commitment ultimately to include the Carvel Collins [editor of the anthology] collection in our series. We cannot permit predators to do so— we owe Caldwell a favor, inasmuch as his royalty rates have remained normal in recent years" (27 June 1960).

Through 1961, when the NAL archival editorial files terminate, Caldwell's overall relationship with the paperback book industry, and NAL in particular, seems to have been remarkably happy.[5] An early example of this contentment occurs in a Penguin promotional letter signed by Caldwell and sent to independent wholesalers across the country.

> Yesterday I met my first magazine wholesaler. It was an exceptionally interesting experience. For the first time I understood how it is that a serious book like mine could sell a million copies in a 25¢ reprint edition. I realized that it is the years of merchandising experience that the wholesaler brings to 25¢ books that made this sale possible. They have made books a business proposition, not merely an artistic one. And I foresee a great future for America, when the most important books are sold on a wide basis throughout the country—in its newsstands and cigar stores and drug counters.
>
> I appreciate what you have done for *God's Little Acre* (a novel in which I personally had something to say and which I am glad has reached an audience of over a million). I hope that you will be able to do the same thing with future Penguin publications of my

5. After Weybright left NAL, Caldwell continued under the editor in chief's guidance. His nonfiction *Deep South* was issued under the Weybright and Talley hardcover imprint in 1968.

own books, and of other serious books, which without the magazine wholesaler, might never have left the library shelf or the bookstore counter. (5 November 1946)

* * *

Throughout the fifties, Signet editions of Mickey Spillane passed from hand to hand in every army barracks, college dormitory, and high school locker room in the country. Replacing Caldwell as the number one author on the NAL list, his worldwide sales rivaled those of Pocket Book's Erle Stanley Gardner in the mass market. In December 1951, an army corporal urgently wrote from the Far East: "It is with deep regret that I heard that Mickey Spillane, the very talented author of the Mike Hammer series, has been killed in an automobile accident. I, along with all other faithful readers of these books, would like that officially verified. Rumors are so very malicious and more often than not, exaggerated, over here that we find the statement very hard to believe since we have no reports of the accident in newspapers" (7 December 1951). Marc Jaffe, Spillane's editor at NAL, replied to this rumor, a phenomenon that today is commonly associated with rock music stars as opposed to more durable detective story writers. "I'm happy to pass along the word to you and to all the rest of Mickey Spillane's fans that America's most popular mystery author is very much alive, and working on a new book. Strangely enough we have gotten many letters from overseas mentioning the rumor that Mickey Spillane is dead. Why don't you start the truth going around?" (9 January 1952).

As with Caldwell, NAL feared poaching from rival publishers. The most immediate and the most logical pilferer again was Fawcett Publications. Through sales conferences and conventions as well as author tours, Spillane had become personally acquainted with the Fawcett executives responsible for NAL's national wholesale distribution and for the Signet sales that engineered his preeminence in the mass market. When Weybright learned in the summer of 1950 that Spillane had dusted off an old unpublished work, *Whom the Gods Destroy*, and submitted it to Dutton for consideration, he was at first elated. On 23 July he informed Spillane's agent, John McKenna, "I confess I am so keen to read the new manuscript that I would drop anything or break any appointment to do so." But the manuscript turned out not to be publishable as then drafted. At a meeting that included the author, his agent, and Dutton's Nicholas Wreden, heavy revision was demanded. When Spillane refused to make the necessary changes, Weybright became concerned that Gold Medal would pick it up. To prevent this, he asked Dutton to "make certain that *Whom the Gods Destroy* is not rejected—and therefore ineligible for submission elsewhere—

but [placed] merely in the deep freeze pending further developments of Spillane works."[6] Weybright must have been aware for some time that there was a quantity of unpublished Spillane material drifting free. Earlier in 1950 he counseled John Edmondson at Dutton.

It is not only important to keep Mickey happy and satisfied, but imperative that his rejected material not be released to any competitive paper bound hands. I sometimes get apprehensive about this, for reasons which need not be included in this letter. I hope you have a firm commitment from Mickey and his agent on this point. If a borderline case should arise in which a rejected manuscript is threatened with placement elsewhere, I think another conference is indicated with Dutton, NAL, Spillane and McKenna. . . . We can cope with the problem by editorial revision, by the use of a pseudonym under any other imprint besides yours or ours, or in whatever manner seems desirable to promote all of our best interests, which are, in the last analysis, identical: the development of Mickey Spillane in the same creative way, by Dutton and NAL, as Morrow and Pocket Books have done with Erle Stanley Gardner (who, incidentally, uses a pseudonym for his lesser mystery output). (29 May 1950)

Clearly hardcover Dutton not only had to keep Spillane happy, it also had to satisfy NAL, the company supplying it with substantial subsidiary income and responsible for having tapped through their Signet paper reprints "the millions" who were Spillane's true audience. And if there was any doubt of this, Victor Weybright was around to point it out, as when he reminded Spillane's agent, John F. McKenna that "as in the case of Erle Stanley Gardner or Erskine Caldwell, whose hardcover sales are comparatively modest, but nevertheless important for a substantial literary reputation, Spillane's genuine potential lies in the 25 cent mass market " (23 July 1950). The reprinter was probably in more frequent touch with the author than the proprietary Dutton. Paperback sales royalties clearly put NAL in a dominant position to influence the author and his agent should either become unhappy with the hardcover publisher. Dutton, therefore, was well aware that NAL could at any time recommend to Spillane and McKenna another, perhaps "more cooperative," hardcover publisher or, as NAL would with its bestselling authors in later years, itself become proprietary publishers for Mike Hammer and company. NAL was a much more serious

6. Reworked, this manuscript was eventually published by NAL in 1966 as *The Twisted Thing*.

threat than Fawcett to Dutton's primary control. To maintain harmony with the reprinter, Dutton, on at least two occasions, arranged publishing licenses for the reprint and sale of Spillane titles in the British Commonwealth that gave NAL export editions competitive advantages over English paper editions. In the summer of 1951, to further diminish tension among author, publisher, and reprinter and to fend off the Fawcett author snatching, NAL and Dutton worked out a contract with Spillane to acquire complete control of all of the author's creations—past, present, and future. During the course of these negotiations, Truman Talley reported to Weybright on some of Dutton's perplexity.

Lunching with the Duttons on Tuesday I had a long talk with Colonel John [Edmondson]. Naturally everything gravitated to Mickey Spillane and the Fawcett overtures. As he talked at great length on our joint problems, he obviously had great confidence in your handling of the situation. . . . They [Dutton] are a little fed up with the idea of Fawcett's overtures—not only by the very fact that Fawcett has gone after Mickey Spillane, but also because Fawcett, in their capacity as our distributor, has access to Mickey's exact sales figures. Colonel John's exact words were, "It's like playing poker with a guy who knows every card in your hand."
While this feeling has nothing to do with winning Mickey Spillane over to a permanent Dutton-NAL contract, it seems to me that in any future letter to Allen Adams [Fawcett's distribution head], the point should be made clear that "even when merely a rumor hearsay competition between publisher and distributor, when circulated among trade houses, can do our publishing program a great deal of harm in the continuing bitter fight for new titles." As people become more and more aware in the trade of any such struggles with Fawcett, the decisions in trade houses as to a book's reprinter—so often based on intangibles— can't help to favor our competitors and their comparatively mute distribution systems over ours. (15 June 1951)

At this time it appears that Spillane himself was reluctant to restrict his Fawcett connections to only those contacts that aided the promotion and sale of his Signet editions. In apparent violation of the 1951 contract that was finally worked out between the three parties, Spillane, Dutton, and NAL, Spillane occasionally lent his name to and prepared promotional blurbs for the covers of Gold Medal titles. One of these Spillane-Fawcett blurbs was especially prophetic. It arrived on newsstands about the same time that Spillane delivered the last manuscript he would write for NAL and Dutton for nine years. The Gold Medal 1952 edition of John D. MacDonald's *The Damned* states simply above a Spillane signature, "I wish I had written this book." And as the decade unfolded, his two principal publishers would come to feel likewise.

Fawcett was not the only outside organization distracting Spillane. Magazines like *Collier's* called on him for short stories. Comic strip offers were made. Throughout the fifties Spillane was the subject of numerous magazine and newspaper interviews ranging from *True* to *Town and Country*. He also appeared on several television programs and accepted numerous speaking engagements, including one sponsored by the *Harvard Law Review*. At least one radio and one television Mike Hammer series was launched in this period. The fifties also saw three of his novels made into films, beginning with *I, the Jury* whose premiere in 1953 was scheduled for Norfork, Virginia, when the "fleet was in." Throughout the fifties Spillane was called in to serve as a "script doctor" for ailing film and television productions, and he set up his own production studio in Newburgh, New York.

Many of the Spillane distractions were sown in the early fifties by NAL itself as the company introduced Spillane to the life of a celebrity and promoted him as a personality. One result was that even before the last of Spillane's first string of bestsellers, *Kiss Me Deadly*, was submitted, NAL became concerned about the author's meeting editorial deadlines. *Kiss Me Deadly*, finally published as a Signet in 1953, was more than a year overdue when a Spillane vacation postcard arrived from an ocean resort. Dated 12 May 1952 it read in part, "Having a stinko time—people recognizing me wherever I go—photogs & reporters on my neck constantly—home soon—next book before long—only don't tell Dutton—Mickey Spillane." Weybright responded somewhat limply, "I do wish that you could spare your energy from all diversions until you have made delivery on *Kiss Me Deadly* to Dutton." But NAL urgings and Spillane promises and delays had only begun. A year later the author, who at one time boasted he could write as many as four mysteries a year, was again being urged by the editor in chief to evade outside distractions and turn in a fresh full-length novel to Dutton. To prod him along, Weybright pointed out that the author and his softcover publisher were in combat with another author-publisher combine.

> Pocket Books people are spreading the word that you have quit writing, and they are putting on a fierce drive to build up Erle Stanley Gardner to take away some of the market which you took away from Gardner when you were writing. The Pocket Books people are claiming that Gardner is the world's best selling mystery writer—they have sold over 50 million copies of Gardner since

1940—and I think it is a pity that they are able to exploit Gardner to this extent only because there aren't a sufficient number of new Mickey Spillane Signet titles with which to compete. Now that your movie program is launched, and that all of your other projects are in the works, I hope that you cannot only finish *Tonight I Die* but catch up with the long overdue titles that will keep your name, fame and fortune secure in the field where it was achieved—books! (31 July 1953)

By the following year, still with no fresh Spillane manuscript in hand, Weybright sourly characterized the author to an English friend as a "whirling dervish and not very cooperative on anything, including deadlines. So you can imagine the background in trying to put him in harness on a project that doesn't appear to emanate exclusively from his own self-centered mentality " (1 December 1954). By the close of 1955, Weybright was seeking assistance in corralling Spillane from whomever he could including the author's agent, John McKenna. The editor reviewed the situation.

Like Dutton—indeed more than Dutton—we need a new Spillane title. Since Mickey has not produced a book-length manuscript for some years, despite many promises of immediate delivery of such manuscripts, the only alternative seems to be a collection of the short stories and novelettes that he has found time to write for first serial sale.

While Mickey has been writing these brief bits, his paperbound book sales have been declining because of the fact that there is no new Mickey Spillane book on the market. To be sure, the sales are still substantial, but one cannot expect them to hold up to the old level through constant reissues of the older titles. (28 December 1955)

There was some disagreement about the quality of the "brief bits." Weybright appears to have seen them as publishable; McKenna and Dutton did not. They appear not to have been gathered in book form.

Throughout the latter half of the fifties, reminders of Spillane's contractual commitment to the company fly after the author. Writing on 2 February 1958, immediately after NAL discovered another Spillane front cover endorsement on a Fawcett paperback, Weybright again tried a direct approach. Slipping into the author's vernacular to get at the crux of NAL's concern, Weybright states plainly that "I'm confident that we can all make a great deal of money out of your works, receipt of which we have long been anticipating. I hope that you will concentrate your efforts on the

completion of your next book. That, after all, is where the real dough is."
NAL apparently made a concerted effort at this time to get back in closer
touch with the writer and to goad him into writing books again. Marc
Jaffe, for instance, holds out a meeting with Ayn Rand as a carrot as he
too seems inspired by the Spillane prose style:

> There is another thing too that I must talk to you about. I don't
> know how you feel about Ayn Rand, but she's pretty keen on you.
> As a matter of fact, in a speech at the Publishers Ad Club the other
> day, she mentioned you along with Dostoyevsky, Victor Hugo and
> one or two other big literary types. And she wasn't kidding! She
> gave very good reasons why she thinks you deserve serious
> consideration. As a matter of fact, she told Jay Tower [promotion
> manager at NAL] yesterday that she's very keen to meet and talk
> with you in the very near future. Can we set it up for next week
> sometime? You, of course, might not be interested in talking to
> Miss Rand—which is okay by me—but we should let her know one
> way or another within the next couple of days.
> Let's get going! (12 March 1958)

Unfortunately there is no confirmation in the NAL files that this particular
meeting ever took place.[7] Regardless, Jaffe's prompting also failed and the
following year found Weybright buoyantly trying to reinforce still another
Spillane delivery pledge, "It's quite a thrill to hear you are bringing in your
manuscript to New York within a week. Although it's a good many years
overdue, it is most welcome—and so are you" (7 July 1959). However,
more delay followed.

During these hiatus years, Spillane had surrounded himself with a
cadre of aspiring hard-boiled detective writers. Jaffe liked to call them
"Mickey's pal-protégés." All seemed bent on emulating the writer's successful fiction formula. From time to time their manuscripts, possessing varying
degrees of writing skill, arrived at the Dutton and NAL offices. All were
soundly endorsed by Spillane. Weybright himself directed dubious praise
at the efforts of one of them, Mike Roscoe, when he observed that he had
one of Spillane's "greatest assets—an uninhibited sense of narrative, which
makes even the most ridiculous situations as interesting, at least, as the

---

7. A meeting between the two did occur. "When Ayn later met Mickey Spillane, she
discovered that the admiration between them was mutual: he had read and loved her novels.
It was a strange sight to see these two together: Spillane, who physically suggested a prize
fighter or a dock worker, was courteous and pleasant, but nonphilosophical in his approach
to writing, and Ayn painstakingly tried to make him aware of the philosophical meaning and
value of what he had accomplished" (Branden 278).

sequences of events in a comic strip" (12 October 1953). Three Roscoe titles were issued in Signet. Another "pal-protégé" was Charles Wells. In 1951 his *Let the Night Cry* was rejected by Dutton which concluded that "it has all the brutality, fighting and killing, but it lacks the real suspense and mystery that Spillane always sustains." In a memo marked "Urgent" and addressed to Enoch, Weybright himself evaluated the manuscript and exposed the problems of outright rejection of the Wells creation.

> This is God-awful trash, without Spillane's vibration and without plausible motivation, but abounding in retribution, lust, violence, booze, in the lower depths of New York and environs.
>
> I suspect a carbon copy has been submitted simultaneously to Gold Medal, although we were assured first look. This creates an awkward dilemma. The manuscript should be rejected, or put in storage until Wells develops. It would be disgraceful for NAL to offer it to a trade publisher as a joint project. *BUT*, Gold Medal could take it and re-write it. Fawcett must be prevented from exploiting Spillane's name on it.
>
> This is urgent. We promised a quick reading. To salvage it by re-writing and editing, and to place it with a trade publisher, is possible—but the best alternative would be to get Mickey's identification with it completely removed, and let it go. I feel that Mickey's hand is in the plot, but not in the writing, which is pedestrian, forced and crude. (8 October 1951)

It must be remembered that at this time NAL firmly believed that its role within the publishing industry required finding a hardcover publisher for original fiction. Eventually the Abelard Press agreed to produce a heavily edited hardcover edition that later appeared in 1954 as a Signet. On the front cover, along with the required blonde and the warning that "she packed a gun—in her garter holster!" was a Spillane endorsement that "this story moves right along with kicks from first to last." The following year, a second Wells novel was also published by NAL.

Passed on by Dutton for reprint review, Earle Basinsky's *The Big Steal* arrived in 1955 with another Spillane warranty (which later appeared on the back cover of the Signet): "This is my buddy's book. He was there when *I, the Jury* was written. We flew together during the war. And, as far as I can see, this guy has it. I like this story. I think you will too." After initial examination, however, Marc Jaffe was less impressed and told Weybright that "under ordinary circumstances, this would be a flat reject, especially since there's nothing we can do about strengthening the various weak spots. But it does carry the Spillane imprimatur, and I doubt that

211

we'd want Popular Library or one of the lesser competitors capitalizing on the great man's name" (16 May 1955). Still another reason for publishing Basinsky may have been Weybright's hope that the writer-friend might influence Spillane to stick to the typewriter full-time. Weybright hinted at this when he wrote to Basinsky: "Mickey is a keen judge of writing in the field in which he has made his great reputation and achieved his own fantastic audience. His praise is an enormous asset. I only wish I knew how to get him to write some more. We continue to reissue all seven of his books but, without something fresh, they will eventually slip into the ordinary sales category—which is bad for him and bad for us, not to mention Dutton who, after all, gave him his start" (6 July 1955).

Throughout the early fifties, NAL was both pleased and puzzled with the success of the Mike Hammer books. Heightened by Spillane's seeming retirement from writing book-length fiction, there was a disturbing concern within the company that his books would soon be out of fashion. Weybright and his staff were constantly on the lookout for detective-suspense writing in a different style. As described in chapter 5, it was an effort to "regrind the image of the private eye." Mike Hammer's real successor on the NAL list was James Bond whose adventures the company first started reprinting in 1958. It is also interesting to note that in 1962 when Spillane finally did deliver his next new book-length manuscript, *The Deep*, as a Signet, Mike Hammer was not to be found. *The Deep* was commercially successful. However, the character of Mike Hammer was revived in succeeding Spillane novels and, along with Perry Mason and James Bond, continues to this day to contend with criminals in a variety of media, including paperback display racks.

* * *

In the late fifties, Irving Wallace in his position as a writer stood somewhat in contrast to Mickey Spillane. A successful magazine journalist and Hollywood scriptwriter, Wallace had also recently published two nonfiction anthologies with Alfred A. Knopf. Yet he felt trapped. The writer had conceived several book-length projects that he did not have the time and/or the resources to carry out. In 1958 Wallace was introduced to Weybright by Ted Loeff, who ran NAL's West Coast scouting and movie tie-in operation, Literary Projects (see chapter 8). Weybright immediately advanced Wallace four thousand dollars to adapt his screenplay of a P. T. Barnum biography into a book. Knopf, whose last contract with Wallace apparently contained no option clause covering this kind of adaptation, was then asked if he was interested in buying hardcover rights from NAL, proprietary publisher for the Barnum work. This was a complete turnaround of publisher roles appreciated by all aware of past trade practice and categorized in book publishing as "buying backwards." The gatekeeper roles of hardcover publishers and mass market paperback publishers were reversed, the softcover house serving as the initial "gate."

Knopf agreed to publish the Barnum hardcover. However, in the spring of 1959, after the contract for the Knopf hardcover edition had been signed, Paramount proposed calling the film "The Fabulous Showman," a title that was unfortunately not on the film adaptation when the Knopf contract was signed and was similar to one of Wallace's Knopf anthologies, *The Fabulous Originals*. It seemed mandatory for further sales promotion that the Barnum editions, hard and soft, carry the same title as the projected film. Knopf's cooperation was imperative, but it was predictable that he would not be anxious to sponsor two volumes by the same author with such similar titles. On top of this, Weybright had just advanced Wallace still more money, twenty-five thousand dollars, to complete two more full-length book projects: the novel *The Chapman Report* and the biography *The Twenty-Seventh Wife*. Weybright reviewed the sticky situation with Ted Loeff and asked him to have Wallace request Knopf for a title change. "Knopf is leaning over backwards not to make any contact with us on this project now that the contract has been signed. We are good friends, we are in the same building, but you understand that it is very humiliating for Mr. Borzoi to license book rights from a paperbound publisher. That's the crux of your diplomatic mission to Wallace. Please, please have Irving make a firm and insistent demand for *The Fabulous Showman*" (22 April 1959). In a letter that arrived on Weybright's desk shortly after the Loeff letter was mailed, Wallace was more relaxed about the potential implications of different titles as it appeared that Paramount was still uncertain about a final film title.

It is unlikely, as I told you, that the final film will ever be called *The Fabulous Showman*. . . . Now going back to Alfred is like going into a lion's cage unarmed—but I don't mind. If I can influence him to go back to the old title or some other, I will be happy to do so. Just say the word. The only danger might be that he would suspect I might be reflecting you—and, in a sense, this would be under-mining his authority. But we can risk that, if you wish. Or—either of us can try some other titles out on him. Or—we can pass and let him use the title he wishes and you can adjust your final title to the movie when it is in the can (I know you don't like to indicate a title change, but from the point of view of tie-up and sales it might be the best thing—and would probably have to be done anyway, no matter what Alfred finally used). At any rate, if you want me girding loins and kneeling before battle—let me know. (21 April 1959)

213

Wallace wrote again to Weybright confirming that he had obtained Knopf's agreement to the title change and that "he didn't sound sore at all, and I was both surprised and pleased." [8]

Wallace's New York agent, Paul Reynolds, sheds some further light on the 1959 two-book deal that followed the original Barnum advance.[9] It seems to confirm that Knopf acceded to the second NAL-Wallace agreement.

> I phoned Alfred Knopf this afternoon and told him that you were offering Irving Wallace a contract for *Twenty-Seventh Wife* of $12,500 of which $2,500 was to be against foreign rights and $10,000 against American. I didn't mention *The Chapman Report* because Knopf is not publishing Wallace's fiction and I didn't see any point in getting him concerned about that. I told him it wasn't entirely clear in my mind who would be handling the rights, but my understanding was that neither you, nor Irving, nor I were going to make a contract at the moment with any hard back publisher, and I saw no reason why he couldn't wait until all or part of the book was written, and that this was an attempt to get Wallace money so that he could afford to write books rather than TV, that you had no intention of trying to deprive him of first publication rights to this book if he wanted to publish the book. Alfred seemed perfectly happy. He expressed his appreciation of being told about this and said he would talk to me about it at some later date. He certainly wasn't mad or irritable in any way.
>
> P.S. I told Alfred that Wallace had approached you. Knopf has no kick. You are doing the financing to make the books possible and giving Knopf a sure reprint edition. (30 March 1959)

Despite the reassurances of Wallace and Reynolds, Knopf's attitude toward his 501 Madison Avenue neighbor was frequently frosty.[10] As proprietor of the new Wallace material, Weybright was not long in seeking a more congenial hardcover imprint, as he revealed in this letter to Edward Kuhn, Jr., then of McGraw-Hill who later succeeded Weybright as NAL editor in chief. "I have signed up world rights on the book (*The Twenty-Seventh Wife*), along with a novel on which Irving Wallace is engaged, not

8. Late in 1959 Knopf published *The Fabulous Showman* in hardcover. Wallace's screenplay, however, was never turned into a film.
9. This second arrangement with Wallace is described at some length in Weybright, *Making of a Publisher* 256.
10. In his biography Reynolds (190) describes Knopf's subsequent attempts to sabotage a hardcover edition of *The Chapman Report*.

to become a dog-in-the-manger of hard-cover publishers, but to enable Wallace to escape the grind of TV script and film play writing and develop his career as a book author. He absolutely must have a first-class hardcover publisher for his books, as he has had in the past " (4 May 1959). Eventually, Simon & Schuster became Wallace's enthusiastic hardcover publisher sponsoring a string of bestsellers, beginning with *The Chapman Report* and *The Twenty-Seventh Wife*. All were followed by NAL softcover Signets.[11] As NAL issued its own edition of *The Chapman Report*, Weybright learned that Knopf had placed its two Wallace anthologies with Berkley, then a comparatively minor paperback rival to NAL. He informed Wallace. "Too bad that Knopf has placed *The Square Pegs* and *The Fabulous Originals* with Berkley. We once expressed interest, in due course, but I imagine Knopf was piqued enough to place the books in less auspicious hands. Let's not cry over spilt milk. . ." (23 May 1961).

For the most part relations between Weybright and Wallace seem to have been most cordial during the few years that remained of Weybright's tenure at NAL. However, major strain occurred during the summer and fall of 1960 following publication of two periodical articles. Each attributed the inspiration for *The Chapman Report* to Victor Weybright. The first appeared in the 7 July issue of the *Reporter*. It was written by critic Malcolm Cowley who contended that Weybright created a "hidden original" by dreaming up the plot and hiring Wallace to carry it out. In fact at this time Weybright, Loeff, and producer Jerry Wald were using Literary Projects to explore and generate potentially lucrative book and film tie-ins (see chapter 8). *The Chapman Report* was not one of these "hidden originals," however. Wallace wrote to the *Reporter* and tried to correct the contention. But a month and a half later, *Time* repeated the same rumor. In a 22 August 1960 article entitled "Era of the Non-Book," *Time* concluded: "Most books thought up by publishers or movie makers are farmed out to authors. Irving Wallace's *The Chapman Report*, old publishing hands insist, was hatched by Victor Weybright of New American Library and reads like the hack job it is." With an advance copy of the issue in hand, an annoyed Weybright wrote to the conservative weekly.

Speaking of non-books (*Time*, August 22nd), odder still are non-newsweekly news magazines, which pick up falsehoods from opinionated weeklies such as *The Reporter Magazine* and spread the lie that anyone except Irving Wallace conceived or created his extraordinary novel *The Chapman Report*. . . .

11. Wallace hardcover novels stayed with Simon & Schuster until 1980 when his *Second Lady* helped resurrect NAL's dormant hardcover line, NAL Books.

You may quote—if you are capable of editing the letter
without distortion—the enclosed communication from Irving
Wallace to *Reporter Magazine* when they first promulgated the
falsehood which you ascribe to "old publishing hands," whoever
they may be. (17 August 1960)

Weybright, abroad for a good deal of the time as this controversy developed, also corresponded with Cowley at the *Reporter* who seems throughout this dispute to have the measured respect of both Weybright and Wallace. In one of a series of letters to Cowley, the editor in chief takes another swipe at *Time* magazine.

Your letter of August 3rd reached me in London where I am very
busy working on a variety of book projects, none of them
prefabricated. We are leaving the fabrication department to *Time*
magazine these days. Harold J. Laski once told me that he invented
Time magazine when he was teaching the founders at Yale. Laski
was the world's greatest liar, so obviously I don't believe a word of
what he said. But obviously he must have given *Time* a transfusion.
Time, Inc. had seen a copy of Irving Wallace's letter to *The Reporter*
before they published their calculated lie concerning *The Chapman
Report*. The trouble with these reckless and false statements is that,
once printed, they go into the reference file and can never be
overtaken.

I pride ourselves on the fact that we have discovered and
encouraged more West Coast talent than all of America's other
book publishers combined in the past six months. Yet the principal
reward for this activity is a sneer from the sidelines as well as from
the front office of the conservative publishing fraternity.

I saw Irving Wallace in Paris—a very pleasant evening with
four of our authors who happened to be there: Bemelmans, James
Jones, Peter Gilman (*Diamond Head*) and Wallace—and I am
assured at least of the loyalty of our authors if not of our critics and
historians. (7 September 1960)

Naturally Wallace was also curious about who the original source of
the misinformation was. From his perspective it was natural to suspect
Weybright as having some part in starting the rumor. It is easy to imagine
the ponderous editor in chief, not unknown for embellishment, expanding
NAL's role in the production of *The Chapman Report*, perhaps to attract a
new writer to his list or to elicit agent cooperation. While Weybright would
frequently deny doing this, the attribution controversy was still brewing

216

in mid-October of 1960 when the NAL executive responded to Wallace criticism of a German translation and publication arrangement that NAL had made on the author's behalf.

> I wrote a brief note to you via dictaphone over the weekend on the controversy inspired by *The Reporter* and *Time*. We urge you, as an author whom I greatly admire and respect, to consider New American Library your publisher. We are appreciative of your enormous talent. We have never made any claim of any sort to having any part of the creative origins of your writing (nor has Ted Loeff), and I am certain that Malcolm Cowley or any other critic will not for a moment concede that a primary contract by NAL has any adverse affect whatever on the reception of a writer's work. I have striven manfully to give worldwide publication in all major languages to *The Chapman Report* and have succeeded. When Bonnier in Sweden stood aside, for example, I immediately persuaded Bergen that they were wrong and he would be wise to publish the book. When Mark Longman, pressured by his educational colleagues, lost his nerve, I personally intervened to give the book the best possible auspices in Britain under the umbrella of Weidenfeld and Nicolson, through their wholly owned subsidiary, Arthur Barker, now directed by James Reynolds who achieved such success with contemporary fiction at Frederick Muller.
>
> It would be very sad if you would continue to deprecate and discount the energy we have put into the works of Irving Wallace. I have told some 50 members of the critical fraternity, literary profession and publishing industry, while abroad, that you are bound to reach the stature of the late Sinclair Lewis as an American novelist with the gift of social criticism and the finest ear for American vernacular now existent. (17 October 1960)

Wallace responded with astringent distilled from the events of the past several months.

> In your two letters of the 17th you "urge me" to consider New American Library "your publisher." I do, indeed. We have a contract and it is being observed. As to all that you have done for me—at Frankfurt, in Sweden, in England—I certainly appreciate it. However, it seems we have reached a stage where everybody I am associated with is telling me what they have done for me—not only your two letters, but also a letter from Ted Loeff on October 19

telling me what *he* has done for me. I feel like a publisher's ward. As a matter of fact, I could write an impressive letter to you telling you what I have done for you—and a more impressive one to Ted telling him, or reminding him, what I have done for him, which has been considerable. I shall not bother with such childish forensics—not make this an off-shore islands debate—but simply tell you that I believe the score is even. If you or Ted doubt this, I will happily elaborate at length and with facts. Suffice it that on March 30, 1959, when we made the two book deal on *Chapman* and *Wife* you were emphatic to assure me that this was cold business, there was no altruism in your advance to me and that you would make a good deal of money on me, and I on you. I should prefer to believe what you said that day—rather than be forced to perpetually regard myself as one beholden to NAL and LPC.

What really made me demand a release from Warner Brothers after four years was their paternalism. And I knew I would have to leave Alfred Knopf because of his paternalism. Like all well-meaning employers you have a tendency to think the same way. In Paris, at the Ritz, you asked Sylvia [wife of Irving Wallace] to tell me a number of things—among them that we were abroad because of you. This is nonsense, but perhaps you did not know it. I had been to Europe, and once for almost a year, three times before I ever laid eyes on you. I drove a Cadillac and owned three homes long before I ever laid eyes on you. In short, Victor, as I wrote Cowley, you did not "invent" me. Not that you claim that in so many words, but the implication of your conversations and letters recently is clear i.e. that I owe you very, very much and should behave. When I went with you I did so with my eyes wide open, voluntarily, even eagerly—*but* I could not then foresee some of the consequences. (29 October 1960)

In the face of this no-frills interpretation of his role as a publishing gate-keeper, Weybright beat a tactical retreat. "I appreciate your letter of October 29. I am not paternalistic, dear old boy—god forbid!—but a great believer in noblesse oblige and of candor between authors and their publishers and vice versa. "I am taking your advice and dropping this discussion right now" (11 January 1960).

But the matter, however, did not stay at rest. On the same date as Weybright's withdrawal, Wallace wrote a long explanation and justification to Malcolm Cowley that not only reviews origins of *The Chapman Report* but also describes, from a writer's perspective, how the lives of author and publisher become entangled in a business that was increasingly complex and oriented to the West Coast.

I was really stunned when *The Chapman Report* sold to the movies —it is not a movie at all—and I was dizzy when I learned, pre-publication, that I might have a bestseller. I had written four books before. None were bestsellers, although one did sell 12,000 copies. One of these was about a sexual problem, and the others also touched upon sex, but none were manufactured to become bestsellers anymore than *The Chapman Report*.

Many critics were kind to *Chapman*. Those who were not were upsetting to me. But nothing was really destructive to my reputation as a writer, until one day when I was abroad, I received your article in *The Reporter* on the subject of paperbacks. Suddenly I was reading that this child of mine whom I loved and hated and lived with so long, was not even conceived by me. It was bad enough to be a pornographer and manufacturer, but now I was not even a writer at all. Now, it appeared, one Victor Weybright, the affable owner of a major reprint house, and one Ted Loeff, the proprietor of an idea factory called Literary Projects, had, between them, an idea, a plot, characters, fed them into a machine named me, pushed a button—and lo, there was a paperback novel that would briefly be disguised as hardback. I, Irving Wallace, was described to the readership that follows you as some kind of word machine, and whatever credit or discredit might accrue to my book belonged to a rotund publisher in New York and a former press agent in Beverly Hills.

There is, indeed, a Literary Projects Company, and there is a Ted Loeff, a one-time publicist I met when we were in the army in the early forties. After the war, Leoff became acquainted with Weybright. He began to suggest book-movie tie-ins to NAL and eventually became Weybright's western representative. Then, gradually, Loeff got the idea for a company that would invent books. This is Literary Projects. He found that there were average hack writers around, and that they had no creative ideas, but if you gave them an idea—sometimes a plot, characters, research—you could get competent books out of them. So Literary Projects was born. Leoff gets ideas by the dozens, works them out, piles in background research, offers the packages to hungry writers—and also offers, most often with Weybright's backing, big advances. It works for Loeff and Weybright—and it also works for uncreative writers who have thick skins and need the cash. I have never, never been a part of that operation. It may be okay for those who can stomach it or need it or are psychologically prepared to live with it. For myself, for me, I regard it as anti-writing and a practice to be avoided. . . . [Wallace then goes on to explain that in 1958 Loeff approached him while he was writing a biography of Phineas T. Barnum and him offered a four-thousand-dollar advance.]

At that point, Loeff called and said that Weybright was coming to Los Angeles and would like to meet with me. I was eager to meet him. We met at the Beverly Hills Hotel. He said that he understood I was working on a novel and planning another biography. He said he understood I was willing to follow the Barnum formula, sell him my reprint rights and proprietorship in advance so that I could have the money to go on with my books and not return to television. I said "yes," I would like that very much, and that my one desire was to write books full time. Weybright asked me the basic ideas—what was *The Chapman Report* about? What was the new biography about? I told him what I was doing, maybe five minutes devoted to each book. And that was it. We agreed on terms, and shortly he sent me part of the advance. He did not know what I had written. He did not know what I was writing. He did not see a word until the novel was delivered complete. He made editorial suggestions, mostly toning down—and soon Simon & Schuster bought it and also made suggestions. I followed some and discarded others, and that is *The Chapman Report* and that is all Weybright and Loeff had to do with it. Neither one dreamed it up or hatched it. To describe their roles properly: Loeff introduced me to Weybright, and that and nothing else; Weybright bought reprint rights while the work was going instead of after it was done period.

But now, I suspect, I know what is wrong. I did something unorthodox. Instead of following usual procedure, as I did with my first three books, that is, finishing the work, selling hardback, later selling paperback, I reversed the classical approach. I sold reprint first and then followed with hardback. This, I suspect, reflects badly on one's work—literary people say—a-ha!, manufactured. Actually, NAL never interfered. I wrote as I pleased, what I pleased, and I always have, and always will. But I begin to see that for the writer this may be a harmful practice. Perhaps this is what influenced you or *Time*. At any rate, before all the bad publicity, I had made another backwards deal with NAL—promised them my next two novels before making my hardback deals. But your article and *Time* made me realize that my new books would be misunderstood, and there might be more of the same about Weybright and Loeff, and distortions would go on. So, I asked Weybright to let me off the hook, let me get out of future paperback reprint deals. He refused, as he had a right to do.

I think I wrote this long letter to get it out of my system—and to let you know the truth as a person I have admired. Nothing I have written or am writing or intend to write will ever be hatched by anyone else or farmed out to me or touched by outside hands. For better or worse, I am my own man. And I wanted you to know. (1 October 1960)

Weybright received a copy of the Wallace letter and immediately wrote to Cowley who, as an editorial adviser of long standing with Viking Press, as well as a critic, might be expected to have a sympathetic ear. "Irving is not particularly grateful to the publisher who emancipated him from the dreary drudgery of Hollywood—but his bark is worse than his bite. All publishers have inspired and instigated books. The hell of it is that, as Irving says, I had nothing to do with the origin or theme of *The Chapman Report*. I simply financed him to the tune of $25,000 so that he could write two books without the intrusion of a job. I do not know why he fails to report that figure when he confides the comparatively modest $4,000 on Barnum" (10 October 1960).

A month later, as the author was working on *The Prize*, destined to be his next fiction bestseller, the *Daily Express* in London repeated the rumors that, as Wallace laments to Weybright: "Once the myth begins it will not stop—not in the life of *Chapman*, and, or you shall see, not in the life of *The Prize*." There was indication that, as with *The Chapman Report*, credit for the conception of *The Prize* would go to Weybright.[12] Wallace concluded this last of the series of letters on the attribution of *The Chapman Report* with bitter resignation.

Yes, Victor, the myth goes on. I had ceased writing of it to you, but it goes on. It does not impair the sales of the books, of course, but it impairs my morale. I don't like trade circles in NYC, Hollywood and London reading and accepting such destructive gossip. In the last three weeks I have received eight more clippings from major newspapers around America carrying on the story of Victor Weybright's creativity in the manner of *Chapman*. Two days

---

12. To counter this new rumor, Wallace may have prepared one of the most elaborate defenses ever constructed by a writer. *The Writing of One Novel* was Wallace's 250-page chronicle on the preparation and publication of *The Prize*.

ago the Preminger-Stuart Agency phoned to say that they had a brilliant idea for a novel and would I be free to write it for them. I said what gave them the idea that I would ever do such a thing? The executive on the phone said, " Well, you are still working for Ted Loeff, aren't you?" I said dammit, no, and told him what he could do, and he apologized and was glad to be corrected, but he said that was the understanding all around this town. Frankly, I feel quite hopeless and discouraged about the whole thing. As I wrote Cowley, it is bad enough being castigated for a book, but then to learn that you hadn't really written the book at all. (17 December 1960)

Despite the tensions it later engendered, the financial arrangement Weybright and Wallace worked out on 29 March 1960 in the Beverly Hills Hotel represents an important benchmark in growth to adult maturity of mass market paperback publishing. As we have seen, Weybright was not shy about letting the book trade know that his company was both financier and proprietary publisher for the bestsellers of the former Knopf author. He summarized his satisfaction to Wallace in the spring of 1961 when he wrote, "I am proud to have been identified with your move from journalism and Hollywood entertainment to the stature of a creative novelist of universal importance." The quarter-book handmaiden had become literary patron, taking the risks and harvesting the profits from subsidiary sales to film and television companies, from overseas sales, and most important and symbolically, from the sale of hardcover rights to trade publishers. The Wallace deal was applauded, albeit not publicly, by many of Alfred A. Knopf's hardcover colleagues, eager to get a piece of the Wallace action that Simon & Schuster eventually won. It inspired NAL and its major softcover competitors, particularly Bantam Books, to new and even more commercially directed business goals. This in turn lead to acquisition by still larger and even more profit-motivated corporations, eventually encouraging the final evolution of mass market houses into fully rounded book publishing operations no longer limited to softcover reprinting.

In 1966, a year after Victor Weybright's complete separation from NAL, Irving Wallace responded to the publisher's request for reflections on their relationship that could be included in the memoirs, *The Making of a Publisher*. Wallace supplied a summary of sorts of his relations with the publisher that aptly and clearly recognizes the culture and the commerce of book publishing. "The fact is—despite our differences of the past, which were the usual differences between a publisher and an author—I have always regarded you as one of the truly creative forces in the publishing field. I've said it before and I'll say it again. I've known and worked with a fair share of publishers, and you were the only one who honestly understood writers, and considered a typewriter as important as an IBM or adding machine" (30 July 1966).[13]

13. This quote is from a Wallace letter in the Victor Weybright Collection, Archives of Contemporary History, University of Wyoming.

11

Epilogue

Victor Weybright's final years with the company—the discord generated with the parent Times-Mirror Company and the rivalry that developed with his copartner, Kurt Enoch—are bitterly chronicled in his autobiography, *The Making of a Publisher*, published in 1967. Events related in these memoirs became archetypal examples within the book industry of probable results from large, corporate takeovers of small, sensitive, and trend-setting book publishing operations.

The NAL editorial records at New York University contain few Times-Mirror interchanges after 1961. However, there is a good deal of information on relations between Victor Weybright and the Times-Mirror Company in the Weybright corporate and personal papers deposited at the University of Wyoming's Archives of Contemporary History. They confirm that through the first half of the sixties NAL was seen by Times-Mirror as the core around which a large book publishing wing would be added to their corporate structure.

At the time of the 1960 merger, it was decided that Weybright and Enoch would annually exchange a seat on the Times-Mirror board of directors. However, it is clear from the Wyoming papers that the parent corporation found it awkward to deal with two spokesmen for the same subsidiary. No matter who held the seat, Enoch's dual responsibilities as both NAL president and treasurer seem to have naturally required his being in constant touch with Los Angeles corporate executives. And while Weybright retained his title of chairman of the board for New American Library, there does not seem to have been a place or function for this position within the larger Times-Mirror corporate structure.

In an effort to streamline the administration and management of NAL and to prepare for successors to Enoch and Weybright, Times-Mirror hired management consultants McKinsey and Company to study the book publisher's operations and to prepare a set of recommendations. Until their report, it had been expected within publishing circles that Truman Talley would eventually succeed Victor Weybright and that Kurt Enoch's son-in-law, Peter Gruenthal, would assume the other half of the company leadership. Both Talley and Gruenthal had been employed by the company since the late forties. Both, through a series of promotions, one matching the other, had moved to positions of major responsibility. However, the McKinsey report, as the consultant's recommendation came to be known, did not allow for the continued tandem leadership. It rearranged the management of the subsidiary by encouraging the hiring of a single chief executive officer from outside the company. This individual would become responsible for all operations including the editorial and marketing functions.

John P. R. Budlong, head of McGraw-Hill's trade book division, was hired to assume this position once the details of the succession could be agreed upon. Kurt Enoch, who appears to have gained the substantial confidence of the management and directors of the Times-Mirror Company, moved out of NAL to offices a few blocks away at 280 Park Avenue. He was placed in charge of a rapidly expanding Times-Mirror "book publishing group." By the mid-sixties Times-Mirror acquisitions included the World Publishing Company of Cleveland (trade and reference books), Harry N. Abrams Company (art books), C. V. Mosby (medical books), Matthew Bender & Company (law books), the H. M. Gousha Company (maps), and Jeppesen & Company (technical books). About the same time, a New English Library was also unveiled in Great Britain; it was based on the acquisition and merger of two existing British paperback houses, Ace Books and 4-Square, and under the general administration of Enoch and Weybright.

In the fall of 1963 NAL issued its first hardcover list. It included one guaranteed bestseller, Ian Fleming's latest James Bond thriller, *On Her Majesty's Secret Service*. The Times-Mirror acquisition of the World Publishing Company also found NAL taking over for a time that publisher's general book program, including the highly successful Meridian trade paperback imprint.

Several senior editors—most notably Truman Talley, E. L. Doctorow, David Brown, and Edward Burlingame—all left NAL within a few months of each other.[1] The hostile recommendations contained in the McKinsey

1. Brown had been a successful Hollywood producer at 20th Century-Fox. Husband of Helen Gurley Brown, bestselling author (*Sex and the Single Girl*) and *Cosmopolitan* editor,

Report appear to have inspired some if not all of these resignations. Victor Weybright also severed his working connections with Times-Mirror and NAL with a series of resignations: as a director in 1964, as editor in chief in 1965, and as chairman of the NAL board in 1966. In late 1966 *Publishers Weekly* announced the formation of a new trade book imprint, Weybright and Talley. Weybright continued this partnership with Truman Talley until his retirement in 1970, when the firm was purchased by book publisher David McKay Company. Truman Talley remained with the imprint until the late seventies when he established a new personal publishing imprint Truman Talley Books in association with the New York Times book publishing arm, Times Books. Four and a half years later, he moved his imprint to E. P. Dutton.

Following his retirement from active book publishing in 1970, Victor Weybright maintained a Fifth Avenue office as a publishing consultant. He remained active in many of the numerous professional and philanthropic organizations that commanded his attention as a publisher and editor. He also continued his world travels. He died 3 November 1978 at the age of seventy-five. Kurt Enoch retired as president of the Times-Mirror book publishing division in 1967 after helping to merge the Harry N. Abrams Company, at that time one of the world's most distinguished art book publishers, into the Times-Mirror publishing division. Following retirement and up until his death in February 1982 at eighty-six, Enoch also maintained an office on Fifth Avenue only a few blocks from that of Victor Weybright. His *Memoirs of Kurt Enoch* were privately issued by his wife in 1984. Unfinished at the time of his death, they unfortunately conclude shortly after his founding of the company with Victor Weybright.

NAL's fortunes in the sixties as a Times-Mirror subsidiary declined despite the large financial resources of the parent company. Several very large royalty advances on major novels do not appear to have been recouped. The merger of the World Publishing Company's trade book program with NAL's hardcover program did not work out successfully. Eventually NAL dropped its own hardcover imprint and the World trade book publishing program was for a time revived. The London-based New English Library never lived up to expectations and ran at a loss for some time. By the early seventies an entirely new management team was running NAL and blockbuster successes like Erich Segal's *Love Story*, Erica Jong's *Fear of Flying*, and the fitness and nutrition titles of Adelle Davis created a rosier profit picture. In the second half of the seventies, NAL began publish-

---

he was hired in 1963 to direct NAL's hardcover program. His stay was short and he soon returned to an even more successful film career as producer of films like *The Sting, Jaws,* and *Cocoon*.

ing the suspense fiction of Stephen King. Since that time his fiction has generated a large portion of NAL's total sales, a domination that resembles earlier company sales of Caldwell, Spillane, and Fleming.

In the spring of 1980, NAL revived its earlier trade hardcover imprint, NAL Books, joining two trade paperback imprints, Meridian and Plume, on the company book list. In 1984, two years after the appointment of Robert G. Diforio as chief executive officer, Times-Mirror sold New American Library for a reported $50 million to a group of investors that included the top management of the company. On 22 February 1985 *Publishers Weekly* announced NAL's purchase of E. P. Dutton, "the 133-year-old hardcover publishers. The new association will give the houses the capability of buying combined hardcover and softcover rights to important titles and, principals say, will strengthen their clout in the marketplace." So Truman Talley's career in publishing, through Dutton's sponsorship of Truman Talley Books, could be viewed as coming full circle. The circle closed for NAL as well when in the fall of 1986 Peter Mayer, chief executive officer of Penguin Publishing, announced that his firm had acquired NAL, thus ending a thirty-eight-year separation from the British publisher. Diforio remarked in the *Publishers Weekly* report, "We've come home again."

Bibliography
Index

Select Bibliography

With few exceptions, the source for all correspondence quoted is the New American Library Collection, Fales Library, New York University. The exceptions, noted in the text, are part of the Victor Weybright Collection in the Archives of Contemporary Civilization, University of Wyoming.

Research into the history of modern paperback publishing requires one to keep Reginald and Burgess' *Cumulative Paperback Index, 1939–1959* constantly at hand. Despite the fact that it oddly contains some dummy entries—titles that were never actually published—its citations for those books actually issued by the major softcover houses are comprehensive and, for the most part, reliable.

John Tebbel's *A History of Book Publishing in the United States* is this century's major contribution to book publishing scholarship. Its fourth volume provides the best sense of hardcover-paperback relationships of any history available. Its carefully prepared and extensive index was the primary source for identification of the book publishing personnel references (editors, publishers, agents, etc.). Hackett and Burke's *80 Years of Best Sellers, 1895–1975* and Haight and Grannis' *Banned Books, 387 B.C. to 1978 A.D.* were also basic reference tools.

I first encountered the "gatekeeper" theme in the Altbach and McVey, and Lane titles, books that I was privileged to review for *Choice*. After this same reviewing journal asked for a review of Coser, Kaduskin, and Powell's *Books: The Culture and Commerce of Publishing*, I became convinced that it was the theme through which I could organize and exhibit the voluminous correspondence that I had begun recording at NYU. Reviewing Powell's subsequent *Getting into Print: The Decision-Making Process in Scholarly Publishing* confirmed the wisdom of this decision. I am most appreciative to have had these provocative examinations at hand.

231

Altbach, Philip G., and Sheila McVey. *Perspectives on Publishing*. Lexington, MA: Lexington Books, 1976.

Bonn, Thomas L., "New American Library." *Mass Market American Paperbacks, 1939–1979*. Ed. Allen Billy Crider. Boston: G. K. Hall, 1982. 183–93.

————. *Under Cover: An Illustrated History of American Mass Market Paperbacks*. New York: Penguin, 1982.

Branden, Barbara. *The Passion of Ayn Rand*. Garden City, NY: Doubleday, 1986.

Coser, Lewis A., Charles Kaduskin, and Walter W. Powell. *Books: The Culture and Commerce of Publishing*. New York: Basic Books, 1982.

Crider, Allen Billy, ed. *Mass Market American Paperbacks, 1939–1979*. Boston: G. K. Hall, 1982.

Davis, Kenneth C. *Two-Bit Culture: The Paperbacking of America*. Boston: Houghton, 1984.

Dzwonkoski, Peter, ed. *American Literary Publishing Houses, 1900–1980: Trade and Paperback*. Vol. 46 of *Dictionary of Library Biography*. Detroit: Gale, 1986.

Enoch, Kurt. *Memoirs of Kurt Enoch*. Privately printed by Margaret M. Enoch, 1984.

————. Paper-bound Book: Twentieth Century Publishing Phenomenon." *Library Quarterly* 24 (1954):211–25.

Hackett, Alice Payne, and James Henry Burke. *80 Years of Best Sellers, 1895–1975*. New York: Bowker, 1977.

Haight, Anne Lyon, and Chander B. Grannis. *Banned Books, 387 B.C. to 1978 A.D.* 4th ed. New York: Bowker, 1978.

Lane, Michael. *Books and Publishers*. Lexington, MA: Lexington Books, 1980.

Morpurgo, J. E. *Allen Lane, King Penguin*. London: Hutchinson, 1979.

O'Brien, Geoffrey. *Hardboiled America: The Lurid Years of Paperbacks*. New York: Van Nostrand Reinhold, 1981.

Powell, Walter W. *Getting into Print: The Decision-Making Process in Scholarly Publishing*. Chicago: Chicago UP, 1985.

Reginald, R., and M. R. Burgess. *Cumulative Paperback Index, 1939–1959*. Detroit: Gale, 1973.

Reynolds, Paul R. *The Middle Man: The Adventures of a Literary Agent*. New York: Morrow, 1972.

Schick, Frank L. *The Paperbound Book in America: The History of Paperbacks and Their European Background*. New York: Bowker, 1958.

Schreuders, Piet. *Paperbacks, U.S.A.: A Graphic History, 1939–1959*. San Diego: Blue Dolphin, 1981.

Sell, Henry Blackman, and Victor Weybright. *Buffalo Bill and the Wild West*. New York: Oxford UP, 1955.

Targ, William. *Indecent Pleasures*. New York: Macmillan, 1975.

Tebbel, John. *Between the Covers*. New York: Oxford UP, 1987.

————. *A History of Book Publishing in the United States*. 4 vols. New York: Bowker, 1972–81.

Wallace, Irving. *The Writing of One Novel*. New York: Simon, 1968.

Walters, Ray. *Paperback Talk*. Chicago: Academy Chicago, 1985.

Weybright, Victor. *The Making of a Publisher: A Life in the 20th Century Book Revolution*. New York: Reynal, 1967.

————. "Paperback Books." *The Readers' Encyclopedia of American Literature*. Ed. Max J. Herzberg. New York: Crowell, 1962.

————. *Spangled Banner: The Story of Francis Scott Key*. New York: Farrar & Rinehart, 1935.

Whiteside, Thomas. *The Blockbuster Complex*. Middletown, CT: Wesleyan UP, 1981.

Index

A 1961 graduate of New York University's Graduate Institute of Book Publishing, Thomas L. Bonn has researched mass market paperback publishing for the past twenty years. He has published articles on almost all aspects of the industry including the design, manufacture, and sales of softcover books. His *Under Cover: An Illustrated History of American Mass Market Paperbacks* was issued by Penguin Books in 1982. He is also author of *Paperback Primer: A Guide for Collectors*. Recipient of the State University of New York Chancellor's Award for Excellence in Librarianship, Mr. Bonn is on the faculty at the State University College at Cortland.